Guilty Aesthetic Pleasures

Guilty
Aesthetic Pleasures

Timothy Aubry

Harvard University Press

Cambridge, Massachusetts
London, England
2018

Library of Congress Cataloging-in-Publication Data

Names: Aubry, Timothy Richard, 1975– author.
Title: Guilty aesthetic pleasures / Timothy Aubry.
Description: Cambridge, Massachusetts : Harvard University Press, 2018. |
    Includes bibliographical references and index.
Identifiers: LCCN 2018002098 | ISBN 9780674986466 (alk. paper)
Subjects: LCSH: Literature—Aesthetics. |
    Literature—Philosophy—History—20th century. |
    Literature—Philosophy—History—21st century. | Literary
    movements—History—20th century. | Literary movements—History—21st
    century. | Criticism—History—20th century. | Criticism—History—21st
    century.
Classification: LCC PN45 .A837 2018 | DDC 801/.93—dc23
LC record available at https://lccn.loc.gov/2018002098

Contents

Guilty Aesthetic Pleasures

INTRODUCTION

Aᴇsᴛʜᴇᴛɪᴄ ᴘʟᴇᴀsᴜʀᴇ ᴄᴀɴ never be innocent. To seek it out is to commit the sin of trying to evade politics—a sin that paradoxically sustains existing political arrangements. Moreover, if aesthetic pleasure is irresponsible, then aesthetic judgment is downright pernicious: under the guise of disinterestedness, it inevitably supports the interests of the privileged, the powerful, and the socially dominant over those of the underserved, the weak, and the marginalized. This, at least, was the view that served to justify efforts to banish aesthetic criticism from academic literature departments in the final decades of the twentieth century, in favor of ideological critique.[1] Ironically, during this period opposition to aesthetics came to be no less axiomatic than the doctrines it displaced. And yet political criticism's hegemonic position within the academy—a position that has only recently faced serious challenges—raises an important question. Namely, why has it been so successful for so long? How did it sideline a set of priorities, concerns, and experiences that were, by its own account, once central to the discipline that it came to dominate? Can its appeal be credited solely to its unassailable validity and persuasiveness? What does political criticism do for those who embrace it in order to remain so inexhaustibly attractive?

In attempting to answer some of these questions, this book will argue that there is considerably more common ground than is generally

1

recognized between the formalists who once determined the direction of English studies and the politically oriented scholars who succeeded them. Surprisingly, one point of continuity is a profound suspicion of the aesthetic, a suspicion already present in the midcentury writings of the New Critics.[2] In their effort to turn criticism into a rigorous academic discipline, the latter in fact defined their approach against what they regarded as the merely impressionistic work of fin de siècle aesthetes such as Walter Pater and Remy de Gourmont. But if the New Critics' disavowal of aestheticism did not prevent them from working to cultivate a sensitivity to the peculiar power of poetic language, nor have the far more vehement attacks that have followed in their wake succeeded at curbing our reliance on reading practices aimed at promoting aesthetic satisfaction.[3] Indeed, even when it was the object of near-universal reproach among academics, aesthetic judgment never disappeared; it simply went underground.

In recent years, dissatisfaction with political criticism has emerged from various quarters. One response, New Formalism, has sought to renew investment in the specificity of literary form—an effort that has won many supporters but without reorienting the discipline in any systematic way.[4] A series of interventions all championing postcritical strategies of interpretation may prove more disruptive. A number of influential scholars, including Sharon Marcus, Stephen Best, Heather Love, Bruno Latour, Rita Felski, and Franco Moretti, have sought to move beyond the "hermeneutics of suspicion"—that is, to stop automatically treating literary texts as symptoms of deeper ideological forces.[5] To be sure, these figures have adopted divergent approaches, with Moretti and his followers employing digital technology to mine thousands of literary works for data, and Marcus and Best attending to individual textual surfaces. Nevertheless, the various new styles of reading they have put forward—"just reading," "surface reading," "flat reading," "distant reading," and so forth—are unified in their repudiation of *both* symptomatic reading, which is typically identified with political criticism, *and* close reading, which is typically identified with formalism. That these modes of interpretation have been joint targets of attack suggests a stronger alliance between the two than has been previously acknowledged. And this may help to explain why New Formalism has not succeeded at revamping the discipline: the appreciation of form has never really been banished from it.[6] Indeed, perhaps only now that political criticism finds itself in jeopardy can we see that one of its functions has been to lend succor and support to its apparent enemy. The political critique of aesthetics has, in other words, paradoxically enabled scholars to promote heightened experiences of perceptual acuity and intensity, which they implicitly treat as valuable for their own sake, while adjudicating which formal or rhetorical strategies are best designed to promote these experiences—to practice, in short, aesthetic criticism, but in covert fashion.

The Aesthetic Unconscious

As an undergraduate English major, I was taught to praise works of literature for the ambiguities, ironies, and paradoxes that I could discover in them. Then, like many aspiring academics, I had to unlearn my recently acquired aesthetic commitments in graduate school, which I began in the late 1990s. Hoping to increase my knowledge of the Renaissance, I enrolled during my first semester in a seminar devoted to early modern London city comedies. The plays we studied ranged from weird to unreadable, and not just because most of them came to us in blurry mimeographed form that suggested a precarious existence barely perpetuated by repeated unofficial reproductions. The question of whether these texts were great works of literature never arose. Instead we asked what ideological functions they performed, what social and political tensions they reflected, and whose identity politics they served. We treated them no differently from how we treated the other archival materials that were on the syllabus, including John Stow's 1598 *Survey of London*, a four-hundred-plus-page documentation of the myriad bridges, habitations, aqueducts, and other structures in London, which I tried—still a nervous first-year PhD student—to read from beginning to end. The course, I should say, was something of a revelation: while I did not enjoy the primary texts, I found the scholarship about them intellectually invigorating in exactly the way I had hoped all of my graduate school readings would be. A preference for the latter kind of work over the former was not, I suspect, mine alone, and perhaps as a result, the two categories of texts we were reading ended up generating entirely distinct modes of critical response. While explicit aesthetic judgments about the plays were inadmissible, it was perfectly acceptable to characterize the academic articles we encountered as smart or banal, interesting or tedious.[7]

In the semesters that followed, persuaded by arguments made by my professors and by the critics I read, I came to focus less on literature's aesthetic effects and more on its ideological purpose. I return now to this transitional moment in my intellectual development not in order to suggest that I was pressured into sacrificing something important. Quite the contrary, I want to consider why this transition felt so totally seamless. As a matter of fact, I had to sacrifice almost nothing. Political criticism offered the same intellectual satisfaction, the same training in discriminating between powerful and ineffectual uses of rhetoric, and the same heady negotiation with ambiguity, paradox, and irony that formalist criticism had offered. Moreover, this new approach brought certain advantages. For one thing, I could defend what I was doing in political terms. I could contend that I was supporting a progressive agenda by participating in debates of consequence. Moreover, I no longer needed to focus my attention exclusively on musty canonical works. The scholarly interpretations I was reading seemed capable of making all variety of objects the springboard for the aesthetic satisfaction that I was seeking. They, rather than the primary texts, were the source of illumination. And they seemed to promise the same power to me, if I could only master their methods: the power, that it to say, to find inspiration for a complex aesthetic response almost anywhere I looked.

In this book I argue that while political or ideological questions have been the conscious focus of much literary scholarship over the past several decades, aesthetic pleasure has served as its unacknowledged motive.[8] Though rarely discussed explicitly, certain tacit aesthetic criteria and the desires they serve have continued to play a central role in shaping the arguments literary scholars produce. At times scholarship has made itself the object of appreciation through displays of stylistic prowess; at other times it has turned both literary works and nonliterary archival artifacts into sources of fascination. Contemporary academic critical practices may therefore call for an inversion of Fredric Jameson's thesis that formalist readings of literature are driven by repressed ideological imperatives.[9] Jameson, of course, helped create the critical conditions that have forced the aesthetic to operate underground. But if the aesthetic has now come to survive paradoxically by means of its own critique, then it is worth returning briefly to *The Political Unconscious* in order to see whether it might subtly nourish that which it purports to eviscerate.

It is important to note first of all that the problem to which Jameson views modern literature as offering a solution is the same one identified by the New Critics: fragmentation at all levels—the disintegration of traditional communities and the individual's experience brought about by the rise of industrial capitalism, the rationalization of the means of production, the division of labor, the increasing specialization of various social functions and forms of knowledge, and the decline of religious authority.[10] According to the New Critics, poetry offers an antidote to this predicament. It exposes the reader to a dense welter of meanings, which are reflective of the chaos and complexity of modern life. Then it resolves these competing ideas into a higher-order synthesis, thereby providing an experience of unity and wholeness that is otherwise unattainable.[11] According to Cleanth Brooks, "The poet, the imaginative man, has his particular value in his superior power to reconcile the irrelevant or apparently warring elements of experience" (*Modern Poetry* 33). Jameson likewise underscores literature's capacity to offer symbolic resolutions to real-world contradictions: "We are first obliged to establish a continuity between these two regional zones or sectors—the practice of language in the literary work, and the experience of *anomie*, standardization, rationalizing desacralization in the *Umwelt* or world of daily life—such that the latter can be grasped as that determinate situation, dilemma, contradiction, or subtext, to which the former comes as a symbolic resolution or solution" (*Political Unconscious* 42). Moreover, though he is far more suspicious of his subject than the New Critics, Jameson readily adopts the latter's self-assigned task of articulating a serious function for literature within a utilitarian society. "The novel," Jameson contends, "plays a significant role in what can be called a properly bourgeois cultural revolution—that immense process of transformation whereby populations whose life habits were formed by other, now archaic, modes of production are effectively reprogrammed for life and work in the new world of market capitalism" (152). If anything, Jameson's critical account, which holds the novel responsible for reprogramming entire populations, actually represents an inflation of the significance that previous generations of formalist critics had ascribed to literature.

Unlike the New Critics, of course, Jameson regards the "purely formal resolution" that literature provides as illusory and inadequate (79). The contradictions it confronts are political, social, and material, and they cannot be resolved merely through a private aesthetic experience. Thus his objective is to read literary works' formal strategies so as to make them yield up their unconscious determinants: the real political conflicts that they are attempting to manage in a merely symbolic register. And yet, ironically enough, Jameson's argument does not simply jettison aesthetic satisfaction in favor of hard-headed political insights; rather, it makes these political insights serve as the basis for the aesthetic satisfaction that they are purportedly designed to supplant, in effect co-opting the function that the New Critics had assigned to literature. Extolling the virtues of his Marxist approach, Jameson proclaims, "What is crucial is that, by being able to use the same language about each of these quite distinct objects or levels of an object, we can restore, at least methodologically, the lost unity of social life, and demonstrate that widely distant elements of the social totality are ultimately part of the same global historical process" (226). It is not poetry, in other words, that can restore the "lost unity" to a wholly fragmented, secular society, as the New Critics had hoped, but Jameson's own theory of history.[12]

The Political Unconscious comes closest to acknowledging that it is appropriating the aesthetic power that it is claiming to repudiate in a famous early passage:

> From this perspective the convenient working distinction between cultural texts that are social and political and those that are not becomes something worse than an error: namely, a symptom and a reinforcement of the reification and privatization of contemporary life. Such a distinction reconfirms that structural, experiential, and conceptual gap between the public and the private, between the social and the psychological, or the political and the poetic, between history or society and the "individual," which—the tendential law of social life under capitalism—maims our existence as individual subjects and paralyzes our thinking about time and change just as

surely as it alienates us from our speech itself. To imagine that, sheltered from the omnipresence of history and the implacable influence
of the social, there already exists a realm of freedom—whether it be
that of the microscopic experience of words in a text or the ecstasies
and intensities of the various private religions—is only to strengthen
the grip of Necessity over all such blind zones in which the individual
subject seeks refuge, in pursuit of a purely individual, a merely psychological, project of salvation. The only effective liberation from
such constraint begins with the recognition that there is nothing that
is not social and historical—indeed, that everything is "in the last
analysis" political. (20)

Notice that while Jameson regards the distinction between political
and nonpolitical texts as a cause of great harm, his curious phrase
"something worse than an error" conveniently enables him to avoid
calling it an actual error. To do so, of course, would be to suggest
that the gap, which this distinction reflects, between "the social and
the psychological, or the political and the poetic," does not in fact
exist. But Jameson regards this gap as "structural, experiential, and
conceptual"—that is, a phenomenon formidable enough to exist on
multiple registers, indeed one that demands the radical intervention
he is advocating. Thus he hesitates to deny its reality altogether. To
attribute reality to this gap, however, is to call into question Jameson's
argument that "everything" is political; the former's validity comes at
the cost of the latter's. At the very least, Jameson seems to recognize
that most people living within a capitalist system perceive a division
between the private and the political and would thus be likely to view
his account of a thoroughly politicized world as counterfactual—that
is, a kind of fiction.

Jameson is of course committed to the notion that fictions, theories, and other intellectual constructs do not merely describe but in fact
shape reality—a position that enables him to distinguish his approach
from vulgar Marxism, which would treat all such phenomena as su-
perstructural emanations of a material base. Thus a mere theoretical
distinction can buttress the "tendential law" that "maims our existence." Moreover, merely "to imagine" is to "strengthen the grip of
Necessity"—though it is reasonable to wonder why a force indomitable
by definition and endowed by Jameson's ominous capitalization with

quasi-mythical power would require any backing from the wayward daydreams of the lost souls living under capitalism. Jameson needs to posit just such an inexorable power in order to deny the possibility of a realm of authentic freedom afforded by religious ecstasy or aesthetic bliss. Yet he also needs to argue that the imagination, though incapable of carving out even a tiny space of autonomy within the existing order, can nevertheless pose a challenge to that order. The latter claim is crucial if he wants to ascribe political agency to his own theory.

The effectiveness of Jameson's methodology hinges, then, on the question of whether the political vision of the world that he offers is any more powerful or any less delusional than faith in the aesthetic or religious spheres whose liberatory potential he categorically denies. The tragedy of the latter is that they offer only a false sense of freedom, leading us to believe that we can transcend history, thereby guaranteeing our submission to the current power structure. For Jameson, the problem is not so much Necessity as our own efforts to stave off its controlling influence, to create "blind zones"—dark, lonely cells of our own making that imprison us precisely by attempting to keep Necessity at bay. Jameson's solution is to work to break down the walls of these prisons not in order to let his readers out but rather in order to let history in. His aim is to give readers the intellectual equipment necessary to see everything as political and thus escape the narrowness of their "microscopic" perspective and the banality of their "merely psychological" concerns.

Although Jameson casts his solution as antithetical to the aesthetic and religious responses that represent a retreat from politics, he can pitch it as a better alternative, a more effective medicine, only by promising the same result that they promise: liberation from constraint. In effect, Jameson acknowledges that his theory provides a service similar to the one advertised by the approaches he rejects. Moreover, the liberation he advocates begins not with anything as drastic as revolution or even political action; rather, it follows immediately upon "recognition," a purely theoretical or intellectual experience. It begins, in other words, with the acceptance of a narrative that, in insisting on the ubiquity of the political, directly contradicts the way most people understand their own experience, and thus cannot help but come across as a fiction, one that promises to enhance their vision, to endow all the seemingly random, banal, personal details of their lives with great significance as elements within a salvific, historical narrative. The goal of *The Political Unconscious*, then, is to replace readers' weak, unsatisfying fictions with a stronger one capable of making the whole world bright and meaningful—an effect exponentially augmented by Jameson's preternatural theoretical dexterity and rhetorical facility. Although Jameson is undeniably advocating a revolutionary political program, he is also offering, under the guise of shattering the aesthetic, a superlative aesthetic experience.

Definitions

To argue that criticism as staunchly political as Jameson's remains invested in aesthetic pleasure is necessarily to raise the question of what exactly the term *aesthetic* signifies. The category first emerges as a subject of intellectual inquiry in the writings of the German philosopher Alexander Baumgarten. At the end of his 1735 *Reflections on Poetry*, he remarks, "The Greek philosophers and the Church fathers have already carefully distinguished between *things perceived* [αἰσθητά] and *things known* [νοητά]. It is entirely evident that they did not equate *things known* with things of sense, since they honored with this name things also removed from sense (therefore, images). Therefore, *things known* are to be known by the superior faculty as the object of logic; *things perceived* [are to be known by the inferior faculty, as the object] of the science of perception, or **aesthetic**" (78; all emphasis in the original). It is Immanuel Kant, of course, who produces the most important conceptualization of the aesthetic, building in *The Critique of Judgment* on Baumgarten's definition in order to investigate how perceptual experiences can serve as a form of pleasure. While Kant uses "aesthetic" rather broadly to characterize judgments "whose determining basis *cannot be other than subjective*" (44), he offers a more specific description of "judgments of taste"—and it is this description that has served to delineate the particular character of the aesthetic for most readers. Significantly, judgments of taste are, for Kant, "disinterested": they are not based on the sense of any future advantage a given object might confer on the observer; their evaluation of the object is based exclusively on the pleasures that arise in the very experience of perceiving it (43, 46, 62–64). They are not rooted in a desire to possess, consume, or make use of the object in question. Moreover, while such judgments may, insofar as they are shared by others, eventually promote solidarity and even justice, they are not motivated by any such agenda; they follow from and refer only to the subject's perceptual experience of the object.[13]

For our purposes, then, *aesthetic pleasure* will designate that which derives from and arises during the mere act of perceiving or contemplating a given thing, a pleasure whose existence does not depend on a recognition of the usefulness of that thing, the purposes it might serve, or the future consequences it might bring about. In the course of considering different methodologies, I should note, pleasure will become a fairly broad category of experience, one that involves masochistic moments of confusion, abjection, and self-denial but that is nevertheless treated as compelling or worth pursuing. An *aesthetic experience* is one in which aesthetic pleasure is a central or defining feature. *Aesthetic value* will refer to the value that audiences ascribe to a text, gesture, or work of art, based on the satisfaction it produces in the moment that it is perceived or examined. While Kant and Edmund Burke have made the beautiful and the sublime the privileged aesthetic categories, numerous subcategories operate now in academic scholarship and elsewhere as a basis for assigning aesthetic value. In this book I will consider the ones that have played a prominent role in contemporary criticism, including the complex, the ambiguous, the opaque, the paradoxical, and the fragmented—to name just a few.[14] *Aesthetic judgment*, a topic we will return to shortly, will indicate those statements about a work's merit based exclusively on its capacity or failure to produce aesthetic pleasure. *The aesthetic*, as a category, will refer to the whole array of critical and creative practices designed to arouse aesthetic pleasure. It is important to note that works already designated as artistic or literary are not the only ones capable of inspiring aesthetic experiences. As Jan Mukařovský, Gérard Genette, and others have persuasively argued, the aesthetic function is as much the product of the kind of attention paid to a given object as it is to the object's intrinsic qualities.[15] Hence criticism can often serve to aestheticize a particular object by the way that it describes or analyzes it, and it can in the process itself become a source of aesthetic pleasure.

Finally, *aestheticism* will refer to any philosophy or project that identifies the pursuit of aesthetic pleasure as the highest or most important human endeavor. It should go without saying that it is possible to argue for the importance of aesthetic pleasure without espousing aestheticism—though critics have not always clearly distinguished between the two.

To define aesthetic criticism precisely, it is necessary to address its relationship to formalist criticism, since the two are often identified. Immediately upon inventing the category of the aesthetic, Baumgarten asserts the dependence of the faculty it designates on outward forms: "The philosopher presents his thought as he thinks it. Hence there are no special rules, or only a few, that he must observe in presenting it. He has no special interest in terms, so far as they are articulate sounds, for as such they belong among the *things perceived*. But he who presents sensate subject matter is expected to take much greater account of terms. Hence that part of aesthetics which treats of such presentation is more extensive than the corresponding part of logic" (*Reflections on Poetry* 78). While it can often be maddeningly difficult, as Genette has argued, to determine which elements belong to the form and which to the content within certain works of art, the distinction is somewhat easier to make in literature (*Aesthetic Relation* 24–25). To consider the formal aspects of a literary work usually means to pay as much attention to the language—the sound and look of the words, the rhythm and syntax, and so forth—as to what that language represents. It can of course also mean concentrating on patterns of images, motifs, actions, or other narrative structures that are not linguistic elements strictly speaking but can nevertheless be categorized alongside the linguistic elements as means of representation, or what Baumgarten calls the "presentation."[16] It is frequently assumed within academic literary studies that attention to form entails aesthetic pleasure and therefore that aesthetic and formalist criticism are synonymous—an equation that makes sense given the centrality of sensory perception to both approaches.[17] In what follows, I will generally assume that formalist and aesthetic criticism refer to a single family of connected interpretive practices, with one often implying the other, but I will simultaneously try to respect the distinct emphases of the two, recognizing that formalism indicates an attention to linguistic or structural

elements, while aesthetic criticism suggests an attention to the immediate pleasures involved in apprehending an artistic or literary work.

Specifically, this book will be examining the aesthetic pleasure that
emerges during the act of reading, but also in the moment of beholding
an object or contemplating an idea or situation. In some cases the
source of pleasure is the thing described by the text, in some cases it
is the language used to describe it, and in many cases the two become
difficult to distinguish. Frequently, the aesthetic effect is one of defa-
miliarization: a given reality suddenly becomes strange, as if the reader
were encountering it for the first time, and this effect can inspire the
feeling that one is temporarily escaping from the everyday world and
the entanglements, worries, and frustrations that it involves.[18] Such features have been documented countless times by other critics and
enthusiasts of art; my purpose in rehearsing them here is to underscore
the central and distinct role they continue to play within political criticism as a motive for the interpretive exercises that it performs.
Jameson's argument, for instance, has been influential at least in part
because of the complexity and rhetorical verve of its analysis. *The Political Unconscious* makes the world change right before our eyes,
creating a new kind of "recognition" by tracing lines of association,
paradoxical knots, and hidden homologies in the social reality it describes. To be clear, I am not contending that such experiences never
lead to actual social change. I am simply suggesting that the prospect
of social change is not the only or, in some cases, the most compelling
reason that contemporary literary scholars value such experiences.

Intrinsic Value

It is often difficult to account for what makes intrinsically valuable
experiences valuable, though people seek and have them all the time.
A good conversation, television show, movie, walk, daydream, fantasy,
podcast, excursion, drive, song, meal, book—all of these can be and are
experienced as worthwhile in the moment that they are being experienced. For better or worse, as Sianne Ngai has argued, contemporary
consumer culture is dedicated to providing a steady diet of low-intensity
aesthetic experiences (*Our Aesthetic Categories* 20–21, 58). Nevertheless, justification requires measurable consequences. It is much easier

to rationalize a given activity based on the benefits it might produce than for its own sake. One can name, anticipate, catalog, and quantify these benefits, whereas the fulfillment of the moment immediately vanishes and then invariably eludes description. What was so great about the book you read last night? Well, it made me think. Made you think what? No answer, it seems, will suffice. Even unequivocally hedonistic indulgences such as binge drinking or television watching are frequently rationalized as cathartic releases of pent-up urges that allow for greater productivity later on.

The tendency to equate the value of all experiences with the practical benefits they confer is especially pervasive in colleges and universities in the United States. This is unsurprising. Although liberal arts programs have historically claimed a commitment to the disinterested pursuit of knowledge for its own sake, they have also tended to present this knowledge as something graduates can take with them and apply in other contexts. The BA is, after all, widely understood as a kind of preparation: for the civic demands of life in a democratic society, but more importantly as training for a future career. Ever since they began admitting middle- and working-class students at the turn of the twentieth century, colleges and universities in the United States have functioned primarily to help the latter secure gainful employment by teaching them marketable skills.[19] This emphasis on transferrable modes of knowledge has only become more pronounced in the postwar decades as universities have increasingly come to serve the needs of massive multinational corporations, which function as donors supporting the development of new programs, particularly in the sciences, as sources of student loans, and as destinations for future graduates.[20] Thus the effort to foster aesthetic sensitivity, an ability to appreciate a given object, text, or idea for its own sake rather than for the uses it might serve, would appear to contradict what is for many students, teachers, and administrators the very mission of higher education.

In the past seventy years, academics have attempted to rationalize literary studies on various grounds. They have sought to present literature as imparting a knowledge of the world distinct from but no less rigorous than what the sciences offer. They have stressed the practical skills their classes cultivate, including the ability to analyze language, to marshal evidence, to think logically, and to communicate effectively.

And in recent decades, they have presented their discipline as a means of critiquing unjust political arrangements, fostering thoughtful social and ethical engagement, and promoting justice. Significantly, as we will see in the chapters to come, these defenses have often insisted on identifying a social purpose not just for literary studies in general but for precisely the kinds of aesthetic experiences that would seem most resistant to being instrumentalized. This insistence, I will argue, is a consequence of the way the New Critics redesigned literary studies, ensuring that certain aesthetic experiences, predicated on the encounter with ambiguity, irony, and paradox, would continue to serve as the defining feature of the discipline. Finding a purpose for these seemingly recalcitrant, elusive moments of aesthetic pleasure has therefore been a part of all subsequent attempts to rationalize the study of literature.[21]

But is it worthwhile or even necessary to distinguish the aesthetic value of literature from its more practical functions? For what reason? One way of answering these questions is merely descriptive: in other words, this book maintains that, whatever outward justifications contemporary literary scholars provide for their work, they are motivated at least in part by a commitment to aesthetic pleasure—a commitment they betray in ways that are occasionally explicit but more often oblique, obscure, or inadvertent. To put it simply, whether or not we should value the aesthetic for its own sake, we already in fact *do* value it. But in this book I will also suggest what we stand to gain from acknowledging our aesthetic commitments. The default assumption underwriting most political criticism is that in order to demonstrate the significance of a particular text or a particular way of thinking, one must describe the political work it performs—its capacity to make sense of or, better yet, influence various struggles for power, prestige, and economic resources that are happening beyond the text, beyond the privacy of the reading experience, *out there* in the real world. This assumption has persisted even among the New Formalists. Caroline Levine's highly touted intervention *Forms*, for instance, acknowledges the litmus test that her preferred method of reading must pass: "For politically inclined readers, a formalist's understanding of social tempos will matter only to the extent that it can help us to effect social change" (68). Her answer? "I want to suggest that a new attention to rhythm has this potential" (68). Indeed her book justifies its attention to form exclusively by locating patterns thought to be specific to literary works within other political and institutional spaces. To be sure, many such arguments presume a capacious definition of the political so as to encompass a wide range of beliefs, gestures, experiences, desires, and so forth. Nevertheless, the deferral to the political as the ultimate measure of importance has often precluded a full understanding of other kinds of experiences, other ideals, and other forms of fulfillment activated by literary works.

Arguably the scholars who have been most forthright in asserting nonpolitical criteria of value and in affirming experiences that exist outside the traditional political sphere have been queer theorists, including most famously Eve Sedgwick, Leo Bersani, D. A. Miller, Lauren Berlant, Michael Warner, and Lee Edelman.[22] Rejecting the either literal or metaphorical procreative ideal that serves within much mainstream heteronormative discourse to justify pleasure, queer theorists have been far more willing than others to defend nonproductive modes of enjoyment, modes that could, by virtue of their status as valuable and fulfilling for their own sake, be read as exemplary instantiations of the aesthetic.

Edelman's *No Future* offers an especially forceful argument for a queer *jouissance* that enacts "a rupturing of our foundational faith in the reproduction of futurity" (17). The contemporary political order, argues Edelman, is wholly invested in the image of the Child, who represents the future of society and the possibility of progress toward a better world. But queer subjects, viewed as rejecting the traditional family, refusing the imperative to engage in biological reproduction, and exerting a corrupting influence on the young, are made to signify a threat to this ideal. While most liberals and progressives have sought to divest queerness of such connotations, Edelman provocatively contends that members of the queer community should in fact embrace their figural status as unregenerate death-driven deniers of a viable future: "Fuck the social order and the Child in whose name we're collectively terrorized; fuck Annie; fuck the waif from *Le Mis*; fuck the poor innocent kid on the Net; fuck Laws both with capital ls and with small; fuck the whole network of Symbolic relations and the future that serves as its prop" (29). Accepting his assigned role with a vengeance, Edelman seeks to expose the collective investment in the Child as itself a deathly attachment to a fantasy, one that endlessly displaces fulfillment to an inaccessible horizon, negating the present, demonizing queer desire, and radically circumscribing the scope of acceptable political discourse.

Edelman calls for a queer assault on what he terms "aesthetic culture—the culture of forms and their reproduction, the culture of Imaginary lures" (48). But his assumption that aesthetic investments are inherently conservative prevents him from recognizing his own advocacy of experiences that contribute nothing to the future as itself an emphatic aestheticism.[23] Strangely enough, it is his radical politics that leads him to this audacious disregard for practical utility. The main target of No Future's animus is the "liberal discourse" that strives to deny the "ascription of negativity to the queer" (4), the "liberal humanism whose rallying cry has always been, and here remains, 'the future'" (106). Edelman's intervention thus exemplifies a curious pattern within contemporary literary studies: while almost all scholarship at present claims to be engaged with politics, radical scholars seem far more willing than their liberal counterparts to assert nonpolitical registers of experience and modes of value, including the aesthetic. To be clear, this book will argue that all different forms of political criticism of the past several decades, from liberal to radical, have been shaped by implicit aesthetic commitments. The difference is that radical theorists, particularly radical queer theorists, are somewhat less afraid to acknowledge these commitments openly. Edelman's contempt for mainstream political discourse yields a helpful explanation: whereas liberals claim a pragmatic commitment to improving the current political situation and thus hope to turn literature and criticism into practical means of exposing its shortcomings and effecting incremental change, radicals like Edelman categorically reject the political order as such and thus celebrate gestures that do nothing to improve or reproduce it.

Edelman characterizes his own political project as "impossible," which raises the question of what exactly he hopes to accomplish (3). The answer may be more modest than his energetically combative rhetoric would suggest. What No Future argues for is a mode of life that exists within the current political order but does not comply with its imperatives, a way of being that contributes nothing to politics, that does nothing to shape the future, that exists in fact adjacent to contemporary political struggles, but is nevertheless recognized as valuable according to nonpolitical criteria. Some will see this as a futile hope, reading Edelman's argument as a doomed effort to imagine a sphere of autonomy within a political order whose influence pervades all realms of experience and thus grants no such sphere. But it is also possible to view his polemic as a revolt against a narrower, slightly less inescapably coercive context—namely, the discipline of literary studies and its discursive constraints—constraints that discourage any positive assessment of a text or practice that does not translate it into a conventionally future-oriented mode of left or progressive politics.

Berlant has expressed a similar urge in her role as the leading figure within both queer theory and the overlapping subfield of affect studies, which, in its attention to the visceral experiences promoted by literature, has proved itself to be far more open to questions about aesthetics than other forms of political criticism.[24] Berlant's recent neologism, the "juxtapolitical," designates a world of emotional solidarity, generally for women, that is not perceived by those who participate in it as political.[25] Describing the aim of her 2008 book *The Female Complaint*, Berlant declares, "In this book the work of critical distance in the context of the reproduction of life focuses on scenes of ordinary survival, not transgression, on disappointment, not refusal, to derive the register of critique. Here, ordinary restlessness appears as a symptom of ambivalence about aspirational normativity and not a pointer toward unrealized revolution. It seeks to understand the flourishing of the social to one side of the political as something other than a failure to be politics" (24–25). Berlant's suggestively ambiguous term, the *juxtapolitical*, seems to validate the nonpolitical conceptualization through which certain nonacademic subjects view their own practices, while also recognizing that in order for this perspective to be brought into academic discourse and taken seriously, its *proximity* to the political—that is, the one register that really matters—must at least be established.

Berlant's searching analysis leads to a question that she stops just short of asking, namely what might result if we bracketed the political, if we made an attempt to understand the significance of a given practice or textual artifact without even trying to place it in relationship

to the political, without granting it the consolation prize of our quali-
fied approval for at least approaching or getting close to the political?
It is important to note that to argue on behalf of nonpolitical criteria
of value does not entail a rejection of political criteria or the premise
that literature can and does serve various ideological functions. It is
only to suggest the need to allow space for other forms of interpretation so as to register the diversity of ways in which both academic and
nonacademic readers appreciate literature, and thus make it possible
to account for certain pleasures of reading that are not predicated on
the text's ability to effect social or political change. The effort to recover the notion of aesthetic value as something embedded and con-
cealed within current scholarship is one strategy for creating that
space, or rather for conferring visibility and legitimacy on a space that
already exists.

To be clear, my argument is that political criticism has, despite
appearances, effectively preserved various kinds of aesthetic appreciation. Thus I am not arguing that a departure from political questions is
necessary in order to cultivate aesthetic satisfaction. Nor am I arguing
that scholars ought to disentangle the political and the aesthetic in
order to capture one or the other in pure form. What I am asserting is
the need to be aware of the multiple, *distinct* components that typically constitute a given act of interpretation, in a way that avoids automatically translating one into the other. Assuming that the meaning
and value of literature cannot be exhaustively described in political
terms, what might the deployment of a critical vocabulary that allows
for open aesthetic evaluation allow us to accomplish? What purposes,
strategies, effects, and responses might we be better able to describe?
What, in our own experience of literature, might we more honestly
account for?

It is important to keep in mind that the aesthetic, as we will see in
later chapters, does not function only as a luxury item, enjoyed exclusively by those in positions of privilege. Indeed, the ability to pursue
aesthetic fulfillment may be more, not less, urgent for those who have
been the victims of oppression. As Cheryl Wall observes, "From its be-
ginnings in the United States, black writing has been defined as
having *only* an ideological importance" ("On Freedom" 286). Wall notes
that in the past quarter century, critics have become more attentive to

"the dual quests for freedom and for beauty in black writing" (287). To take African American writers as seriously as their white compatriots, Wall implies, it is necessary to ascribe to their works aesthetic qualities that are distinct from political objectives. To value the work of black authors only insofar as it serves a political purpose, in other words, is to deny it the full range of yearnings, ideals, and satisfactions that is typically ascribed to any great work of literature. Moreover, the aesthetic, as we will see, can serve as an indispensable resource precisely for those who lack political agency, who have no way of improving their material and social conditions. And it does so *not* because it promises future political progress but because it is valuable in itself, in the moment of its emergence, as a nonpolitical source of solace or satisfaction when other forms of support are absent.

Needless to say, it is not always easy to distinguish between aesthetic and political value. In many instances, it may be difficult to separate out the pleasure produced merely by perceiving a particular artistic work from the pleasure rooted in a sense of that work's political usefulness. But this is not a reason to deny the distinction altogether. In order for there to be moments of entanglement, after all, there have to be two distinct phenomena. To put it in more everyday terms, it ought to be possible to read a book and deem it politically compelling but aesthetically disappointing, or aesthetically compelling but politically disappointing. To make such distinctions, of course, it is necessary to resist the temptation, a powerful one for literary scholars, to treat our different criteria as collapsible into one, to assume that a satisfying aesthetic effect necessarily entails a salutary contribution to the political sphere or that an attachment to a reactionary politics automatically makes a work unpalatable at all levels, including formally.

Impure Aesthetics

A paradox of my approach is that I argue for the aesthetic as a distinct experience and mode of evaluation but then search for it in unlikely places, recognizing it as always enmeshed with other agendas, appearing under false pretenses, often hidden or disguised within institutional projects or initiatives that claim a more practical purpose. A central discovery of my research has been that, at least within postwar American academic culture, the aesthetic cannot exist in isolation. To survive, it needs to hitch itself in quasi-parasitic fashion to some more concrete and justifiable enterprise capable of achieving legitimacy within the university in accordance with the larger economic and political imperatives that it serves. The aesthetic needs to present itself as a means to some more practical end while surreptitiously offering a kind of pleasure that eludes instrumentalization. This means that the aesthetic will often assume an unexpected form, one that contradicts prevailing conceptions of it as radically autonomous. In *Cultural Capital*, John Guillory persuasively asserts the need to rethink the aesthetic in order to acknowledge its impurity, observing, "There is no realm of pure aesthetic experience, or object which elicits nothing but that experience. But I shall nevertheless argue that the *specificity* of aesthetic experience is not contingent upon its 'purity'" (336).

To maintain that the aesthetic is inevitably impure is to recognize that it is not in fact categorically innocent. The aesthetic can and must be put to all kinds of uses, some more defensible than others. The production and assertion of aesthetic value can be employed to rationalize the high prices of luxury commodities. Aesthetic techniques can serve to construct brand identities themselves designed to augment the social status of certain types of consumers. As Sarah Brouillette has cogently demonstrated, the expanding creative economy is capable of enlisting various modes of aesthetic training and artistic production in order to promote markets for new kinds of immaterial commodities, to accelerate gentrification under the guise of urban renewal, and to foster neoliberal social policies (*Literature and the Creative Economy*). Aesthetic practices and values can of course be harnessed to serve more progressive ends, as means, for instance, of attracting people to social movements. They can also help cultivate fulfilling intellectual or emotional experiences whose social impact is negligible. What is important to recognize is that the aesthetic does not designate a privileged autonomous realm. It does not suggest a special capacity for critique or subversion. To argue that an object or gesture has aesthetic value is merely to say that perceiving or contemplating it produces satisfaction without implying any judgment about the longer-term consequences it may produce. To respect the specificity of the aesthetic is to recognize that this satisfaction entails no claims about the political value or uses of the objects to which it responds.

One way of articulating the specificity of the aesthetic is in temporal terms. The literary work, we might say, yields moments of satisfaction as it is being read that are aesthetic in nature, but then the dispositions cultivated in these moments may subsequently produce actions that are more accurately described as ethical or political. That a particular experience of a text can be situated within a causal sequence that ultimately yields social or political consequences does not require a denial of the aesthetic value realized in the initial moment in the sequence. Another way of capturing the specificity of the aesthetic is spatial: one can imagine a text emanating beams of influence, some political, some aesthetic. At times the beams overlap or merge together, but they each make a distinct contribution to the overall effect of which they are a part. Critics of the aesthetic may reject all such temporal and spatial schemes on the basis of their view that there are in fact no truly nonpolitical modes of experience and no nonpolitical criteria for judging the value of literature. In this book I seek to refute such claims by finding evidence of aesthetic appreciation precisely within the work of those who seem most emphatically opposed to it, by demonstrating that even the most thoroughly committed political critics, whether deconstructionist, Marxist, feminist, or New Historicist, tacitly attribute intrinsic value to the encounter with ambiguity, irony, and paradox that was originally institutionalized as the defining experience of literary studies by the New Critics.

In what follows, I defend the position that literature and criticism contribute something valuable to the experience of readers that is not political; I argue further that a failure to recognize the specificity of the aesthetic can lead scholars to misread aesthetic effects as political ones. Such a claim will no doubt be unacceptable to those who believe that the best way to further a left-progressive vision is to politicize all areas of experience. While this approach to the political derives in part from a particular interpretation of Karl Marx, the social movements of the 1960s and 1970s, most notably the second-wave feminist movement, extended it further, demonstrating how various contexts that did not necessarily appear political—the bedroom, the therapist's office, the classroom—were very much the product of ideological mechanisms and thus crucial sites of struggle.[26] While it would be misguided, in the wake of the great advances propelled by these movements, to question the validity of their efforts to expand our understanding of the political, it is also worth noting that to view everything as political a priori actually deprives these gestures of their particular force and meaning.

The problem with the view that everything is political is not only that it can foreclose our capacity to describe the way most people experience their lives, automatically translating into ideological terms certain moments whose felt particulars require a different vocabulary. The problem with this view is also that it tends to conflate several distinct definitions of the political. In some moments, the political is used to designate all phenomena that are enabled by, structured by, or implicated in the various forms of social affiliation and the ways that power is allocated within a given context. But the political can also be a term of praise, a way of indicating that a particular literary work or mode of interpretation represents an effective means of critiquing a given power structure. Moreover, the political can also be used more forcefully to designate those texts that not only critique particular ideological arrangements but also inspire protest and resistance. If the first definition of the political, indicating embeddedness within power relations, justifiably entails a broad application of the term, its ambiguity—the uncertainty as to which meaning is in play— allows it to be deployed in order to mischaracterize all variety of gestures as agents of transformation. The overuse of the term, in other words, makes it difficult to determine which gestures actually stand a chance of effecting real change in our society. Thus, the argument for distinguishing the aesthetic from the political ought to appeal not only to those who want to ascribe aesthetic value to literature but also to those who are politically engaged and want to distinguish those textual and critical practices that can truly contribute to the realization of justice and collective well-being from those that we value only because they produce satisfying aesthetic experiences.

While English departments obviously perform important political work, promoting a capacity to think critically about a variety of social realities and fostering cross-cultural understanding, scholars have a habit of overstating the capacity of both literary texts and criticism to

subvert or reinforce hegemonic power structures. The aesthetic strategies that contemporary scholars tacitly favor, including defamiliarizing, unsettling, making strange, and the like, are especially susceptible
to being treated as sources of political change, insofar as they involve perceptual transformations that appear, at least momentarily, to
remake the world. This sudden alteration in the way the reader appre-
hends reality can be misrecognized as the very onset of concrete political change or as a form of political engagement in itself.[27] To be
sure, the aesthetic can in many situations mobilize political involvement, but it is important to recognize that, in so doing, it can also con-
strain the forms that this involvement assumes. An unacknowledged
commitment to certain privileged aesthetic criteria can, for instance,
entail an overvaluation of the political efficacy of certain sophisticated
rhetorical strategies and a disregard for other, less complex but more
effective modes of political action. Thus parody, irony, and strategic
ambiguity have often been treated as more worthy of attention among
scholars than passionate affirmation or collective protest organized
around simple and explicit goals.[28] This does not mean that there is
no place for aesthetic complexity within politics; but acknowledging
the indebtedness of political criticism to aesthetic criteria may allow
for an understanding of how exactly these criteria shape the kinds of
interventions that scholars are inclined to make, thus potentially
opening up alternative ways of thinking about and engaging with
politics.

Inescapable Judgments

As may already be clear, I will be treating aesthetic criteria—the
standards that dictate which sensations, perceptions, and modes of
contemplation become a source of pleasure—as the product of contingent historical developments. Indeed, this book seeks to track subtle
changes in the aesthetic criteria that academic literary scholarship has
deployed over the past eighty years, based on the particular institutional and societal demands that have emerged at different historical
moments. It has often been assumed that to expose the contingent
status of aesthetic judgment is to undermine its very possibility. Kant,
after all, argues that judgments of taste can function as valid claims

about how other people should respond to particular objects because they are rooted in transhistorical, universally shared cognitive dispositions (*Critique of Judgment* 87–90, 159–162). And yet, even as the ever-shifting fashions within art, literature, and criticism would seem to imply the impossibility of any transcendental grounding for aesthetic judgments, this impossibility does not deprive such judgments of validity as a register of the poetic effects that a given work can produce for certain audiences. It simply means that a particular aesthetic judgment will be valid only to the extent that others already share or can be persuaded to adopt the criteria on which that judgment is based. Insofar as the members of a particular reading community are shaped by the same historically rooted psychological urges, cognitive tendencies, and emotional yearnings, it is likely that they will also share certain aesthetic criteria.[29] Indeed, underlying the apparent diversity of methodologies, ideological positions, and theoretical premises within academic literary studies are, as I hope to demonstrate, several more or less uniformly held, but underdiscussed, aesthetic preferences.

But even if it is true that certain criteria are widely shared within the academy, one might object that such criteria have frequently served as the disguised expression of reactionary, patriarchal, classist, racist, or colonialist ideologies and are thus not worth propagating or defending. The first thing to say in response is that aesthetic criticism has no exclusive monopoly on these particular tendencies; any interpretive statement about literature, whether aesthetic or anti-aesthetic, can smuggle in the same dangerous baggage. The solution to this problem, then, is not to scapegoat aesthetic criticism—as if, by imposing a quarantine on it, one could somehow stop the spread of undesirable ideologies. The solution is to subject any given aesthetic assessment to the same scrutiny as other acts of interpretation—so as to determine what ideological premises underlie it and whether these premises are sufficient grounds for rejecting its validity. But it is important to resist the urge to treat particular aesthetic criteria as if they were forever synonymous with particular political agendas, given that alliances between stylistic preferences and ideological commitments have invariably proved to be contingent rather than transhistorical. The aesthetic criteria embraced within literary studies tend to be the complex product of myriad influences, cultural and institutional, global, national, and local. In some cases these criteria endure longer than the historical pressures that first helped to construct them, and thus they acquire a life independent of any single ideological purpose. This is especially likely to happen when they are nurtured and sheltered within the semiautonomous space of the English department.

Probably the most devastating exposure of the ideological bases for aesthetic judgment is Pierre Bourdieu's *Distinction*, which famously argues that an individual's artistic taste is a form of cultural capital—the product, in other words, of that individual's social status and thus a means of reaffirming invidious class divisions. And yet, while he underscores the strong correlation between taste and class, Bourdieu also refuses to translate the former into purely economic terms. Doing so, he recognizes, would entail a disregard for the semiautonomy of the artistic sphere and a failure to understand the operations specific to it. "The literary and artistic field," remarks Bourdieu in his 1983 essay "The Field of Cultural Production," "is contained within the field of power, while possessing a relative autonomy with respect to it" (319). Moreover, the forms of aesthetic appreciation that serve to support that field cannot be regarded solely as a means of establishing economic status; nor can the claims they make about art be entirely dismissed. Bourdieu observes,

> The work of art is an object which exists as such only by virtue of the (collective) belief which knows and acknowledges it as a work of art. Consequently, in order to escape from the usual choice between celebratory effusions and the reductive analysis which, failing to take account of the fact of belief in the work of art and of the social conditions which produce that belief, destroys the work of art as such, a rigorous science of art must, *pace* both the unbelievers and iconoclasts and also the believers, assert the possibility and necessity of understanding the work in its reality as a fetish; it has to take into account everything which helps to constitute the work as such, not least the discourses of direct or disguised celebration which are among the social conditions of production of the work of art *qua* object of belief. (317)

Aesthetic value, that which gets asserted in "celebratory effusions," has a paradoxical status in Bourdieu's analysis. It is an illusory mode of fetishization, but it also serves as the very condition for the existence of the artistic field and the works that constitute it. To reject or reduce it would be to "destroy the work of art as such," since the latter depends for its reality on a certain historically produced way of perceiving it. The aesthetic, then, is an illusion that is also a foundation for and constituent feature of an important social reality. Though it is possible, writes Guillory in his analysis of Bourdieu, "to translate the (false) philosophical problem of 'aesthetic value' into the sociological problem of 'cultural capital,'" there is, Guillory insists, a "remainder, which is nothing other than aesthetic experience" (*Cultural Capital* 327). When an individual appreciates a canonical work of art, in other words, he or she does not merely think, "This work makes me feel very high-status right now, and that is why I like it." Even simply to function as a persuasive source of prestige, the viewer's response must involve a fulfilling experience, one that justifies itself in noneconomic terms.[30]

Although an aesthetic education obviously does serve to reinforce the class position of those who receive it, the same accusation could be leveled at any form of knowledge currently offered by English departments, including the left critique of aesthetics. Indeed, a suspicion of so-called high art and the ideological role it performs has become a powerful form of cultural capital in its own right.[31] Moreover, English departments have always offered resources that allow individuals to feel more cultured than others. But they have—particularly those in public universities—also functioned during the past half century as a means of democratizing forms of cultural knowledge, including a capacity for aesthetic pleasure, disseminating them to a wider swath of the population than ever before. To be sure, such a task does presuppose a hierarchy according to which certain texts and experiences are regarded as intrinsically better than others. But almost all scholarly approaches to literature have in one way or another subscribed to this view. Perhaps, then, a better goal than pretending to eradicate hierarchies of taste in a futile effort to eschew aesthetic judgment would be, as Guillory has suggested, to delink these hierarchies as much as possible from class categories and the disastrous material and social consequences they entail for those positioned at the bottom (*Cultural Capital* 340). One of the more effective strategies for doing so is to work to disseminate the aesthetic experiences that English departments favor as widely as possible, thus making them less rare, less monopolized by a particular subclass, and therefore less dependent for their perceived value on the social status they confer.

A central premise of this book is that while aesthetic judgment may be difficult to justify, precariously grounded, and in many cases problematic, it is also inevitable, even if it frequently assumes a disguised form in contemporary scholarship.[32] If this premise is correct, then the best strategy for scholars, whether they seek to defend aesthetic judgment or expose its ideological function, is to make it as explicit as possible. Doing so will open up questions that have been mostly neglected in the past several decades—namely, what kind of work are the aesthetic criteria that prevail within the academy doing? What political projects are these criteria enabling or foreclosing, and what pleasures? What are they allowing us to appreciate in the texts we study, and what are they preventing us from appreciating?

* * *

In Chapters 1, 2, and 3, I examine the methodologies that have provided many of the governing assumptions and critical methods to academic literary study over the past eighty years—first New Criticism, then deconstruction, and finally New Historicism—in order to understand better how each methodology served to both repress and tacitly preserve the aesthetic, thus forcing it into the disreputable and subterranean position that it has occupied for several decades. New Criticism, I argue, unwittingly laid the groundwork for its own replacement; deconstruction provided a bridge between formalism and political criticism, smuggling the former into the latter; and New Historicism, which facilitated the assimilation into academic scholarship of the various left political causes of the late 1960s, including both Marxism and the identity-based movements, nevertheless maintained a formalist commitment in the way that it served to curate the historical archive. These chapters offer an analysis of theories and critical practices and an institutional history of English, but told from a new vantage point, with the aesthetic as the complicated, morally ambiguous, and embattled but stubbornly resilient protagonist.

It is important to note that in focusing on these three methodologies, this book does not seek to offer an exhaustive account of literary studies in the postwar era; rather, I am simply exposing a set of strategies through which the aesthetic has been able to survive, using several important examples, with the implication that analogous patterns are likely discoverable within other methodological approaches. New Criticism, deconstruction, and New Historicism actively competed with, borrowed from, and influenced multiple other schools of interpretation, including Chicago formalism, structuralism, psychoanalytic criticism, postcolonialism, feminist studies, African American studies, queer theory, and ethical criticism, to name just a few. I have chosen to emphasize the three that I have because each was a central formation whose dominant position enabled it to dictate strategies across the discipline, whose name often came to stand in for the diversity of critical practices that prevailed during the time of its ascendancy, and whose success, as I will argue, depended on its commitment, whether open or covert, to fostering certain privileged aesthetic experiences. That said, I recognize that giving priority to these necessitates many exclusions. Though no satisfying remedy to this problem has seemed possible, short of producing a book many times the length of this one, I have tried, at least, to acknowledge the vast critical terrain that adjoins or overlaps with the intellectual movements studied here, identifying in each chapter instances of confrontation and confluence between New Criticism, deconstruction, and New Historicism and their rivals in order to understand how their debates were shaped and their successes or failures influenced by their differing approaches to the aesthetic.

In Chapters 4 and 5, I focus on the academic reception of two of the most celebrated American novels of the postwar era, Vladimir Nabokov's *Lolita* and Toni Morrison's *Beloved*—canonical flashpoints in the opposition between aesthetics and politics. I offer these case studies in order to illuminate how the academy participated in the process of assessing the "greatness" of two literary works whose status, in the years immediately following their publication, was still up for grabs. Focusing on the criticism these novels inspired has given me the opportunity to consider New Criticism, deconstruction, and New Historicism as practiced not just by their vaunted founders but also by the relatively more obscure multitude of scholars whose work exemplifies these methodologies in their everyday operation. Significantly, *Lolita* seems perfectly designed to satisfy aesthetes and formalists, while

Beloved appears to do the same for political critics. Yet the readings of *Lolita* betray a profound anxiety about the aesthetic—a desire to yoke it to some more consequential ethical or political goal in order to justify its existence. Meanwhile, the confidence evinced by scholars of *Beloved* in its political significance nevertheless betrays an attachment to aesthetic pleasures—buried but still discernible within the descriptions they offer of the novel's political function.

Since literary studies appears now to be experiencing yet another moment of self-redefinition, with multiple camps vying to establish the next dominant critical fashion, in the conclusion to this book I consider what some of these approaches might mean for the future of aesthetic criticism. Will the repudiation of the hermeneutics of suspicion allow for a more explicit embrace of aesthetic pleasure or simply find a new way of disguising its presence? Does the method of distant reading championed by those working in the digital humanities represent the final eradication of the aesthetic in the name of purely scientific goals, or could it promote a different kind of aesthetic pleasure, perhaps one predicated on new criteria?

Before proceeding, I want to offer a few clarifications about my own critical method. In my approach to New Criticism, deconstruction, and New Historicism, I have adopted strategies from all three. As I consider the texts that exemplify each methodology, I offer close readings of particular passages in order to discover their ambiguities as a New Critic would, but also, like a deconstructionist, their moments of self-contradiction and aporia; and I situate all of them within their local ideological and institutional context, in keeping with New Historicism. Insofar as my goal is to demonstrate that these methodologies have more in common than is generally recognized, I have opted not to take sides, pragmatically using one or the other or combining them as necessary in order to produce the clearest understanding of how a particular interpretive approach works, but also, in keeping with the aesthetic imperatives that continue to shape academic scholarship, in order to produce as satisfying an interpretation as I can.

Finally, I should say that in identifying unacknowledged motives for academic criticism, I am not offering anything like a conspiracy theory. My argument does not try to identify the existence of a secret illicit agenda on the part of the scholars I examine; nor does it posit unconscious desires in a psychoanalytic sense. I am simply trying to reveal what I see as a *function* that literary scholarship performs, or, to put it another way, an experience it promises to academics and students. Admittedly, such a project comes with risks. Although in looking for traces of the aesthetic I may have occasionally overread the texts I examine, I would say that such a gesture may be necessary if only as a corrective to the equally strenuous overreadings that have heretofore strived, but failed, to eliminate any such traces within the task of describing literature's importance. At the very least, I hope that assessing the validity of my claims will give readers the chance to examine their own motives for engaging in the never fully justifiable task of criticism: what brought them to it and what keeps them at it.

1

The Intellectual Critics and the
Pleasures of Complexity

In a 1943 essay for *The American Scholar*, Darrel Abel warns his readers that certain "intellectual critics" are plotting to sabotage truth, knowledge, poetry, and beauty, at least in the forms that anyone might recognize. "For the intellectual critics, the world of experience is not a comprehensible logos, an orderly action of embodied principles, 'an army of unalterable law,' but a perceptible chaos, a mighty maze without a plan" (420). He elaborates,

> Their most tentative assertions are perplexed by the shadows of many doubts. This is what *knowledge* and *cognition* mean in the vocabulary of the intellectual critics: viewing facts in such ironic relations that their implications do not agreeably contribute their forces to a common center, but instead oppose and destroy each other.
>
> *Knowledge* is usually supposed to mean affirmation based on reality; the intellectual critics use it to mean negation—or, rather, abnegation, for their knowledge means renunciation of a once acceptable world of simple certainties. (421)

Abel is referring, of course, to that den of nihilistic renegades—John Crowe Ransom, Allen Tate, and Cleanth Brooks—otherwise known as the New Critics. One sign of the latter's extraordinary influence over

31

current critical practices in the academy is just how difficult it is to
see them as the iconoclastic figures that Abel describes.

If Abel's outrage now seems inexplicable, it is not only because the
New Critics have, in the years since he issued his screed, acquired the
reputation as stodgy defenders of traditional values. It is also because
the apparently subversive interpretive habits that Abel attributes to
them—a refusal of "simple certainties," a capacity to entertain mutually negating facts or ideas, an ironic awareness of the contingency of
all truth claims—have come to represent the very proof of rigor for a
good deal of scholarly work produced within English departments and
the humanities in general. Indeed, the New Critics were so successful
in reshaping the common sense of the discipline, naturalizing strategies of reading initially regarded as highly controversial, that the radical
character of their intervention has been all but erased. The purpose of
this chapter is to retell the story of the New Critics so as to recover a
sense of the difference they made, emphasizing both the break they
initiated with earlier modes of interpretation and generally unrecognized continuities between the methodology they championed and
those that supplanted it. At stake in this reevaluation is the capacity
to recognize contemporary approaches within literary studies to all
variety of subjects, including history, politics, and culture, as the expression of a particular *aesthetic*, one the New Critics successfully
popularized in the face of significant opposition.

According to the story endlessly told by its enemies, New Criticism
treats literary works as a source of private aesthetic satisfaction, insti-
tuting an approach that prevails within American English departments
as part of the postwar culture of consensus. Eventually, however, it falls
out of fashion as a consequence of the heroic efforts of politically
minded critics to establish the social relevance of literature. A central
argument of this book is that efforts—favored by the New Critics and
denounced by observers such as Abel—to cultivate heightened aesthetic experiences centered on paradox, irony, and ambiguity endure
within academic scholarship today, albeit in unrecognized forms. In
this chapter, I explore how the New Critics served to ensure this result. One of their central agendas was to legitimize a sensitivity to
poetic form by assigning it a function designed to satisfy the require-
ments of a university culture increasingly organized around scientific

criteria of intellectual rigor. But this meant presenting their own critical work as a mode of serious knowledge production and not merely a
source of aesthetic satisfaction. Aimed at both perpetuating and disguising aesthetic criticism by lending it an institutionally acceptable
form, the New Critics' efforts can be read as continuous with those of
more recent schools of interpretation that claim to repudiate the aesthetic altogether.[1]

Remaking English Studies

A central goal of the New Critics was to establish a secure disciplinary
setting that could insulate and nurture the careful reading of literature within an American social climate otherwise hostile to such ostensibly impractical pursuits. Thus they worked relentlessly during the
1930s and 1940s to turn the criticism of poetry, which had thus far been
the province of journalists and other unaffiliated writers, into a systematic discipline so as to qualify it for inclusion within the university curriculum. While they clearly sought to cultivate a sensitivity to
the aesthetic power of literature, they regularly expressed misgivings
about the category of the aesthetic—at times defining themselves
against the very critical tendencies that have most often been ascribed
to them.[2] Reflecting on his early years of teaching, for instance, Brooks
remarks: "[Robert Penn] Warren and I were not out to corrupt innocent
youth with heretical views. Our aims were limited, practical, and even
grubby. We had nothing highfalutin or esoteric in mind. We were not
a pair of young art-for-art's-sake aesthetes, just back from Oxford and
out of touch with American reality" ("New Criticism" 593). Insofar as
"aesthete" is, as Brooks slyly suggests, code for un-American, decadent,
homosexual corrupter of the young, it is a designation the New Critics
are compelled to disavow in order to avoid jeopardizing their academic
ambitions.[3] But aestheticism is a dangerous posture not only because
it suggests a transgression of social taboos. It was, by the time the New
Critics entered the scene, as René Wellek recalls, already a fashionable
trend in the United States, inspired by Walter Pater and Remy de Gourmont and exemplified by the socialite wit James G. Huneker. The
problem with this mode of criticism, according to Wellek, was that it
was merely a form of "appreciation," entirely "impressionistic" and

devoid of method or rigor ("New Criticism" 613). A stylized recording of subjective responses to art, aesthetic criticism did not involve making claims based on objective standards, and thus it failed in the eyes of the New Critics to meet the criteria necessary to be part of an academic discipline.

In order to establish their own brand of criticism as intellectually legitimate, the New Critics challenged the tendency, which they associated with the aesthetes, to regard reading poetry as fundamentally a passive or sensual activity. A poem's power, they argued, does not consist of an easily observable quality; detecting it requires careful analysis. Moreover, no particular subjects are inherently poetic. The inclusion of waterfalls, stars, flowers, and the like does not make a poem beautiful. "Things are not poetic per se," observes Brooks, and "nothing can be said to be intrinsically unpoetic. . . . At all events, the emphasis must be placed on the poet's *making*" (*Modern Poetry* 11–12). Subjects conventionally regarded as ugly can serve just as well; what matters is how the poet handles these subjects. A brilliant writer like John Donne can make a thing as irritating as a flea or prosaic as a compass a worthy source of contemplation. His poetry is worth reading not because of the intuitive appeal of its imagery but because of the intellectual work embedded in its composition—and the appreciation of this composition demands further intellectual work from readers. Moreover, if a poem's interest does not derive from the simple beauty of its subject matter, nor does it derive from the gracefulness or elegance of its formal structures. Far from celebrating beauty for its own sake, the New Critics maintain that poetic forms merit attention only insofar as they are integrally connected to the content that they serve to both express and embody.

Yet it is important to observe that while they reject fin de siècle aestheticism, the New Critics offer an account of reading poetry remarkably similar to Immanuel Kant's description of the aesthetic response to a beautiful object. According to Kant, this experience consists of the intuition of a unity, a purposiveness that holds together and lends coherence to the chaotic manifold of intuitions that the beautiful object yields (*Critique of Judgment* 20–32). Fond of quoting Samuel Taylor Coleridge's claim, partially inspired by his reading of Kant, that the poet's power "reveals itself in the balance or reconcilement of opposite or discordant qualities" (*Biographia Literaria* 166), the New Critics regard the poem as a higher-order synthesis of heterogeneous or contradictory impulses.[4] Moreover, the devices capable, in their view, of effecting this synthesis—namely, paradox, irony, and ambiguity—are valuable primarily as a basis for aesthetic apprecia-tion. These devices do not communicate a proposition or truth that can be detached from the poem; on the contrary, they support a struc-ture in which any given idea is balanced by an opposing idea, in which assertions and counterassertions harmoniously coexist.[5] The poem therefore dispenses no categorical moral precepts or spurs to action; indeed, one cannot take anything useful away from the poem at all. The ambiguous statement leads perpetually back to itself as it draws attention away from any of its potential meanings and onto its own power to sustain rival interpretations. Unable to separate an unequiv-ocal argument from the poem's network of elements, the reader is, the New Critics aver, obliged simply to concentrate on the text itself, to appreciate the strenuous experience of perceiving it for its own sake. In apprehending a beautiful object, as Kant put it, "We *linger* in our contemplation of the beautiful, because this contemplation rein-forces and reproduces itself" (*Critique of Judgment* 68).

Poetry, the New Critics insisted, is complex. This statement may seem so unexceptionable now as to be hardly worthy of mention, but it was not received as such when Brooks, Ransom, and their British counterpart William Empson first attempted to defend it.[6] To appreciate a work's complexity generally required a careful search for ambigui-ties or ironies that might qualify or trouble its seemingly straightfor-ward sense. However automatic such procedures have become, espe-cially in the college classroom, midcentury critics and scholars vehemently opposed them on a variety of grounds. The most irreverent of their enemies, Max Eastman, accused the New Critics of turning literature into an arid parlor game. "[They] find so little in real life to exercise their understandings upon," he argued, "that they develop a devout passion for conundrums, riddles, rebuses, acrostics, logographs, and games of solitaire and twenty questions" (*Literary Mind* 72). Douglas Bush, president of the *MLA*, complained, "In emphasizing complexity and ambiguity the critic has often been unwilling to ac-cept anything else. Starting from the premise that a poet cannot mean

merely what he appears to mean, the critic tries to see how many meanings, allusions, and overtones he can force into the text. . . . When
complexity and ambiguity have become a fetish, there seems to be no
check upon interpretive irresponsibility except the limits of the critic's
fancy" ("New Criticism" 18–19).

While Bush worried that the New Critics saw too much in certain
poems, many critics argued that they saw too little in others, by employing a method that eclipses the aesthetic power of simplicity.
"Attitudes can be relatively simple and valuable and they can be very
complex and of little value," observed Arthur Mizener. "[Richard]
Crashaw's 'In the Holy Nativity of our Lord God' is much more complex in attitude than Milton's 'On the Late Massacre in Piedmont,' but
the latter is probably the better poem" ("Desires" 468). Herbert J. Muller
cited further examples: "The *Twenty-Third Psalm*, the opening lines
of the Prologue to *The Canterbury Tales, The Song of Roland*, Celtic
romance, the poetry of Pushkin—I cannot believe such poetry of relatively simple sentiment is of as low an order as it appears by Mr. Brooks's
standard" ("Relative" 360–361). The Chicago formalists argued that the
New Critics paid too much attention to the multiple dictionary definitions of individual words in order to fabricate ambiguities and paid
too little attention to the generic conventions that served, in their view,
to limit the possible meanings of a given text.[7] Even the New Critical
disciple Murray Krieger admitted, "We are led to imply that the more
complexity the better, so that this theory easily lends itself to the sanc-
tioning of complexity for complexity's sake" (*New Apologists* 132).

But the New Critics did not merely fetishize complexity for its own
sake; they used it to further an array of institutional and practical
agendas. What the notion of complexity does, first and foremost, is to
open up the meaning and aesthetic power of literature to rational
analysis, discussion, and debate. The belief that a poem is the simple
expression of a recognizable emotion or that its value consists in the
simple beauty of its images is intuitively appealing; it would seem to
free the work of literature from the apparatus of explanation. The text's
significance under this assumption is immediately perceivable to anyone
who reads it. But this seemingly democratic premise curtails the possibility of aesthetic education. If the beauty of a poem is simple—an
elementary property like color, shape, or size—then it is difficult to

know how to help the individual who fails to perceive it. An invidious division would seem to follow between those who are aesthetically sensitive and those who are not.[8] If, by contrast, the poem's aesthetic power is not merely a quality that inheres in its individual images or in the simple emotion that it communicates but rather is dependent on the relationships between a diversity of heterogeneous elements, then grasping its power may require explanation. To help others appreciate a poem, one must at least identify all of its important elements and try to explain how they are related to each other. In asserting this seemingly basic but once controversial doctrine—that poetry is complex—the New Critics furnished scholars and critics with an abundance of expository and pedagogical tasks, giving academic English departments a raison d'être and guaranteeing their perseverance.[9]

By seeking to explain exactly what makes various literary works worth reading, the New Critics were offering something of particular use in the midcentury college classroom, as numerous observers have pointed out.[10] Before their intervention, English departments consisted primarily of historically or philologically oriented scholars and belle-tristic generalists. The former, according to Gerald Graff, devoted their lectures to tracing the etymologies of words, without ever explaining why a given literary work was valuable or worth reading in the first place; the latter delivered impassioned jeremiads about the degeneration of contemporary culture and evinced great enthusiasm for certain authors, but provided no systematic methods for reading and interpreting the works they assigned.[11] Neither was especially well equipped to meet the needs of the first-generation college students who were matriculating at an unprecedented rate in the early twentieth century and whose numbers would grow even more dramatically following the passage of the GI Bill after World War II.

The New Critics developed their methods as a better answer to the problem of how to teach literature to these relatively underprepared students. As Brooks explains, "When in the early 1930s Robert Penn Warren and I found ourselves teaching 'literary types and genres' at a large state university, we discovered that our students, many of whom had good minds, some imagination, and a good deal of lived experience, had very little knowledge of how to read a story or a play, and even less knowledge of how to read a poem" ("New Criticism" 592–593). Making sense of the forms of knowledge cultivated by traditional literary scholars demanded cultural capital, which these students lacked, and it presupposed exactly what New Critics wanted to disseminate: an ability to appreciate difficult literary works. The New Critical method of close reading, which consisted of reproducible procedures focused on short passages of literary works severed from any broader historical context, was, by contrast, relatively easy to teach even to those without any significant literary or historical education. Close reading, in other words, gave English departments a set of skills that they could actually impart to students, and it gave professional literary critics a steadily remunerative, institutionally secure career as university professors.[12]

The New Critics' largely successful efforts to institutionalize their practices of reading can be read as a deeply contradictory response to various social and economic developments in the early twentieth century. In general, the New Critics lamented what T. S. Eliot had called the "dissociation of sensibility" allegedly brought about by the decline of Christianity, the breakdown of traditional communities, and the rise of a secular scientific worldview ("Metaphysical Poets" 64). Whereas in earlier eras, according to the New Critics, a set of universally accepted, aesthetically and morally coherent doctrines, narratives, and symbols had provided a unity of purpose both to the community and to the individual, modernity had wrought only fragmentation. As Brooks put it, "Childhood—the childhood of a race or of a culture—gives a suggestion of what such unity can be, but development into maturity, and specialization, break up the harmony of faculties and leave intellect at war with emotion, the practical life with the life of sentiment, science with poetry" (Modern Poetry 90). Particularly horrifying to the New Critics, given their southern agrarian roots, was the rise of corporate capitalism, which led to the prioritization of productivity and efficiency over all other goals and promoted a division of labor that reduced the individual to a narrowly defined function within an inhospitable bureaucratic structure. Their complaints were, as Ransom wearily acknowledged, the generic ones typically provoked by modernity:

> It is a common opinion that business as a self-contained profession
> has created business men who are defective in their humanity; that

the conduct of business has made us callous to the personal relations
and to social justice; and that many of the occupations which business has devised are, in the absence of aesthetic standards, servile.

All these exclusions and specializations, and many more, have
been making modern life what it is. (*World's Body* 68)

But poetry, the New Critics argued, could provide an antidote, addressing the individual in his or her wholeness as a human being, appealing simultaneously to reason and feeling so as to harmonize the
two, offering an aesthetic experience that was valuable in itself and not
as a means to some other end.[13]

Yet, ironically, it was precisely the growth of corporate capitalism
that was providing the students whom Brooks and Ransom were hoping
to educate. In the early twentieth century, a new class of white-collar
professionals emerged to manage the large corporations that were assuming a central role in the U.S. economy.[14] A college degree, which
had not been required for entrepreneurial endeavors or positions in
small, family-run businesses, was becoming a necessary credential for
entrance into the corporate managerial sector.[15] While many among
the rapidly growing ranks of first-generation college students sought
vocational training in engineering, law, business, agriculture, medicine, and so forth, most colleges and universities continued to require
courses in the humanities, often as a prerequisite for more specialized
tracks. Relieved of the obligation to prepare students for a specific
career, but guaranteed enrollments by their status as a gateway to the
vocationally oriented disciplines, humanities departments were, as
Louis Menand has observed, able to remain dedicated to the disinterested pursuit of knowledge for its own sake while simultaneously presenting themselves as a nonspecific preparation for the diversity of
challenges entailed by adult life in the twentieth-century United States
(*Marketplace* 45–50).

Offering a method well suited to the new generations of college students, the New Critics benefited enormously from the growth of enrollments driven by the expansion of managerial capitalism, which
they otherwise found so distasteful.[16] Moreover, they sought not only
to educate but, as Stephen Schryer has convincingly argued, also to become white-collar professionals themselves, turning literary criticism

into a specialized, institutionally delimited field—exactly the kind of formation responsible for the social and psychic fragmentation that they incessantly lamented (*Fantasies of the New Class* 29–54). Somehow, they hoped, by insulating the careful study of literary forms from other endeavors and focusing on the text, severed from any broader historical context, they could inspire aesthetic experiences that would transcend the very divisions on which their critical work depended.

It is not surprising that the New Critics should desire for themselves the privileges that come with professional status. In addition to financial stability and the opportunity to influence young minds, full-time jobs in universities meant the freedom to produce work based on internally developed intellectual standards, without regard for the potentially compromising demands of the market. In seeking this freedom, of course, the New Critics were no different from the millions of other Americans who also hoped to enjoy the security of working within the white-collar professional sphere. An explicit goal of professional organizations, even as they promoted specialization and contributed to the division of labor, was to produce a measure of autonomy from the market, proscribing certain practices for failing to meet ethical or intellectual criteria even if they might be profitable, while protecting members from competition by limiting the number of people who could enter a given profession.[17] Large corporations, it is worth noting, offered additional shelter to many of their employees. The separation of ownership and management, first analyzed by Adolf Berle and Gardiner Means in their seminal study, *The Modern Corporation and Private Property*, was a crucial development. During the early twentieth century, companies came to depend for their capital on a large number of individual stockholders, while the task of running these companies fell to corps of salaried managers with no financial stake in the company, an arrangement that gave white collar employees significant power and autonomy, protecting them from the short-term vicissitudes of the market and allowing them to consider factors other than profits and losses in making decisions. Significantly, a central task for managers was to ensure that those working for them were happy and fulfilled.[18] The urge to construct or inhabit a sphere relatively insulated from economic calculations, within which other priorities, including the desire for community, for intrinsic goods, and for intellectual and emotional satisfaction, might thrive, was shared, in other words, by the New Critics and by those involved in building the professional managerial sector whose existence they deplored.

The dramatic expansion of managerial-corporate capitalism during the first half of the twentieth century facilitated, it would seem, the systematic delivery of a basic aesthetic education to millions of Americans in academic English departments across the country. To be clear, the structural dependency of these two developments is not necessarily a reason to regard the work of the New Critics with suspicion. It is worth considering, first of all, to what degree the protocols of close reading instituted by the New Critics actually served the needs of corporations. Considering the function of midcentury English departments in the United States, Richard Ohmann observes,

> Complex industrial firms needed a corps of managers who could size up needs, organize material, marshal evidence, solve problems, make and communicate decisions. Government and other bureaucracies had similar need for exposition and argument and allied skills. Writing was no longer mainly a private and public art, but a tool of production and management. (*English in America* 93)

While it is undeniable that English departments have played a central role in teaching students how to write since their inception, the careful analysis of poetry is certainly not the only or most efficient way to prepare students to "organize material, marshal evidence, solve problems, make and communicate decisions," as the now widespread focus on nonliterary texts in composition classes testifies. John Guillory offers a different hypothesis: by defining literature as difficult—that is, distinct from mass cultural forms—the New Critics offered cultural capital to college students seeking to become members of the educated middle and upper-middle classes (*Cultural Capital* 172–174). Undoubtedly, the knowledge, taste, and linguistic facility that literary training imparted were appealing in part because they functioned as markers of status. Insofar as they suggest a freedom from material necessities, impractical pursuits, according to Pierre Bourdieu, confer prestige on those able to engage in them (*Distinction* 54). The creation of a discipline organized around the close reading of poetry was, as we have seen, just one expression of an urge to construct elite corporate-professional spheres. But if the New Critics worked to foster certain privileged, even rarefied experiences, they also paradoxically sought to make these experiences as widely available as possible. Notwithstanding their staunch defense of a rigid hierarchy of taste, the New Critics attempted not to restrict but to expand access to cultural capital.

What makes the New Critics' success peculiarly unaccountable is the fact, only obliquely acknowledged by Guillory, that the cultural capital they were disseminating was, by the time they achieved hegemony in the university, already rapidly decreasing in value. Guillory attributes the decline of English studies' popularity to the rise of a "professional-managerial class which no longer requires the (primarily literary) cultural capital of the old bourgeoisie" (*Cultural Capital* xii). But the professional-managerial class to which he alludes was already in existence by the 1930s and a dominant force by the immediate postwar years, which raises the question of why a discipline set up to provide literary cultural capital during this period would be at all attractive or necessary. As Guillory notes, "With few exceptions, it is only those students who belong to the financially secure upper classes who do not feel compelled to acquire professional or technical knowledge as undergraduates. The professional-managerial class, on the other hand, many of whose members have only recently attained to middle and upper middle-class status, depends entirely on the acquisition of technical knowledge in order to maintain its status, or to become upwardly mobile" (46). Assuming this schema is correct, New Criticism might make sense as a reactionary vestige of an earlier age, aimed at teaching the dwindling percentage of old-money elites who had the luxury to devote themselves to literature. Indeed, Guillory surmises that close reading was originally designed precisely for this class of students (168). But Brooks's claim that his approach to criticism came out of his encounters with unlearned students at a "large state university" suggests otherwise. Though influenced by aristocratic ideals, New Criticism was from the outset a way of imparting a difficult mode of cultural knowledge to a new category of first-generation students who, ironically enough, did not really need it in order to advance socially or economically.

New Criticism is thus a conundrum: an imperfect fit for any of the social functions that might be attributed to it, related obviously to midcentury economic developments, but successful in ways that these developments cannot fully explain. Systems are never perfectly efficient, of course, and the success of New Criticism may simply have been one of the more fortuitous inefficiencies fostered by midcentury American capitalism. After all, what the New Critics helped to support was the democratization, on an unprecedented scale, of nonproductive forms of aesthetic sensitivity that had been mostly reserved up until that point for members of the leisure class. To see this result as both enabled by the growth of corporate capitalism and at the same time commendable for its own sake is to require a somewhat novel conceptualization of the aesthetic, one that rescues it from both implausible valorization and radical denunciation. Aesthetic experiences of the kind that the New Critics encourage, in other words, are in no way independent of ideological or economic pressures, and as such their value does not consist in their ability to resist the social structures in which they are embedded. But they are not therefore reducible to ideology. Rather, they are simply impure: haphazard, gratuitous moments of emotional and intellectual fulfillment within larger economic and political processes to which they somehow lend only minimal support, allowed to exist—generally in disguised or even muddled form—because of their obscure positioning within socially productive mechanisms, but valuable only for their own sake, fugitive way stations along a path leading somewhere else.

Critical Power

Arguably the most significant consequence of the intervention spearheaded by Ransom, Brooks, Warren, and Tate was a position of markedly greater institutional prestige and power for the critic. The premise that poetry is complex means that an appreciation of its power will depend as much on the critic as it does on the poem. The middleman becomes indispensable, his analysis no less necessary than the literary text for creating the aesthetic effect that he identifies, his language no less subtle and lyrical than the language he aims to illuminate.[19] And this new status will, as I will shortly argue, influence the willingness of subsequent generations of academics to make aesthetic discriminations in rather unexpected ways.

Brooks acknowledges that his approach requires critics to model their methods on the work of poetry itself in his famous essay "The Heresy of Paraphrase":

> We have precisely the same problem if we make our example *The Rape of the Lock*. Does the poet assert that Belinda is a goddess? Or does he say that she is a brainless chit? Whichever alternative we take, there are elaborate qualifications to be made. Moreover, if the simple propositions offered seem in their forthright simplicity to make too easy the victory of the poem over any possible statement of its meaning, then let the reader try to formulate a proposition that will say what the poem "says." As his proposition approaches adequacy, he will find, not only that it has increased greatly in length, but that it has begun to fill itself up with reservations and qualifications—and most significant of all—the formulator will find that he has himself begun to fall back upon metaphors of his own in his attempt to indicate what the poem "says." In sum, his proposition, as it approaches adequacy, ceases to be a proposition. (*Well-Wrought Urn* 197–198)

At first glance, Brooks appears to be describing a heretical path down which nobody should venture; he appears to be humbly asserting the "victory of the poem over any possible statement of its meaning." But if he is questioning the adequacy of the "simple proposition" that attempts to encapsulate the poem's meaning, Brooks's attitude toward the more elaborate kind of proposition, whose complexity is aimed at overcoming his own objections, is more ambiguous. This latter hypothetical proposition, steadily acquiring new "reservations and qualifications" in its struggle to exemplify the virtues of paraphrase, seems doomed to fail and prove Brooks's point. But it does not actually fail; instead, it becomes something wholly different. It ceases to be a proposition. With its metaphors and its complexities, it becomes akin to the poetic rhetoric whose meaning it is seeking to approximate, and thus it no longer functions as a demonstration of the impossibility of paraphrase. Instead of two equally inauspicious examples, Brooks is actually offering two different *options*. Since Brooks is outlawing paraphrase, what strategy remains available to the critic? A better alternative, clearly, is to produce criticism that employs the same rhetorical devices as poetry itself.[20]

To put it another way, propositions *about* a poem will necessarily fail to articulate its meaning, and thus a more effective strategy for the critic is to produce a kind of mimetic imitation of the poem that she is seeking to characterize. But given this urge to use poetry as a model for how criticism should operate, it is important to remember what exactly a strong poem, in Brooks's view, does. It does not depend for its aesthetic power on the object that it is describing; it does not merely reflect something worthy of notice outside itself. A poem *makes*. It takes an object that cannot on its own be inherently worthy of attention and makes it poetic. And this, I would suggest, is precisely what the New Critical close reading, through its quasi-poetic rhetoric and its relentless search for submerged metaphors, ironies, and ambiguities, does to the poem itself; the close reading makes the poem worthy of critical interest.

The New Critics demonstrate this capacity to project aesthetic value onto literary works no more clearly than in their repeated efforts to remake the literary canon. Though we typically identify the canon wars with the late twentieth century, they have been raging for over a century, and the New Critics launched two important campaigns. The first aimed at marginalizing neoclassical, romantic, and Victorian literature in favor of metaphysical and modernist poetry. The second, which demonstrated even more clearly the extraordinary authority they sought to invest in the act of criticism, aimed to readmit precisely those authors and literary modes they had previously banished—a task Brooks famously accomplished in *The Well-Wrought Urn*. The purpose of this exercise was to demonstrate that New Critical interpretive strategies were flexible enough to be of use in considering all variety of poetic works, and not just a cherry-picked set of preferred authors, but it simultaneously revealed the seemingly limitless power of the New Critical method to find what it was looking for in any given text. Considering, in *The Well-Wrought Urn*, poems that were, according to his own premises, banal, sentimental, and simple minded, Brooks used the interpretive methods that he and his fellow New Critics had perfected in order to *recast* those poems as aesthetically compelling.

Very early on, *The Well-Wrought Urn* introduces a difficulty familiar to anyone who has attempted to teach poetry to undergraduates. Considering William Wordsworth's sonnet "Composed upon Westminster

Bridge," Brooks remarks, "I believe that most readers will agree that it is one of Wordsworth's most successful poems; yet most students have the greatest difficulty in accounting for its goodness" (5). Brooks goes on to consider and then reject several possible reasons for admiring the poem:

> The attempt to account for it on the grounds of nobility of sentiment soon breaks down. On this level, the poem merely says: that the city in the morning light presents a picture which is majestic and touching to all but the most dull of soul; but the poem says very little more about the sight: the city is beautiful in the morning light and it is awfully still. The attempt to make a case for the poem in terms of the brilliance of its images also quickly breaks down: the student searches for graphic details in vain; there are next to no realistic touches. (5)

In fact, Brooks concludes, "the sonnet as a whole contains some very flat writing and some well-worn comparisons" (5). Significantly, Brooks is dramatizing the actual pedagogical dilemma that first mobilized New Criticism's most important innovations: how to help the untrained student appreciate poetry.[21] And yet his initial account of the poem's resistance to analysis is sufficiently persuasive so that when he asks, "Where, then, does the poem get its power?" he seems to be invoking a difficulty faced not just by the untrained reader but by anyone who seeks to understand Wordsworth's poetry, including the well-educated professor anxious to offer guidance to his ill-equipped students.

One might read this initial gambit as Brooks's effort to acknowledge and overcome his disdain for the romantics. But his curiously convincing posture of bewilderment might also be regarded as indicative of a more intractable dilemma—one that only an encounter with a literary form relatively resistant to New Critical methods could bring to the surface. How do we explain what makes a particular poem powerful? On what grounds? Why exactly does a certain sequence of words and images arouse cognitive satisfaction or pathos? Reading Brooks's book more than half a century later, it is important to recognize something that he himself takes pains to emphasize from the outset. However basic they may sound, these are *difficult* questions.[22]

And Brooks's admission may yield a clue as to why the New Critical enterprise eventually falls out of fashion. Among the reasons for the turn away from aesthetic considerations in favor of historical, political, and ideological concerns, in other words, might be the simple fact that aesthetic judgment—that is, explaining why a given text or passage produces satisfaction, pleasure, exhilaration, and the like—is peculiarly hard—and hard in a way that prompts reflexive resistance. What has followed New Criticism might be read, in other words, not as a rigorous repudiation but instead as an evasion of the difficult task of aesthetic judgment.

To be fair, Brooks sets the stage for this retreat almost as soon as he identifies the problem—as if to demonstrate how the very effort to raise this particular question entails its own refusal. Immediately after dramatizing the dilemma of the reader who cannot say why Wordsworth's poem is powerful, Brooks describes the analogous dilemma of the speaker within the poem, who cannot explain why he finds the city beautiful: "It is odd to the poet that the city should be able to 'wear the beauty of the morning' at all. Mount Snowden, Skiddaw, Mont Blanc—these wear it by natural right, but surely not grimy feverish London" (6). Ultimately, Brooks concludes, the speaker does make a convincing case for London's status as a beautiful place worthy of poetry. And in doing so, he achieves what the romantic poets saw as their primary goal. Brooks observes, "Coleridge was to state the purpose for him later, in terms which make even more evident Wordsworth's exploitation of the paradoxical: 'Mr. Wordsworth . . . was to propose to himself as his object, to give the charm of novelty to things of every day, and to excite a feeling analogous to the supernatural, by awakening the mind's attention from the lethargy of custom, and directing it to the loveliness and the wonders of the world before us. . . .' Wordsworth, in short, was consciously attempting to show his audience that the common was really uncommon, the prosaic was really poetic" (7). It is important to note here that the imaginative procedure performed by Wordsworth, the poet, on the prosaic, ugly city of London is exactly the same as the one performed by Brooks, the critic, on the dull, hackneyed language of the poem. The two gestures are perfectly analogous.

In both cases, the beauty does not seem to belong, strictly speaking, to the observed object, whether that object is London or the poem about

London, but depends for its existence on the transformative scrutiny of the observer. The function of the latter, according to the quotation from Coleridge, is "to *give* the charm of novelty to things of every day." What Wordsworth appreciates in London and what Brooks appreciates in "Composed upon Westminster Bridge," in other words, is not a simple property unproblematically possessed by the object and easily perceivable by the senses. What they both find compelling is precisely the tension between the object's prosaic or common and its poetic or uncommon aspects. Paradox emerges as the very source of the object's interest. Both the city and the poem merit admiration only to the extent that they are constituted by a contradiction and thereby come to be what they are not—uncommon because they are common, poetic because they are prosaic. But if these objects are dependent for their aesthetic power on what they are not, or on what they do not themselves possess, then one might also say that they require the kind of transfiguration that only an observer, a poet or a critic, might be capable of bestowing on them. The paradox of Wordsworth's poem, which is, in Brooks's view, responsible for its success, consists of a question about whether the object—London or the poem itself—is in fact beautiful, and whether that beauty is intrinsic to the object or projected onto it. The positive aesthetic judgment the poem elicits, in other words, is predicated on its capacity to call into question the very possibility of aesthetic judgment.

All throughout *The Well-Wrought Urn*, it is in fact difficult to decide whether the complexities that emerge are internal to the poems or the product of the interpretive work performed by the critic—and this confusion is magnified by Brooks's tendency to model his own rhetorical strategies on those of the poems he is reading. Just after stating that paradox is the defining feature of poetry, Brooks immediately admits, "I overstate the case, to be sure; it is possible that the title of this chapter ["The Language of Paradox"] is itself to be treated as merely a paradox" (3). Thus he attributes to his own language the feature that, in his view, distinguishes poetry from all other discourses. In other places, Brooks more directly imitates the postures of the poets he is considering. In suggesting, for instance, that the line, "Hairs less in sight, or any Hairs but these!" in Alexander Pope's "The Rape of the Lock" may reference Belinda's pubic hairs, Brooks employs the very strategy of witty indirection that he attributes to Pope, remarking coyly, "Belinda would doubtless have blushed to have her emphasis on 'any' interpreted literally and rudely" (94). In a later chapter, immediately after arguing that the speaker in Wordsworth's "Intimations of Immortality" makes a shift from "sight to sound" in order to participate more fully in a scene of mirth from which he feels excluded, Brooks turns his own attention away from the poem's imagery and onto its meter, making an analogous shift, remarking, "The metrical situation of the stanza, by the way, would seem to support the view that the strained effect is intentional" (135).

The relationship between the critic and poet, as Brooks imagines it, consists of both mimicry and rivalry. Over and over again, in discussing Pope, Wordsworth, Alfred Lord Tennyson, Thomas Grey, and Eliot, he identifies nuances, ambiguities, or paradoxes, of which, he suggests, the author is "unconscious"—thus endowing himself, rather than the poet, with a full understanding of the work's meaning (98, 103, 126). A fixation on the author's biography, motivations, and conscious intentions, the New Critics argue, impedes efforts to interpret the literary work—a position W. K. Wimsatt defends most famously in "The Intentional Fallacy." According to Brooks, "Wordsworth's great 'Intimations' ode has been for so long intimately connected with Wordsworth's own autobiography, and indeed, Wordsworth's poems in general have been so consistently interpreted as documents pertaining to that autobiography, that to consider one of his larger poems as an object in itself may actually seem impertinent. . . . It may actually surprise some readers to see how much the poem, strictly considered in its own right, manages to say, as well as precisely what it says" (*Well-Wrought Urn* 124–125). The phrase "how much" subtly registers what is at stake. He intends to read the poem as a repository of multiple meanings, and before his intervention the treatment of Wordsworth's autobiography as the key to understanding his poetry had served to foreclose this possibility by presuming that the meaning of the work could be equated with a single, discoverable intention in the mind of its author. The practical consequence of Brooks's argument here is obvious: the more ambiguities one can attribute to Wordsworth's poetry, the more it lends itself to multiple readings, the more work there is for critics to perform.

According to many of New Criticism's enemies, disregarding the author's intention eliminates poetry's vitality, its status as a human form of expression. "The effect of such devices," concludes Abel, "is to cut the poet off from his readers by making the poem a 'highly visible' construction which speaks for itself, not for its maker. Thus readers lose the exciting consciousness of being in communication almost immediate with hearts of alien circumstances, but hearts wonderfully the same as their own" ("Intellectual Criticism" 419). Mizener remarks, "When you take a poem out of that context provided by what Coleridge called the primary imagination, you take it out of familiar experience, and that is what Mr. Brooks's analyses tend to do" ("Desires" 465). Under the dispassionate scrutiny of the New Critics, argues John Paul Russo, the poem becomes "tranquilized" ("Tranquilized Poem"). Alfred Kazin goes further, suggesting, "On the obvious level this criticism resulted in a literature of decadence, a literature specializing in isolated ecstasies, a literature cut off from the main sources of life and floundering in the sick self-justifications of estheticism" (On Native Grounds 429–430). Echoing these concerns, Mark Spilka seems to recognize the agenda behind the apparent act of murder perpetrated by New Critical procedures: "If . . . we minimize the author's role, as we persistently minimize response, the penalties are these: the critic will become the author, he will supply his own intention (plus his own emotions) and rewrite the story" ("Necessary Stylist" 285). The New Critics, in other words, euthanize the poem only in order to revive it through their own interpretations, performing, as it were, a kind of critical CPR. The act of divesting the poem of the contextual and biographical material that had served for previous readers to constitute its meaning and interest, in other words, extends extraordinary power to the critic to fill in the void.

Poetry versus Science

While irony and ambiguity obviously served important institutional purposes for the New Critics, the latter generally attempted to defend these properties in a disinterested fashion, pointing to their intrinsic value. They enshrined the now widely accepted view that the capacity to entertain multiple contradictory attitudes or ideas within a single text is unequivocally good. But what, they asked themselves, makes it good? I. A. Richards had famously offered a psychological justification informed by Coleridge's theory of poetry. Most individuals' minds, Richards suggested in *Principles of Literary Criticism*, are poorly organized; their impulses interfere with each other, and thus the satisfaction of one urge prevents the satisfaction of others. "In order to keep any steadiness and clarity in his attitudes the ordinary man is under the necessity on most occasions of suppressing the greater part of the impulses which the situation might arouse. He is incapable of organizing them; therefore they have to be left out" (184). The poet, by contrast, is able to reconcile his opposed impulses through a finer, more comprehensive mental organization, and he transmits this mental organization to the reader through the work of literature. "The equilibrium of opposed impulses, which we suspect to be the ground-plan of the most valuable aesthetic responses, brings into play far more of our personality than is possible in experiences of a more defined emotion" (251). This equilibrium, which reading poetry fosters, allows readers to satisfy a greater number of their psychological impulses in any given moment, thus making them healthier, happier, more effective human beings.

While they accept Richards's argument that great poetry produces a reconciliation of opposed impulses, the New Critics worry that an emphasis on literature's therapeutic capacity will serve to diminish its perceived importance, especially compared to the increasingly central role that the scientific disciplines are assuming as a form of knowledge production within modern society. Considering Richards's justification of poetry, Ransom observes, "Poetry is needed as a complement to science because it is prepared to give to the emotions, and through them to the attitudes, their daily work-out; science intends to suppress them in order to map the objective world without distraction. Science is for use in our overt or gross practical enterprises, but poetry ministers directly to the delicate needs of the organism" (*New Criticism* 22). The problem with this division between science and poetry, according to Ransom, is that it is invidious; it places literature on the wrong side of a series of oppositions, between rationality and feeling, between work and play, and between seriousness and triviality. "The theory of poetry as agitation," writes Ransom, "gives us a muscular or gymnastic view of poetry: the poem resembles a gymnasium with plenty of dumb-bells and parallel bars for all the member interests; and what the member interests obtain from it is pure or abstract exercise, which does not pretend to have any relation to affairs." But "to be interested," Ransom continues, "is to try to obtain a cognition, to do what Mr. Richards wickedly denies to poetic experience and grants exclusively to science: to seek the truth" (*World's Body* 154–155).

The New Critics' fears about science's growing power will turn out to be painfully prophetic.[23] Although the sciences already represented a dominant paradigm by the 1930s, it was during World War II and after that they assumed a hegemonic role within the universities, reshaping the way administrators conceived of the value of academic research to the great disadvantage of English departments and other liberal arts disciplines. Buoyed by government grants aimed at mobilizing technological developments necessary to gain a military advantage first over the Axis powers during World War II and then over the Soviet Union during the Cold War, the academic sciences experienced dramatic growth in the 1940s and 1950s. As Jennifer Washburn observes, money granted to scientists under the Office of Naval Research and the National Institutes of Health increased from $3.4 million in 1946 to $50.5 million in 1951. Meanwhile, in response to *Sputnik*, support from the National Science Foundation increased from $16 million in 1956 to $480 million just a decade later. During the same period, as Washburn notes, private companies began investing large amounts to endow university laboratories, hoping to extract profits from developments in medicine, chemistry, and engineering—a trend that only accelerated through the final decades of the twentieth century (*University, Inc.* 59–71).

The New Critics' attitude toward science reveals the conflicting institutional imperatives that they were trying to answer. As we have seen, one of their central agendas was to create a community organized around aesthetic experiences whose noninstrumental, holistic character might provide a salutary alternative to an increasingly technocratic, profit-obsessed, socially fragmented American society—of which the scientific disciplines, in their view, represented a prime symptom.[24] And yet the New Critics were also aware that science was increasingly determining the criteria by which all of the academic disciplines were measured. Hence Ransom's admission, "Criticism must become more scientific, or precise and systematic" (*World's Body* 329). To establish literary criticism as a legitimate academic field, the New Critics knew that they needed to present it not just as a source of pleasure or psychological support but as a form of knowledge. In doing so, they constructed procedures for analyzing the text that bore a remarkable resemblance to the scientific method. In particular, Wimsatt's famous admonition against the "intentional" and the "affective" fallacies attempted to sequester the feelings and thoughts of both the author and the reader from the act of criticism, in order, like any rigorous scientific practice, to isolate the object under investigation from all extraneous phenomena and to reduce the influence of the investigator's own bias.[25] As Christopher Herbert has noted, "Only the limitless prestige of the scientific could possibly have rendered acceptable so drastic an insult to the natural interplay of readers' personalities and literary texts" ("Conundrum" 198).

The New Critics were also aware, however, that they could never compete with science on its own terms, since nobody was going to read Shakespeare to learn about anatomy or John Donne to learn about astronomy, and thus they presented literature as a fundamentally different kind of knowledge, one that was, at least by certain measures, preferable to science. Scientific accounts of reality, Ransom argues, are "its reduced, emasculated, and docile versions. Poetry intends to recover the denser and more refractory original world which we know loosely through our perceptions and memories. By this supposition it is a kind of knowledge which is radically or ontologically distinct" (*New Criticism* 281). Science approaches the individual objects that it seeks to describe as examples of broader taxonomic categories, thus translating concrete objects into abstract concepts, under which various particulars can be subsumed. "The work of science," concludes Ransom, "is a work of classification in terms of universals, not a work of imitation in terms of particulars" (*World's Body* 199). Literature, by contrast, according to the New Critics, seeks to represent objects in their wholeness and their particularity. Because of its texture, its rhythms, its incongruous connotations, its metaphors, and its capacity to yoke together contradictory qualities, poetry is able to offer an ontologically richer sense of reality: "The density or connotativeness of poetic language," argues Ransom, "reflects the world's density" (*New Criticism* 79). While Richards had argued that the capacity of poetry to balance contradictory impulses allows it to meet the emotional needs of readers, Ransom and his fellow New Critics contend that this capacity actually reflects the complex and contradictory nature of reality.

Ransom rejected the attribution of a therapeutic function to poetry because he believed that poetry's superiority to science as a form of knowledge depended on its resistance to being instrumentalized: "Art exists for knowledge, but nature is an object both to knowledge and to use; the latter disposition of nature includes that knowledge of it which is peculiarly scientific, and sometimes it is so imperious as to pre-empt all possibility of the former" (*World's Body* 197). The defining purpose of science, in other words, is to make use of nature, and this sometimes precludes its capacity to know or understand nature. Literature, by contrast, suffers from no such conflict of interest. Its knowledge is untainted by any concern for the purposes it can make nature serve. Indeed, no search for the immediate or long-term consequences that literature might yield is necessary; its value is not displaced onto a scene of action external to its own being; literature, as a form of pure knowledge, is its own justification.

While such an impractical conception might seem like a futile attempt to push back against the utilitarian tides that had overtaken the United States, the New Critics were actually in part motivated by a pragmatic agenda. As we have seen, they were invoking an ideal central to the mission of most liberal arts colleges: the disinterested pursuit of knowledge for its own sake—one to which the sciences also subscribed, at least in theory. "We may define a chemical," Ransom suggests, "as something which can effect a particular cure, but that is not its meaning to the chemist" (343). While Ransom generally positions literature in direct opposition to science, in certain moments he suggests that literature merely pursues a purer version of what science, in its true essence, also pursues—as if literature were somehow science's better half—better at performing what science would also seek to perform if it could only avoid getting ensnared in utilitarian calculations. Uselessness, then, is a mark of poetry's peculiar power as a form of knowledge and a means of justifying its need for institutional protection inside the academy.

But how exactly can one verify the claim that poetry offers a form of knowledge equal to or greater than that produced by science? The New Critics respond to this challenge by rejecting scientific truth criteria as a means of judging the knowledge that poetry offers. Science searches for tendencies that recur in various circumstances; it aims to abstract from a particular situation rules or principles for predicting the behavior of larger categories of phenomena, and the scientific community deems propositions true only after the tendencies it identifies are shown to be repeatable in multiple experiments. Poetry, by contrast, celebrates "incessant particularity" (*New Criticism* 25), focusing on elements that are specific to a given situation or experience, thus refusing the broad patterns that science equates with truth. Poetry, in other words, represents phenomena that are by definition nonrepeatable and thereby produces a kind of knowledge resistant to verification via scientific methods.

Since the two operate according to entirely different standards and represent ontologically distinct phenomena, science and poetry can never meet on the same playing field to decide which offers a better account of the world. If we read John Keats's "Ode on a Grecian Urn" correctly, avers Brooks, "we shall not feel that the generalization"— that is, the final sentence of the poem—"is meant to march out of its context to compete with the scientific and philosophical generalizations which dominate our world" (*Well-Wrought Urn* 165).[26] By what criteria, then, can the truth of a poem be measured? Brooks places extreme limits on what the reader is allowed to consider in making such judgments: "The poem is *not* to be conceived of as a statement, 'clear,' 'beautiful,' or 'eloquent,' of some truth imposed upon the poem from without" (265). Here Brooks is refusing to treat the poem's meaning as a paraphrasable content separable from the poem itself. The truth that a poem offers must be dependent on the formal devices, the metaphors, the images, and the ironies, through which it is conveyed.[27] But in denying that a poem articulates a "truth imposed upon the poem from without," Brooks seems to be imagining a form of truth entirely internal to the poem, one that inheres within its texture but nowhere else, suggesting, in other words, that the poem does not actually represent an external state of affairs.[28] Tate goes further, arguing, "[The poem] is not knowledge 'about' something else; the poem is the fullness of that knowledge. We know the particular poem, not what it says that we can restate. In a manner of speaking, the poem is its own knower, neither poet nor reader knowing anything that the poem says apart from the words of the poem" (*Reason in Madness* 135).

Ransom does try to mitigate the solitary confinement to which New Critical definitions sentence poetry, arguing that it describes a world "which we know loosely through our perceptions and memories" (*New Criticism* 281). But even this statement assumes a vague sense of reality before the intervention of poetry, thus assigning to the latter considerable power to construct the knowledge that it purports to "recover." Poetry, it would seem, actually teaches us how to perceive and understand reality. The poems the New Critics prefer—metaphysical and modernist—insist that the world is dense, contradictory, and protean, and they thus dictate the very ontological assumptions according to which readers are expected to judge the truthfulness of literature, providing a justification for the use of ambiguity, irony, and paradox. Refusing to have its content "imposed from without," good poetry, according to the New Critics, substantiates its own authority.[29] The poem simulates reality, as Brooks suggests, "by *being* an experience rather than any mere statement about experience" (*Well-Wrought Urn* 213).

While the New Critics often assert the superiority of poetic knowledge to scientific knowledge, they never seek to invalidate particular scientific theories. Their rhetoric is best read as a strategic response to an inescapable institutional reality. Given the advantages enjoyed by science, the New Critics are content merely to carve out a space for the study of poetry alongside it—in part by borrowing some of its rigor for their own discipline. Aware of their own precarious position, they pragmatically reject positivistic assumptions that require an either-or decision between poetry and science, refusing the premise that reality lends itself to a single description, the truth of which entails the negation of other descriptions.[30] Their philosophical premises allow them to avoid any direct confrontation with science and to reject any empirical test through which their views about the deep ontological truth of poetry might be examined or discredited. In lieu of proof, the New

Critics offer an intense aesthetic experience, a defining feature of which is a conviction in its own validity as a way of understanding the world.

The close reading of poetry, when done right, will necessarily inspire a commitment to its methods by means of the exhilarating encounter with the dense, dark, complex reality of the world that it appears to produce. It is worth noting that what the New Critics present here as knowledge of the world's fundamental nature is of course a historically conditioned point of view—a specifically modernist lens shaped in part by the dramatic upheavals and social changes of the first three decades of the twentieth century, one that privileges fragmentation, uncertainty, and flux. Moreover, a belief in the poem's truth depends entirely on its aesthetic force—something felt with particular intensity in the moment of reading. And yet, as a perception entirely bound up with the temporally delimited experience of reading poetry, this form of knowledge in no way precludes assent to other, more "docile" accounts of the world, including scientific descriptions, in other moments. Indeed, the only practical consequence entailed by the knowledge that poetry offers may be a desire to read more poetry. Whether the world truly is paradoxical, dense, and multivalent or whether it is simply intellectually satisfying to read poems that present it in this way is something the New Critics are never able to determine definitively.

Aesthetic Commitments

Both Richards and the New Critics simultaneously entertain and resist the idea that the experience of ambiguity produced by poetry is valuable in itself, independent of any longer-term function it might perform. Richards predicates the value of this experience on the intrinsic pleasure it affords; but he also seeks to augment its perceived significance by underlining its power to strengthen overall psychological health. The New Critics suggest that the experience of good poetry is about nothing other than itself, but they also cast this experience as a serious form of knowledge capable of rivaling science. Moreover, they present this knowledge as a necessary bulwark against an increasingly utilitarian and profit-obsessed social landscape. In assigning these functions to poetry, the New Critics work hard to distinguish the forms of close reading they prescribe from aesthetic appreciation, from the urge to enjoy literature merely for its own sake, and in this regard, as I have been arguing, their efforts can be read as continuous with, rather than opposed to, the methodological camps that come after them. Though the standard narrative aligns New Critics with aestheticism and later scholars with its repudiation, almost all of the major schools of interpretation of the past century, including New Criticism, have been characterized by a similar ambivalence. The specter of the merely aesthetic, in other words, has functioned for academic literary scholarship as a persistent scandalous possibility, one that continually resurfaces and must be continually disavowed.

The forms of thought favored by the New Critics necessitate a capacity to concentrate single-mindedly on the formal properties of certain canonical poems. While later schools of political criticism have purportedly rejected formalist analysis and the traditional canon, they have never successfully sidelined the experience of irony, ambiguity, and paradox that the New Critics sought to encourage. Indeed, as we will see, it is because these politically oriented methodologies have preserved this experience that they have been able to gain traction within the academy. Moreover, the technique that has allowed them to accomplish this—to reject attention to a privileged set of literary works while still producing the kinds of rich aesthetic experiences that those literary works were once viewed as exclusively equipped to generate—is the ever-versatile method of close reading pioneered by the New Critics.

Alarmed by the rise of deconstruction, Brooks responds in 1979 to an essay by J. H. Miller as follows: "Though I of all people have to feel abashed at quibbling over other people's discoveries of paradoxes, I confess that I find absurd some that tumble forth in Miller's exegesis" ("New Criticism" 603). He goes on to argue, "Granted an agile mind and a rich stock of examples from the world's literature, granted modern theories about the doubleness of the human mind and the ways in which secret meanings can underlie surface meanings (and one can sometimes 'mean' one thing by uttering its opposite), it is possible to construct readings that make a kind of glittering sense. The real trouble is that the game is almost too easy to play" (603). The claim that Miller's analysis makes "a kind of glittering sense" echoes a passage from the classic textbook *Understanding Poetry*, which Brooks and Warren first published in 1938. Seeking to refute the misgivings inspired by the work of one of their cherished metaphysical poets, Andrew Marvell, Brooks and Warren observe, "As we have said, this poem is built on paradox. Is this paradox merely a piece of glittering rhetoric but finally specious? Or does it embody a truth?" (*Understanding Poetry* 225). While Brooks seems to equate "glitter" with shallow sophistry, his use of the term first to describe Marvell's language play and then forty years later to describe the rhetorical tricks of the deconstructionists suggests that a transfer of powers has occurred. If it was once the prerogative of poetry to "glitter," it has become, by the time the New Critics have finished reshaping the discipline, one of the central functions of literary criticism. Moreover, Brooks's reluctance to "[quibble] over other people's discoveries of paradoxes" suggests an awareness that the excesses of deconstruction represent a logical consequence of New Critical methods.[31]

What the New Critics accomplished, both through the theoretical claims they made about literature and through the practical method of close reading that they disseminated, was to empower several generations of critics, including many of the American deconstructionists, to subject practically any text they encounter to a rigorous analysis so as to bring out its hidden ambiguities and paradoxes and thus make it worthy of interest. This capacity, which the New Critics hoped would allow readers to recognize the virtues of a limited set of great works, has actually served to endanger the very possibility of aesthetic discrimination. The robust, highly intellectual strategies of analysis that they developed, designed in part to establish criticism as a rigorous discipline akin to the sciences, make it difficult to determine, as we have seen, whether the aesthetic satisfaction that is produced results from the literary work or from the act of interpretation. But aesthetic judgment also becomes unnecessary. If critics can, through the power of their own analysis, make a diverse range of texts the springboard for the desired aesthetic response, then there is no need to distinguish between good and bad works of literature. Canon construction, in other words, becomes a needless endeavor.

As I have suggested in this chapter, the New Critics set the precedent for challenges to the canon by quickly opening their own list of favored poets to admit the romantic and Victorian writers whom they had excluded. In doing so, they demonstrated how it might be possible to examine works viewed initially as unpromising and banal, including the poetry of Grey, Wordsworth, and Tennyson, so as to discover, as Brooks puts it, "the secret meanings" that "underlie surface meanings" and thus recast those works as complex and intellectually stimulating. Later scholars who argue that other purportedly undervalued writers outside the canon deserve consideration are only following the example set by the New Critics. The point here is not that such previously marginalized authors are unworthy of our attention; the point is that the New Critics unwittingly devised a set of aesthetic criteria and a mode of interpretation that would allow for a limitless expansion of the literary canon, indeed a limitless expansion of the scope of our critical interest.[32]

The focus of literary scholarship has of course come to extend beyond the boundaries not only of the traditional canon but of "literature" altogether, as critics now subject a seemingly endless variety of historical documents within the archive, including advertisements, legal briefs, journal entries, letters, and the like, to the close reading methods that the New Critics instituted.[33] And in recent years posthumanist and new materialist scholars have begun to ascribe unknown depths to mere objects, to things that were not even designed to be appreciated by humans.[34] The ability to find aesthetically rewarding paradoxes and ambiguities in such seemingly unpromising materials has allowed several generations of scholars to reject any firm distinction between literature and other texts, while bracketing questions about aesthetics in favor of historical or ideological questions. But if the drift of academic work has featured a repudiation of specifically literary values, it has not entailed a rejection of New Critical aesthetic priorities. Quite the contrary: as I will seek to demonstrate in Chapters 2 and 3, literary scholars have continued to seek out the experience of ambiguity, irony, and paradox; they have simply made a wider range of subjects, materials, texts, and intellectual problems serve as the basis for that experience. Thus they have been able to foster the satisfying cognitive responses that the New Critics treated as the exclusive province of poetry, while turning their attention to political, historical, and ethical problems—thereby endowing their work with a political significance that an explicit focus on aesthetic questions would have precluded.

When contemporary literary scholars attempt to justify their decision to focus on a particular text, they almost always do so now in terms of its relevance to broader political or historical issues, and rarely on the basis of its aesthetic merit. But such ideologically oriented rationales frequently mask unacknowledged aesthetic preferences. If these preferences remain undeclared yet still faintly decipherable, this demonstrates, strangely enough, the indirect influence of the New Critical method. Recall Brooks's dictum in "The Heresy of Paraphrase" that statements *about* a poem's meaning will never do it justice and thus any attempt to approximate the poem's meaning will ultimately end up imitating the very techniques that it is seeking to describe. A lasting legacy of the New Critics' emphasis on the complexity of literary language is the uneasiness that invariably attends efforts to summarize the meaning of a particular work, along with the sense that this meaning must somehow be *evoked* rather than simply stated. This uneasiness has prompted some heroic efforts on the part of scholars to produce a mode of rhetoric no less complex and textured than the language of the literary texts that they are examining. Thus, one result of the attack on paraphrase is that post–New Critical literary scholarship tends to reveal its aesthetic commitments less in the statements it makes about literature than in the rhetorical techniques that it deliberately or unwittingly imitates. Even if contemporary scholarship does not seem to be *about* aesthetic questions, in other words, it inevitably reveals preferences for certain kinds of formal strategies by means of the devices that it has borrowed from the literary works to which it is, either directly or obliquely, responding.

Ironically, the very tendency that has appeared to undermine the possibility of aesthetic judgment among contemporary academics also signals an implicit preference for a particular poetic mode. The critical practice first introduced to the academy by the New Critics of turning any text, however ostensibly banal, into a repository of intellectually rewarding complexities makes objective judgments about a given text's intrinsic merits almost impossible. But this practice simultaneously betrays attachment to a very specific aesthetic criterion, one that assigns great value to those forms of writing, whether critical or literary, capable of performing the same kind of intellectual operation—that is, recasting an unpromising object so as to make it strange and thus worthy of interest. The inspiration for the New Critics' brilliant analytical exercises was the heady formal conceits of the metaphysical poets. And one might say that the interpretive strategies of many contemporary academics, whatever the explicit focus of their attention, are both modeled on and reveal an aesthetic preference for metaphysical poetics, for rhetoric that can, through elaborate metaphors and ironies, transfigure our perception of the dull, everyday world, turning whatever object happens to be at hand—whether a flea, an ugly city, a bad poem, or a random archival fragment—into a source of aesthetic satisfaction.

To be sure, there are many ways to refigure the world, and to say merely that contemporary literary scholarship values this rhetorical effect is not to pinpoint with any precision the particular aesthetic commitments at work in shaping the discipline. Indeed, a variety of contradictory aesthetic values continue to exert a subtle influence over scholarship, and arguably the best strategy for identifying these specific values is to attend to the particular forms and styles through which academics articulate their arguments, rather than the explicit positions they take. Moreover, despite their heterogeneity, the various formalist investments and implicit aesthetic criteria that underwrite contemporary literary scholarship are all more or less unified by a shared, reflexive attachment to complexity. Though this attachment may now seem like simply an essential, transhistorical feature of any mode of serious intellectual thought, it is only one option among many; it is, in other words, a culturally specific aesthetic. At other moments, as the enemies of New Criticism remind us, critics have admired literary works on the basis of their simplicity, clarity, and conviction rather than their complexity, ambiguity, and irony, and one could easily identify other alternatives as well. Ironically, the New Critics' victory in that debate was so total, at least within the academy, that their understanding of intellectual sophistication no longer seems debatable, and this has allowed it to persist as an uncontestable, well-nigh invisible aesthetic motive, shaping a variety of scholarly projects that seem far removed from aesthetic or formal concerns.

Among the many reasons that New Criticism still functions today mainly as the bad father of modern academic criticism, invoked only to be disowned, is the egregious gender politics of its practitioners. Almost all of the New Critics are male, as are the authors they celebrate, and they never hesitate to laud what they see as the masculine and denigrate what they see as the feminine qualities in the literary works they study. The question Brooks poses in "The Heresy of Paraphrase" is not auspicious: "Does the poet assert that Belinda is a goddess? Or does he say that she is a brainless chit?" (*Well-Wrought Urn* 197). Whether Pope or Brooks deserves the blame, neither of the two possibilities allows this character to escape traditional stereotypes of femininity. Brooks does, however, recognize the problem with the options he has presented, stating a sentence later, "Whichever alternative we take, there are elaborate qualifications to be made" (197). And in this moment, notwithstanding his failure to recognize the limitations of his own patriarchal values, Brooks unwittingly maps out a particular path for feminist literary criticism, one that happens to be aligned with New Critical aesthetics. For those scholars interested in portrayals of women that challenge gender stereotypes, neither of the first two options Brooks proposes is viable, and thus the only other strategy is to embrace the need for "elaborate qualifications," the need, in other words, for irony and ambiguity. What Brooks offers here is only a hint, one whose aim is simply to define a particular kind of critical intelligence, but his definition has proved useful in ways he never could have foreseen. Despite their hostility to formalism, the next generation of critics will work hard to align New Critical aesthetic values, including ambiguity, irony, and undecidability, with particular political causes—left, feminist, antiracist, and queer. The deconstructionists are central to this effort, and the work they perform to bridge traditional formalist values and radical political goals is the subject of Chapter 2.

2

Appetite for Deconstruction

A$_T$ $_{THE}$ 1968 Modern Language Association Conference, Louis Kampf was arrested for refusing to take down a poster he had taped to the wall of the Americana Inn declaring, "The Tygers of Wrath are Wiser than the Horses of Instruction" (Kampf and Lauter, introduction 36). He and fellow scholar-activists Paul Lauter, Richard Ohmann, Florence Howe, Frederick C. Crews, and Noam Chomsky were in the process of "stirring things up," and the arrest was an auspicious beginning (34). The next day, five hundred people attended Chomsky's teach-in on the Vietnam War. It precipitated a march to the lobby of the Americana, where demonstrators held an impromptu debate with MLA representatives and demanded that the charges against Kampf and three other protesters be dropped. Meanwhile, the members of the Tactics Committee, convened to persuade the MLA to adopt a series of resolutions opposing the Vietnam War and racially discriminatory policies in the United States, rapidly swelled as disaffected academics from around the country found their way to marathon sessions held in an upstairs room at the City Squire Motel. The committee ultimately succeeded in passing all but one of the resolutions it sponsored and in electing Kampf to the position of second vice president of the MLA—a radical addition to a still conservative governing body.[1]

A central aim of the protesters was to challenge the MLA's efforts to sequester literary studies from contemporary political struggles. The teaching of literature, they held, necessarily performed a political function, whether or not its practitioners acknowledged this fact. Within the contemporary social order, it generally served to perpetuate class inequalities by disseminating knowledge to the already privileged and to reinforce racial and gender hierarchies by upholding a white male literary canon.[2] Although Kampf and Lauter admitted in *The Politics of Literature*, the collection inspired by the protests, that there were no "simple, direct, one-to-one relationships between literature and action," they nevertheless sought to promote approaches to scholarship and pedagogy that could help create "a humane and socialist society" (introduction 50–51).

Among the targets of attack for the growing ranks of politically minded literary scholars of the late 1960s were the New Critics, who, according to Ohmann, "see art as freeing man *from* politics by putting him above his circumstances, giving him inner control, affording a means of salvation, placing him beyond culture" ("Teaching and Studying Literature" 142). Indeed, the MLA protest can be seen now as an early campaign in the decades-long struggle to discredit the formalist approach to literature championed by the New Critics in favor of the explicitly political modes of scholarship that now dominate the discipline. Several factors initially favored the New Critics in this conflict, among them the great number of tenured professors prepared to defend the principles that had served as the basis of their training, as well as the unmatched efficacy of close reading as a pedagogical tool in the classroom. But another development also served to buttress formalist interpretation, extending its life well into the 1970s and early 1980s: the emergence of deconstruction.[3] Though greeted with horror by the New Critics, the Yale deconstructionists, including Paul de Man, Geoffrey Hartman, J. H. Miller, and Barbara Johnson, were no less committed than their forebears to abstracting canonical works from specific historical contexts, to scrutinizing the rhetorical and stylistic devices of individual passages, and to finding hidden ambiguities and paradoxes within the text.[4]

The question this chapter takes up is how exactly the deconstructionists were able to recast ahistorical, formalist interpretation so as to make it attractive to scholars and students increasingly interested in connecting literature to political problems. How, in other words, did deconstruction compete with other schools of criticism more directly involved in the political struggles of the day—against U.S. imperialism, capitalism, racism, and sexism—so as to maintain the viability of formalist analysis while also developing strategies of interpretation that would eventually be adopted within political criticism? My aim is to shed new light not only on the functions performed by deconstruction during its heyday but also on a variety of scholarly assumptions and practices that continue to shape the discipline. A significant consequence of the deconstructionists' efforts, I argue, has been the persistence of unacknowledged aesthetic values even within the politically oriented methodologies that came after midcentury formalism.

Radical Continuity

It is not hard to see why left intellectuals of the late 1960s were initially seduced by deconstruction. Its roots in the French Marxist movement Tel Quel lent it credibility as a subversive mode of thought.[5] Moreover, its leading practitioners, Jacques Derrida and de Man, appeared intent on destabilizing not just particular power structures but the very foundations of Western thought, modern rationalism, and language as a means of understanding the world—an ambition perfectly pitched to satisfy the desire for systematic revolution shared by many within the New Left.[6] But perhaps more important than the specific claims forwarded by the deconstructionists was the style in which their claims were couched. Their disregard for the conventions governing academic debate, their tendency to leap over steps in their arguments without explanation or apology, their habit of overreading seemingly insignificant textual details and then using their readings as the basis for extravagant and sweeping pronouncements, their avant-garde defiance of clarity, their irreverent, pugilistic tone—all of these rhetorical gambits announced their movement as an anarchic revolt against the prevailing order. At the same time, their extraordinary erudition and microscopically close attention to canonical texts, alongside their passionate if perverse commitment to the very intellectual traditions they seemed to be questioning, allowed them to present deconstruction as a legitimate scholarly enterprise, one that academics could embrace without renouncing the protocols on which their professional advancement depended.[7]

Notwithstanding its iconoclastic rhetoric, deconstruction was well equipped to meet the institutional imperatives that academic literary studies faced in the late 1960s and 1970s.[8] A brief review of the state of the discipline during the period will help to illuminate why deconstruction was such a good fit for English departments. The years just after World War II had been a time of unprecedented growth for the humanities, with significant increases in enrollments spurred by the GI Bill and growing numbers of employers who treated the BA as a prerequisite for entry into white-collar professions.[9] As we saw in Chapter 1, the New Critics had reshaped English departments to meet the needs of first-generation students, the majority of whom came to college without significant prior knowledge of literature or history. During the 1960s, English found itself in an institutionally secure position, offering composition courses to a majority of matriculating students and advanced literature courses to a smaller, but still significant, percentage of undergraduates.[10] By the end of the decade, however, the very growth of enrollments was beginning to produce a serious problem. PhD programs had been expanding in order to meet the growing demand for teachers, but funding from both university administrations and the state had not kept pace.[11] Thus many departments found themselves dealing with severe budget constraints and unable to hire as many full-time professors as they needed to staff their courses. This challenge produced the conditions that have continued to vex English departments up to the present moment: a massive overproduction of PhDs, an absurdly competitive job market, and a sizable pool of disgruntled, poorly paid adjuncts.[12]

As competition for jobs intensified at the beginning of the 1970s, English departments needed ways to distinguish between strong and weak candidates, and thus publications became increasingly significant as a criterion. In previous decades, it had been possible to get a job and tenure on the basis of teaching ability, service, or connections, but this state of affairs was rapidly coming to an end. According to a 2006 MLA Task Force report, during the 1970s English departments sought to disrupt the influence of "old boys' networks," limit the power of chairs, and minimize factional biases in their decisions on hiring and promotion, and thus they frequently deferred to quantity of publications as a purportedly objective standard (*MLA Task Force* 30–32). During the same period, the struggle between universities for prestige escalated, with the ever more powerful sciences vying for lucrative government contracts and aggressively touting the socially beneficial advances in knowledge they were producing. Though humanities professors had nothing commensurate to advertise, the prestige market had come to hold sway over all areas of academic life, and thus they too felt pressure to underscore their scholarly contributions.[13] As the market tightened further, job candidates were increasingly expected to have a record of significant scholarship before they were hired for their first job, and at many universities the monograph became a prerequisite for tenure. A Carnegie study reported that while only 21 percent of faculty strongly agreed that it was difficult to get tenure without publications in 1969, that number had doubled by 1989 (Boyer, *Scholarship Reconsidered* 11).

In the face of such pressures, deconstruction proved to be an extremely effective engine of scholarly activity, enabling a proliferation of articles and books.[14] One of its central interventions, after all, was to challenge the assumption that the primary task of interpretation is to discover the author's intention so as to produce a single, definitive reading of a text, or to arrive at what Roland Barthes refers to as an "ultimate meaning"—a result that would obviate the need for further interpretation (*Image, Music, Text* 147). The deconstructive tendency to treat literary works instead as divided, contradictory, polyphonic, endlessly enigmatic, and capable of yielding multiple contradictory readings served to rationalize a dramatic increase in scholarly essays, as Michael Fischer has observed (*Does Deconstruction?* 104–106). By the lights of deconstruction, any given text becomes a perpetually renewable resource for those needing to produce new scholarship. To be sure, the New Critics were already moving in this direction, as de Man observed when he applauded William Empson for demonstrating poetry's capacity to accommodate an "infinite plurality of significations" (*Blindness and Insight* 236). But far more than the New Critics, the deconstructionists sought to maximize this statistical potential, aggressively searching for bizarre angles on classical works, justifying

the seemingly endless proliferation of criticism by treating the multitude of idiosyncratic and contradictory interpretations as proof of a
given text's inexhaustible richness. Deconstruction served, in other
words, to increase the power that the New Critics had conferred on
scholars to translate any textual detail into a source of interest and
aesthetic satisfaction.[15]

Moreover, in numerous ways, the discourse of deconstruction
served a legitimizing function for the practice of literary criticism. John
Guillory has discussed how the emphasis on technicity, on rhetoric as
mobilized by particular interests, aligned deconstruction with the
values of the corporate-bureaucratic administrations that were coming
to dominate the university (*Cultural Capital* 257). But one might also
note how the reliance on obscure jargon (*supplementarity, logocentrism, catachresis, aporia, metonymy*, and so forth) betrayed a desire
to emulate the sciences. Though this style of discourse obviously alien-
ated many, it served for that very reason to substantiate the status of
literary criticism as a serious academic discipline, one that required
lengthy training and conferred on those who had mastered the requisite vocabulary an appearance of expertise. If New Criticism had sought
to democratize the capacity to understand difficult literary works in
order to appeal to the growing population of undergraduates, deconstruction answered the painful imperatives of a rapidly constricting
academic job market by giving the discipline a tool for winnowing professional critics from mere enthusiasts, privileging a select group of
hypercompetent students willing and able to negotiate a forbidding
technical jargon.

And yet, even as it served the various institutional needs of English
departments, rationalizing the increased emphasis on publications and
conferring prestige on individuals capable of deploying its terminology
effectively, deconstruction simultaneously provided academics a rhetoric of subversion and estrangement. Understood affectively, the
defining goal of its practitioners was to shatter people's complacency:
the faith that literary works could be understood, that language could
deliver meaning in a transparent fashion, that reason could transcend
the specific rhetorical structures through which it functioned. While
deconstruction's posture of radical skepticism appealed, as I have already indicated, to the oppositional urges of countercultural and left

intellectuals, it also functioned as a useful attitude for navigating the inhospitable conditions of life within academia. As Donald Pease eloquently puts it,

> For a profession whose disheartened members are subject to the anxieties provoked by the increasing competition for an increasingly reduced number of jobs, a method able to re(-)read their competitive anxiety as a fundamental basis for interpreting canonical texts and able to reevaluate their disillusionment with both their logocentric culture and their profession as the prerequisites for entrance into the "ideal space" of a society of intellectuals related through their shared sense of alienation seems a compelling if not an inevitable choice. Although deconstruction cannot now be viewed as the implicit recovery of a single critic's self-consciousness *through* the self-reflexivity of the text, through the increasing popularity of deconstruction for a generation of disillusioned young critics, this post-structuralist strategy will have the effect of legitimizing their common sense of powerlessness, insignificance, and instability by leveling all of these moods into effects of the "free play" of *différance,* the only viable counter-discourse to the "mastery"-oriented discourse of the logocentric tradition. ("J. Hillis Miller" 88)

What made deconstruction so adept at performing these contradictory functions was the radical ambivalence—the aporia—that structured its own defining strategy of critique. Derrida emphasized this strategy as early as 1967 at the famous Johns Hopkins Conference, "The Languages of Criticism and the Sciences of Man: The Structuralist Controversy": *"There is no sense* in doing without the concepts of metaphysics in order to attack metaphysics" ("Structure, Sign, and Play" 250). As its proponents endlessly repeated, deconstruction relied on the very traditions that it called into question. It dramatized the incoherence of logocentrism by means of logocentric arguments. Thus deconstruction served as a perfectly effective form of intellectual equipment for those interested in attacking the academic institutions on which they depended, or hoped to depend, for a livelihood.[16]

The position of English departments in the university during the 1970s made them particularly receptive to this kind of thinking. It had been more than two decades since New Criticism had effectively rewritten the discipline; as a result of the extraordinary success of these changes, what was once innovative had become automatic.[17] Meanwhile, hints of a full-fledged crisis of the humanities were just beginning to appear. English departments, in short, were sufficiently secure in the present and sufficiently anxious about the future to welcome the opportunity to rethink the methods that had put them in that position. Doing so was also a convenient way of satisfying the demand for continuous innovation rooted in the market-oriented ideology that was increasingly dictating the administration of higher education. Deconstruction allowed English departments to engage in an apparently radical self-critique and to refurbish their operations—to answer the call for self-reinvention coming from both left radicals and corporate administrators—without discarding the values or procedures that had served to define them. It helped to preserve the formalist methodology that the New Critics had instituted by turning that methodology against itself, allowing formalism to survive in the face of political agitation and institutional upheaval on the basis of its own incessant self-destruction and reconsolidation.

Figures of Truth

To be clear, deconstructionists were not able to perpetuate formalism without at the same time transforming it; in particular they offered a markedly different account from the New Critics' of what constitutes the aesthetic value of literary forms and what function these forms serve. To clarify the shift in perspective that deconstruction brought about, I turn briefly to de Man's exemplary essay "The Rhetoric of Blindness" (*Blindness and Insight* 102–141).

Recall that the New Critics justify poetry's ironies, metaphors, and ambiguities on ontological grounds: its strange and difficult formal devices are necessary, they hold, to represent the full complexity of reality. Poetry and its criticism are important because they offer a fuller knowledge of the world than other disciplines, including the sciences. It is precisely this position that de Man rejects. A literary text, he maintains, "leads to no transcendental perception, intuition, or knowledge but merely solicits an understanding that has to remain immanent because it poses the problem of its intelligibility in its own terms" (*Blindness and Insight* 107). Literature promotes understanding, but only about itself, about its own failure to deliver a definitive meaning. Seeking to elucidate Jean-Jacques Rousseau's theory of how signs function—a theory he endorses—de Man argues, "The sign is devoid of substance, not because it has to be a transparent indicator that should not mask a plenitude of meaning, but because the meaning itself is empty; the sign should not offer its own sensory richness as a substitute for the void that it signifies" (127). In absolute contrast to the textured, full-bodied evocation of the real imagined by the New Critics, what literature designates, according to de Man, is "the void."

John Crowe Ransom's reading of how poetic metaphors work exemplifies the New Critics' ontological assumptions. Precisely because it is figurative, argues Ransom, the phrase "The oak, ancient, moaning its splendors gone" (World's Body 157) reveals a truth about the depicted object that scientific accounts overlook. While poetry seems to embellish the things it describes, adding, in this case, a tragic disposition to the tree, thus granting the world a measure of grandeur, beauty, and mystery, this is not a mere projection. Poetry is actually telling us something true about reality, which we might be more willing to accept if we were not under the influence of a modern scientific paradigm. De Man considers a similarly counterfactual figure of speech in Rousseau's *Essai sur l'origine des connaissances humaines*. When primitive man first encounters another person, he may respond, "I see a giant," in which case his expression will function, according to de Man, as a "metaphor for the literal statement, 'I am frightened'" (Blindness and Insight 134). But de Man denies the usefulness of this example, because it fails to illuminate Rousseau's sense of how language operates, either in literature or in everyday contexts. The problem is that it translates too easily into a basic, "utilitarian" emotion and thus belies the purpose that language was invented to serve: "Fear is on the side of hunger and thirst and could never, by itself, lead to the supplementary figuration of language" (134–135). According to de Man, a much more revealing subject than fear would be love. He quotes from Rousseau's *Nouvelle Héloïse*: "Love is mere illusion. It invents, so to speak, another universe; it surrounds itself with objects that do not exist or to which only love itself has given life" (135). Here, de Man appears to be in agreement with the New Critics. Figural language, when it is working to fulfill its true purpose, does not deal with mere material needs or utilitarian calculations; rather, it describes useless, impractical passions such as love, and as such it creates "another universe," introduces an added dimension to reality, which we might call the aesthetic.

But for de Man figural language does not actually reveal a truth about reality; it does not refer to any real phenomenon in the world.[18] "The metaphorical language which, in the fictional diachrony of the *Essai*, is called 'premier' has no literal referent" (135). Literature may invite the mistake that the New Critics make, tempting readers to treat its figures of speech as if they signified something real: "The rhetorical character of literary language opens up the possibility of the archetypal error: the recurrent confusion of sign and substance" (136). But at the same time, literary language signals a recognition of its own vacuity: "We are entitled to generalize in working our way toward a definition by giving Rousseau exemplary value and calling 'literary,' in the full sense of the term, any text that implicitly or explicitly signifies its own rhetorical mode and prefigures its own misunderstanding as the correlative of its rhetorical nature; that is, of its 'rhetoricity'" (136). If literary language enriches our sense of the world, making everyday objects strange or beautiful, it simultaneously asserts that such gestures of aestheticization are illusory. Moreover, it self-consciously enacts a property of all language, demonstrating how the figures we use inevitably entail misinterpretation, leading us to believe that they meaningfully refer to some truth beyond themselves.

Significantly, denying literature's ontological function does not entail the loss of its privileged position. Literature, according to de Man, is especially capable of deconstructing itself, thus illuminating the logocentric delusions that thwart our ability to perceive the void.[19] And this conception of literature offers a clue as to why deconstruction, despite its repudiation of New Criticism, fares better in American English departments than its immediate predecessor, structuralism, another European export that also vied for influence but without ever gaining a solid foothold in the United States. Whereas structuralists reject the piety that confers a special status on literature, treating it instead as the predictable product of semiotic codes and generic rules also at work in shaping all language production, deconstructionists such as de Man and Miller persist in attributing unique deconstructive powers to literature, thus preserving its favored status, as well as the rationale for a specific discipline designed to study it.[20]

Moreover, while de Man seems bent on dispatching the traditional romantic illusion that literature can function as a source of truth and beauty, he obviously finds literature attractive precisely for the deceptions that it perpetrates. Literature demonstrates the unreliable character of language through its own unreliability; the errors in interpretation that it inspires are central to the work that it performs. "In accordance with its own language, [the text] can only tell this story as a fiction, knowing full well that the fiction will be taken for fact and the fact for fiction; such is the necessarily ambivalent nature of literary language" (136). Though de Man seems to be demystifying certain illusions, he acknowledges their necessity. He is, in short, compelled by the detour through rhetorical figures—giants, moaning oaks, or love—which literature offers. The difference between his approach and the New Critics' is that he appreciates the aesthetic or figural dimension that literary works add to reality only insofar as this dimension is presented as an absolute fiction, a misreading whose seductions neither the writer nor the critic can entirely escape.[21]

In some ways, de Man's response to Rousseau resembles Cleanth Brooks's reading of William Wordsworth, which we encountered in Chapter 1. In both cases, the literary work seems to misread the world, projecting beauty or love where it is absent, which precipitates a corresponding misreading by the critic. And for both de Man and Brooks, it is the paradoxical quality of the text that makes it compelling. But for Brooks the paradox in the poem, the combination of beauty and banality, reflects the paradoxical nature of its subject: the grimy yet remarkable city of London. For de Man the "ambivalence" is present only within Rousseau's literary language, which both posits and denies the truth of its own figures. To suggest that this ambivalence might actually reflect a corresponding ambivalence or contradiction in the world beyond the text would be to attribute to literature the very plenitude of meaning, the mimetic or referential power, that deconstruction categorically refuses.

While de Man comes across in this debate as a tough-minded skeptic unwilling to fall prey to the delusions that ensnare the New Critics, in doing so he invites precisely the doubts about the purpose of academic literary studies that the New Critics were desperate to silence. Ransom presented literature as a rational form of knowledge that could rival the sciences in order to make criticism into a legitimate discipline capable of satisfying the positivist criteria increasingly prevalent within academia. According to de Man, what literature offers is merely an illusion, which it simultaneously serves to deconstruct. It does yield an important insight about language, but this very insight entails the conclusion that literature cannot offer any kind of transcendental truth. Moreover, literary works cannot even state this insight directly; they reveal it only by seeming to convey the opposite impression, by leading the reader into error. De Man's argument deprives poetic devices—metaphor, irony, paradox, ambiguity, and so forth—of any ontological function, any claim on objective knowledge. Deconstruction's success is especially remarkable, in other words, given that it undercuts the rationale constructed by the New Critics for close reading, a rationale aimed at both ascribing a serious function to aesthetic pleasure and preserving the long-term viability of literary criticism as an academic discipline.

Good Vibrations

One reason deconstruction ends up winning adherents within English departments across the United States, despite the apocalyptic warnings issued by the New Critics and other like-minded gatekeepers, is that its methods yield something quite similar to what is offered by its predecessors: cerebral pleasure. In performing this function, deconstruction appears to reaffirm the mission championed by I. A. Richards, who also denied literature's capacity to produce truth claims about the world. As we saw in Chapter 1, Richards argues that complex literary works allow readers to satisfy a far greater number of mental urges than is possible in ordinary life. And the device that Richards identifies as especially well equipped to serve this purpose is the same one most frequently celebrated by deconstructionists: irony. According to Richards, "Irony . . . consists in the bringing in of the opposite, the complementary impulses; that is why poetry which is exposed to it is not of the highest order, and why irony itself is so constantly a characteristic of poetry which is" (*Principles* 250). Irony is effective because it activates not merely one particular mental impulse but also its opposite in the very same moment; it is a way of creating a balance between the reader's contradictory urges, allowing for the expression of both.

Curiously enough, deconstructionists embrace irony for what would seem to be the opposite reason: not for its capacity to promote harmony but for its role in activating interpretive confusion. It is the device, according to Geoffrey Hartman in his preface to *Deconstruction and Criticism*, that "subverts all possible meanings" (viii). Generally speaking, the deconstructionists seem intent on promoting anything but tranquility, comprehension, or mental balance. Reading W. B. Yeats, Hartman happily asserts, "These questions add up to a *hermeneutic perplexity*" (*Criticism in the Wilderness* 24). J. H. Miller is more graphic: "This might be called the aporia of interminability. It is not the encounter with the blank wall beyond which one cannot go, but the failure ever to find an end to the corridors of interpretation. Since no movement backward through the woven lines of the text will reach a starting place with explanatory power to run through the whole chain, it is equally impossible in the other direction ever to reach a definitive explanatory end" (*Fiction and Repetition* 173). Johnson characterizes the experience that literature inspires in one of those breathless lists of abstractions for which deconstruction is famous: "Division, contradiction, incompatibility, and ellipsis thus stand as the challenge, the enigma, the despair, and the delight both of the lover and of the reader of literature" (*Critical Difference* 20). If, as Wayne Booth observes, the deconstructionists seek a "new vitality," then it is clearly a somewhat masochistic variety ("'Preserving the Exemplar'" 417).[22]

While they obviously do not share Richards's goal of promoting psychic balance, deconstructive strategies of interpretation do meet one of the central criteria that he outlines in determining what constitutes a rich aesthetic experience. Of greatest importance to Richards is the sheer number of urges or appetencies that get satisfied: "What is good or valuable, we have said, is the exercise of impulses and the satisfaction of their appetencies. When we say that anything is good we mean that it satisfies, and by a good experience we mean one in which the impulses which make it are fulfilled and successful, adding as the necessary qualification that their exercise and satisfaction shall not interfere in any way with more important impulses" (*Principles* 58). Explaining this in a slightly different way, he observes, "To put it briefly the best life is that in which as much as possible of our possible personality is engaged" (288). Such a life involves minimal suppression, which is why tragic works are especially valuable. "It is essential to recognize that in the full tragic experience there is no suppression. The mind does not shy away from anything, it does not protect itself with any illusion, it stands uncomforted, unintimidated, alone and self-reliant" (246). This state of absolute openness to all possible thoughts, however dangerous, unprotected by false illusions, would seem to be exactly the mode of responsiveness that deconstruction seeks to foster. What the deconstructionists implicitly wager, however, is that no moment of synthesis is necessary to promote the requisite aesthetic pleasure. Unlike Richards, they seem to hold that it is possible to entertain a well-nigh limitless array of contradictory meanings in the mind without ever reconciling them.

Richards's account is highly neurological; it is essentially an argument about how particular texts influence the neural organization of the brain so as to yield satisfaction. While such scientific aspirations would seem to place him entirely at odds with the deconstructionists, the latter characterize the rewards of reading in terms remarkably similar to Richards's. In the same essay in which he attempts to refute the latter's theory of poetry, de Man celebrates the effect of the textual ambiguities discovered by Richards's student Empson—whom de Man treats as a protodeconstructionist: "Instead of setting up an adequation between two experiences, and thereby fixing the mind on the repose of an established equation, [the metaphor] deploys the initial experience into an infinity of associated experiences that spring from it. In the manner of a vibration spreading in infinitude from its center, metaphor is endowed with the capacity to situate the experience at the heart of a universe that it generates. It provides the ground rather than the frame, a limitless anteriority that permits the limiting of a specific entity. Experience sheds its uniqueness and leads instead to a dizziness of the mind" (*Blindness and Insight* 235). As with Richards, it is the multiplicity of unsuppressed mental impulses triggered by the poetic image that constitutes a heightened aesthetic response—described by de Man as a "dizziness of the mind." Moreover, the image of vibration, though lacking an obvious reference, also seems to characterize the experience of ambiguity as one of bodily or neural pleasure, a palpable tingle of the brain.

Images of vibration, oscillation, and kinesis recur in the deconstructionists' essays. Describing Percy Bysshe Shelley's *Triumph of Life*, Derrida remarks, "Such is the arrhythmic pulsation of the title before it scatters like sand" ("Living On" 115). Referring to the competing meanings unleashed by Wordsworth's poetry, J. H. Miller observes, "They are held suspended in a vibration among alternative ways of thinking that is impossible to fix in a single unequivocal formulation" (*Linguistic Moment* 44). Later in his analysis, Miller extends his metaphor, offering a more physically exact description: "Such language says two things at once. In this double saying the poem establishes vibrations of meaning that resonate outward in diffusive circles of sense. If the source of the sonnet is a boundless breath, it moves through the limitations imposed by its form back to another openness" (68). While Miller's reference to breath explicitly underscores the connection between the operations of the poem and the operations of the body, "vibrations . . . that resonate outward in diffusive circles" resembles nothing so much as the euphemistic evocations of sexual pleasure employed by romance novels.

Introducing an interview in *Diacritics* with Derrida in which the latter describes "the turbulence of a certain lack" that serves to "break down the limit of the text" ("Positions" 37), Richard Klein predicts that "anyone who has wrestled with the monstrous difficulties of reading Derrida will probably feel a shiver of anticipation at the prospect of having him interviewed" ("Prolegomenon" 29). However monstrously difficult Derrida's work, Klein's "shiver," along with the preponderance of obliquely somatic figures in deconstructive criticism, suggests a fairly simple answer to the question of what makes it so appealing. Though they often seem to be referencing some unlocatable space in between the text and the reader, the deconstructionists are also arguably registering modes of cognitive, emotional, and bodily response. To recognize this, of course, it is necessary to read such figures of vibration, in violation of fundamental deconstructive prescriptions, *literally*, as straightforward descriptions of viscerally enjoyable, bodily experiences.

Richards of course believed that he was taking the first step toward a scientific understanding of what happens in the brain when an individual reads a complex work of literature. The deconstructionists clearly harbor no such ambitions. Moreover, one could argue that their criticism serves not to describe but in fact to construct the interpretive pleasures to which it alludes. The deconstructionists, in other words, do not merely find a vocabulary for understanding aesthetic responses that preexist their intervention; they actually rethink the goal of reading, promoting entirely new states of cognitive complexity while validating and thereby making it possible to enjoy experiences of disorientation and bewilderment that might otherwise be a source of frustration. Indeed, the rise of deconstruction would seem to suggest that a given mode of aesthetic pleasure is historically and culturally produced, and not, as Richards suggested, the result of innate neurological structures.

That said, the resemblance between Richards's and the deconstructionists' accounts of reading is worth noting, insofar as it suggests a motive for literary criticism shared, albeit tacitly, by the two. Notwithstanding their deliberately ambiguous reference, the far-fetched metaphors that the deconstructionists employ to describe the act of interpretation seem to insist at every turn: you should be enjoying this; your brain should be buzzing right now. Whether this pleasure is an intrinsic neurological side effect of complex thinking, a consequence of utopian political dreams activated by the loss of familiar bearings, or just a form of pride upon demonstrating a facility for a newly fashionable form of sophistication, it is clearly an essential ingredient—indeed, the most oft-repeated promise that deconstruction makes to its readers.

In some sense, of course, the claim that deconstruction promotes pleasure is entirely obvious. Pleasure, after all, is what Roland Barthes, forefather and fellow traveler of the deconstructionists, explicitly advertises as the effect of confronting the text in all of its refractory textuality.[23] But he invariably celebrates pleasure as a mode of radical liberation or revolt and thus fails to anticipate the contradictory functions served by the incessant encoding of pleasure within the language of deconstructive criticism. It is important to note, first of all, that the terms in which the promise of pleasure is made are rarely easy to decipher. As I have suggested, the figures in deconstructive rhetoric that suggest bodily gratification can also sound impossibly abstract. If they sometimes read like the euphemisms of romance fiction, they more often appear to be elements within a hypertechnical jargon designed to depict a space scoured clean of any traces of humanity, where unreal entities collide, combine, collapse, and re-form, without ever resolving into any recognizable shape or scene, like those fractal screensavers ubiquitous in the 1990s. Guillory has suggested that this rhetoric aims to affirm the extreme *rigor* of deconstruction, so as to meet the disciplinary standards of a university increasingly shaped by a "technobureaucratic" ethos (*Cultural Capital* 264). To interpret this same rhetoric as an expression of bodily pleasure is to recognize the conflicting functions that deconstruction is required to serve: both as a means of reconfirming the capacity of English studies to meet criteria of disciplinary rigor and as a libidinal release from those same standards—the sign, in a word, of a discipline that can preserve only by seeming to subvert itself. Significantly, deconstruction's tendency to embed the suggestion of bodily satisfaction within its moments of greatest abstraction and terminological obscurity amounts to a utopian gesture perfectly resonant with New Left revolutionary fantasies. What deconstructive rhetoric represents is a field of struggle saturated with pleasure, a vocabulary that both calls for mastery and incites submission to a state of unknowing bliss, thus enabling an experience that appears to collapse work and play, labor and leisure, discipline and liberation, expressing a vision of social well-being through its very style.

But this paradoxical dream is not, over the long term, enough to sustain deconstruction in its role as the protector of literary studies. For one thing, as we have seen, pleasure is not generally viewed as a sufficiently serious goal for an academic discipline. Richards's argument, according to the New Critics, turns literature into a trivial workout for the emotions.[24] While deconstruction's rejection of New Critical doctrines allows the former to establish itself as a new and radical form of criticism, its skepticism regarding the referential powers of language places its adherents, as I have observed, in the same dangerous position that Richards had occupied. Moreover, by the mid-1970s, pleasure had mostly lost its credibility as a vehicle of social transformation with the conspicuous failure of various countercultural sexual and aesthetic practices to bring about revolution. As a result, many tactics that had once seemed revolutionary came to seem merely self-indulgent. The accusations of irresponsible hedonism, first directed at deconstruction by left critics such as Frank Lentricchia and Fredric Jameson, gradually achieved widespread acceptance, and the latter's aura of rebelliousness ceased to satisfy those who wanted literary studies to be a force for concrete political change. While the revelation of de Man's wartime fascist newspaper articles has assumed center stage in the drama of deconstruction's decline, it was already in crisis well before this episode.[25] By the mid-1980s, deconstructionists realized that in order to ensure that their work would continue to be taken seriously, they needed to establish its ability to exert influence on the world beyond the text.[26]

In the face of these pressures, deconstruction turned in the 1980s and early 1990s explicitly toward ethical and political concerns.[27] While the goal of its proponents during this period was to demonstrate how the interpretive strategies that deconstruction fostered could serve as a means of challenging dominant political structures and promoting justice, I intend to offer a different reading. This new strategy, in my view, served another, less obvious agenda: namely, finding a new justification for a particular set of aesthetic pleasures centered on irony, ambiguity, uncertainty, and paradox. Having built their reputation by refuting the ontological function that the New Critics had ascribed to literature, the deconstructionists needed to find a new rationale for the strategies of close reading that they employed, and political and ethical ideals were, by virtue of their growing importance in the academy, well suited to play that role. While many observers understand this second chapter in deconstruction's history as an effort to politicize a school of theory that had been lambasted for its purported aestheticism, it also represents, curiously enough, a way of reconstituting certain aesthetic values so as to grant them a secure place within political criticism.

In the final sections of this chapter, I consider three defenses of deconstruction offered in the mid-1980s by Miller, Henry Louis Gates Jr., and Johnson. While all three rely in various ways on the assumption that the deconstructionist project of critiquing logocentrism and binary thinking can play an important role in subverting the dominant order, they all seem to recognize that this philosophical conceit is no longer enough to demonstrate deconstruction's potential as a socially responsible or politically engaged mode of criticism. Thus all three seek to rewrite deconstruction, extending its logic into new contexts. In doing so, ironically enough, they also imagine new rationales, new political and ethical functions for the aesthetic pleasures that deconstruction fosters, thereby facilitating the preservation of these pleasures in the decades that follow.

Miller's Ethics

"What do I mean by the ethical?" Miller asks near the beginning of *The Ethics of Reading* (1987). "And what do I claim is gained by shifting the ground from the much more common, in fact almost universal, topic of literary study these days, namely investigations of the political, historical, and social connections of literature?" (4). What is gained is a return of attention to the subject that Miller believes political criticism inevitably overlooks: the act of reading. "Reading itself is extraordinarily hard work. It does not occur all that often. Clearheaded reflection on what really happens in an act of reading is even more difficult and rare" (3–4). By the mid-1980s, in Miller's view, a majority of literary scholars are no longer doing their job: they are no longer reading the text or seeking to understand what it means to read a text. By abdicating their responsibilities, they run the risk of relinquishing the specificity of literary studies, thus undermining the ground necessary to support the discipline's continued existence. Echoing a worry voiced by Ransom almost fifty years earlier, Miller considers the consequence of the increasingly widespread assumption that literary works are the products of history or ideology: "If this view of literature were true, it would make the study of literature a somewhat dreary business, since what would be found in literature would be what is already known by the interpreter and what can more clearly be known and seen elsewhere, for example by the study of history and society as such" (8).[28] Miller's implicit argument is that a return to the task of trying to understand what happens in the moment of reading will reassert the discipline's distinctiveness. But this point of emphasis also happens, not coincidentally, to be the one that defines deconstruction and mobilizes its particular strengths.

Miller recognizes that any call for a return to formalism will seem reactionary. Whatever justification of deconstruction he offers must effectively answer the "guilt in occupying oneself with something so trivial, so disconnected from 'life' and 'reality,' as novels and poems, in comparison with the serious business of history, politics, and the class struggle" (5). The term he selects, *ethics*, is aimed at refuting the view of deconstruction as self-indulgent, hedonistic, or nihilistic. At the same time, however, as a measure frequently applied to individual acts in isolation from broader political structures, the ethical allows Miller to zero in on the scene of reading. There is, he maintains, "a necessary ethical moment in that act of reading as such, a moment neither cognitive, nor political, nor social, nor interpersonal, but properly and independently ethical" (1).

Reading, it turns out, is not only ethical, in Miller's view; it is actually the very source of ethics. He extrapolates this claim by subjecting Immanuel Kant's *Groundwork of the Metaphysics of Morals* to a deconstructive interpretation. The process wherein, according to Kant, we arrive at universal moral laws, depends on the production of a fictional narrative: I must ask myself what would happen *if* everyone were to behave in the same way that I am behaving now. What, for instance, would be the result if everyone who made promises eventually broke them? The very notion of a promise would, Kant suggests, lose all meaning, and it would be impossible to make a promise in the first place. The act of violating a promise, if instituted as a universal law of action, in other words, would entail a self-contradiction, and therefore we are all subject to a categorical imperative to keep our promises (*Groundwork* 70–71). In this example, the imperative is founded on what Miller takes to be linguistic grounds. We derive the moral law from a fictional scenario—the imagined world in which everyone behaves in the same way that we do. Moreover, the primary reason we must keep our word is to preserve the meaningfulness of a specific kind of utterance: the promise. Hence what appears to be a moral law is in fact a linguistic law, one whose purpose is merely to ensure the proper functioning of language. "An agreement to keep the rules of language the same would then be the foundation of civil order, not the law as such" (*Ethics* 35).

Miller's notion that ethical principles are merely the product of language—grammar masquerading as morality—would seem only to corroborate the view of deconstruction as nihilistic. The reading that he has performed, Miller admits, opens the possibility that duty is "an ungrounded act of self-sustaining language, that is, precisely a vain delusion and chimerical concept" (38). Moreover, if his interpretation of Kant is any indication, careful reading, particularly of the deconstructive variety, would seem to be the enemy of the ethical rather than its instantiation. Nevertheless, Miller does not admit defeat. In an audaciously ironic maneuver, he endeavors to show how reading can indeed supply the foundation for ethics, which his analysis of Kant, an enlightenment humanist, has apparently undermined, by turning to Paul de Man, skeptic *par excellence*.

In *Allegories of Reading*, de Man, according to Miller, asserts that ethical truths are the product of a misreading. "One of the primary ways that the failure to read manifests itself at the allegorical level is in the making of value judgments, the uttering of ethical commands and promises ('You should do so and so'; 'You will be happy if you do so and so.') for which there is absolutely no foundation in knowledge" (48). He quotes de Man: "Morality is a version of the same language aporia that gave rise to such concepts as 'man' or 'love' or 'self,' and not the cause or the consequence of such concepts. The passage to an ethical tonality does not result from a transcendental imperative but is the referential (and therefore unreliable) version of a linguistic confusion" (*Allegories* 206, qtd. in Miller, *Ethics* 49). While it is hard to see how such an argument can fend off accusations of nihilism, the belief in the referential truth of ethical statements is, according to Miller's reading of de Man, an error to which everyone, including deconstructionists, is necessarily susceptible: "It is a necessity to be in error or at least confused, as always happens when I attempt to make language referential, and I *must* attempt to make it referential. I cannot do otherwise. In the case of ethics it is a necessity to make judgments, commands, promises about right and wrong which have no verifiable basis in anything outside language" (49–50). In fact, within the interpretive sequence that de Man imagines, the erroneous assertion of ethical truths occurs not before but *after* the deconstruction of the language designed to produce that error. As Miller explains, "The ethical does not come first. It intervenes, necessarily intervenes, but it occurs at a 'later stage' in a sequence which begins with epistemological error, the error born of aberrant metaphorical naming" (45). Remarkably enough, asserts Miller, "ethical judgments and demands are one major example of that committing again of the linguistic error already deconstructed" (48). To make valid ethical judgments, in other words, we must first deconstruct the language of morality, recognize its failure to refer to any kind of reality, and then knowingly *misread* that language, treat it as valid, and accept it as binding on us, despite our knowledge of its groundlessness. This, ultimately, is what Miller means by "the ethics of reading."

An obvious question raised by Miller's analysis is why ethical statements are dependent on this peculiar deconstructive process wherein one first affirms, then denies, and then ultimately accepts their truth. Why would a pre-deconstructive, naïve reading not be enough to ensure the operation and validity of ethical principles? To put it another way, why is the deconstructive doubter more ethical than the naïve believer? Miller never offers an adequate explanation, but he does provide some clues. What makes the deconstructor's response an exemplary ethical achievement is his or her confrontation with a radical contradiction between what de Man calls "two distinct value systems" (*Allegories* 206). Miller observes, "Surely one should want to dwell within the truth, and surely one should want to do what is right, but according to de Man it is impossible to respond simultaneously to those two demands" (*Ethics* 49). When those who have subjected an ethical imperative to a deconstructive reading nevertheless submit to that imperative and accept its validity, they are acting against their knowledge. Because they know that the imperative is "linguistic rather than subjective or the effect of a transcendental law" (49), they are actually sacrificing something—their knowledge—and thereby testifying to the strange necessity of the ethical more powerfully than a person who just naïvely subscribes to its truth. "A categorical obligation is absolute and unconditional. We must do it, whatever the cost" (49). This cost, this sacrifice of knowledge, is what lends ethical rigor to the deconstructor's relationship to the law.

De Man's take on ethical language, in Miller's account, is almost identical to his take, in "The Rhetoric of Blindness," on the metaphors that operate within literary works and generally perform an aesthetic function, lending beauty to the described object. In both cases the deconstructive reader experiences an inescapable ambivalence between denying and assenting to the truth of certain figures of speech; in both cases those figures offer a more appealing vision of reality than the one we would have to accept in their absence. That Miller focuses only on one, the ethical and not the aesthetic, is telling. One purpose of *The Ethics of Reading* is to identify a value in reading literature that can be described without reference to the practical or instrumental purpose of that experience—that is, an intrinsic value—exactly the value frequently referred to as aesthetic. A central function that the category of the ethical is performing in his analysis, then, is to mask Miller's commitment to the aesthetic. This is not to say that he is wrong to assert that reading may have an ethical value; it is only to suggest that his reliance on the term enables him to avoid using the other term, *aesthetic*, and thus to dissociate deconstruction from the latter's negative connotations.

Miller's evasion of the category of the aesthetic betrays itself most conspicuously in his analysis of George Eliot. Motivating Eliot's project is a rejection of art that offers an idealized representation of reality—most notably Christian portrayals of angels, saints, prophets, and the like—which she views, according to Miller, as mere "irrealism," "a detour into the fictive from which there is no return to the real world" (*Ethics* 66–67). Implicitly, according to Miller, Eliot is challenging the Kantian analogy between God and the artist as genius, rooted in the view that both introduce into the world "the plus value of a new beauty which is beyond price" (67). Eliot, by contrast, seeks to reproduce the world as it actually is: "Rejecting an aesthetic of the sublime, the beautiful, the ideal, the rare, the distant, George Eliot affirms with great persuasive power a counter-aesthetic of the ugly, the stupid, the real, the frequent, the statistically likely, the near" (70).[29] In one of his rare invocations of the category, Miller ascribes aesthetic value to Eliot's fiction, but this value depends largely on her work's repudiation of all traditional aesthetic aims. Later he complicates this reading, exploring Eliot's unacknowledged commitment to the very goals that she claims to reject. And yet, significantly, in doing so he redescribes these goals in terms strangely divested of any reference to aesthetic power.

Eliot's chief purpose, according to Miller, is to arouse sympathy for individuals who may be unappealing, which she accomplishes through the use of figural language: a "renaming one's ugly, stupid, inconsistent neighbors as lovable" (74). Despite its pretense of straightforward fidelity, Miller argues, "the language of realistic fiction is not based solidly on any extra-linguistic entities. It transforms such entities into something other than themselves, as your ugly, stupid neighbor is made lovable when he or she has passed through the circuit of representation in a 'realistic' novel" (75). According to Miller, the figural work that Eliot performs is simply another version of the misreading that, in de Man's view, constructs ethics: "My reading of George Eliot's reading of his (or her) own writing has revealed an unsettling rift between the knowledge that writing gives in its resolute commitment to truthtelling, and the power to love one's neighbor the truthtelling story is supposed to give. This fissure is not too different, after all, from the gulf between the epistemology of metaphor and the necessary moment of 'ethicity,' in Paul de Man's account of his 'paradigmatic' text, Rousseau's *Julie*" (80). Moreover, Miller observes that, in recasting the stupid, ugly characters whom she describes, Eliot plays a role similar to the one that Kant ascribes to the artist: "There is more than simple opposition in the relation between the closed circuit economy of realism, on the one hand, the ugly mirroring the ugly and returning the ugly to the ugly, and, on the other hand, the infinite economy of genius, the beautiful (angels and Madonnas, prophets, sibyls) mirroring nothing but the inventive soul of its creator, flying off into the inane ideal without possibility of return. Realism also adds a fictive plus value, and Madonnas or angels also make us admire human motherhood and self-denying aspiration" (79). Eliot's fiction, in other words, performs precisely the aesthetic function—namely, misrepresenting the world so as to make it appear beautiful—that she claims to disavow.

Remarkably, Miller's deconstruction of the opposition between art's traditional aesthetic function as described by Kant and the counteraesthetic propounded by Eliot leads somehow not to a synthesis but to a total effacement of the two, in order to foreground the ethical work her fiction performs. And yet, his effort to attribute ethical value to Eliot remains incomplete, a change in terminology rather than substance, as if his own governing interpretive commitments allow for only a partial shift away from the aesthetic. Eliot's rhetorical figures make a "break in the remorseless chain of cause and effect" and thereby "perform into existence feelings, a will, a resolution" (73). In this progressive series, from feelings, to will, to resolution, Miller seems to stretch toward but stop just short of naming the consequence that would allow him to treat Eliot's work as justifiably ethical: some real, practical action. Though a resolution must be directed at something particular, Miller cannot complete the gesture he begins, because there is no specific action that he can name, and even if there were, it would remove him from the scene of reading that he is committed to valuing for its own sake.

Miller employs the rhetoric of agency and action to give his argument the appearance of engaging with ethical questions, but without specifying any particular content. What Eliot's fiction performs into existence, according to his own interpretation, is not an action but a state of admiration, an affective revaluation of everyday life, and this is a function more accurately described as aesthetic than ethical. Miller uses the word "ugly" continuously in referring to the individuals that Eliot hopes to recast, but he abstains from invoking its opposite, "beautiful," in describing the results of her narrative transfiguration—a term that would seem to designate that "something other than themselves" that they become through her efforts. He obliquely acknowledges that Eliot's work creates beauty when he deconstructs the opposition between realism and "the infinite economy of genius, the beautiful" (79), but he never articulates this function directly, as if he is afraid to be caught in the act of explicitly valuing Eliot's work by ascribing to it a traditional aesthetic function.

The reason Miller stops short of designating the practical modes of action that reading Eliot's fiction might inspire is of course that he is committed to presenting reading as ethical in itself. He says so explicitly near the end of the book: "I have performed acts of reading of my own which are both responses to an ethical demand made by the texts I have read and at the same time ethical acts themselves" (102). But more important than this direct statement is his tendency, shared by other deconstructionists, to present the work of interpretation and thinking as dangerous and heroic. Trying to read Kant, one must navigate "an opaque mist" or "an impenetrable thicket of thorns around the sleeping beauty" (15). Meanwhile, Kant himself "is like a man walking a knife-edge on a mountaintop, with an abyss on either side" (19). Here Miller is of course drawing on a set of associations and metaphors that the deconstructionists have spent years developing. While the New Critics never denied that reading could be hard, they emphasized its capacity to inspire aesthetic fulfillment, suggesting that certain texts, when read in accordance with the protocols they prescribed, could produce experiences more complete, harmonious, and satisfying than any other within ordinary life. By recasting these same experiences as difficult, painful, and terrifying, the deconstructionists present their work as part of a weighty struggle—against someone or something—without specifying a social or political context. Recall: what makes reading ethical, according to Miller, is the moment of undecidability that it produces between two irreconcilable value systems, which in turn requires a painful sacrifice. However dramatic Miller's account, this is simply ambiguity renamed ethics, aesthetic richness viewed as a knife-edge above an abyss.

In assigning deconstruction a central role within the ethical turn of literary criticism, Miller is of course simply doing what other political critics are also doing during this period: enlisting the romantic image of criticism as heroic, which the deconstructionists have helped to create, in order to affirm the discipline's worldly importance. The effect of this rebranding is to give aesthetic appreciation the appearance of ethical or political struggle. Indeed, even while other schools of criticism ultimately reject deconstruction as insufficiently invested in real social and political problems, they appropriate these strategies of self-valorization in order to present their own readings as legitimate political acts; the strenuous negotiation with contradictions modeled by the deconstructionists furnishes the very mode of argumentation through which political criticism proves the depth and courage of its engagement with history.

Gates's Theory

Although he taught at Yale in the early 1980s and enjoyed mutually influential relationships with Hartman, Miller, and Johnson, Gates would never have called himself a deconstructionist. The closest he came was to acknowledge grudgingly that for certain critics, his "name and [his] work have become metonyms for 'structuralism,' 'poststructuralism,' and/or 'deconstructionism' in the black tradition" ("'What's Love?'" 346)—suggesting a misperception based on a contingent proximity to, rather than membership within, the deconstructionist school. And yet when called on to defend it, he did so vigorously. His goal, particularly in his notorious debate with Joyce A. Joyce, was to persuade naysayers that poststructuralist theory could be an effective tool for interpreting the black literary tradition. And yet many of the criticisms he confronted were the same ones being leveled at deconstruction from all different quarters—that it was "sterile," insular, cut off from reality, nihilistic, a symptom of widespread narcissism and irresponsibility, and so forth.[30] Thus, in working to refute these arguments, Gates was, as Joyce observed twenty years later, addressing not only her and other scholars of black literature but also "the numerous other scholars who were questioning the validity of deconstruction" ("Tinker's Damn" 373). Indeed, while Gates frequently claimed he was merely "signifying upon" white critical traditions, repeating them with a difference, translating them into a new context for his own purposes, his use of deconstruction offered a powerful validation to the latter, actively recuperating its residual aesthetic commitments while simultaneously demonstrating its political efficacy.[31] Although Joyce accused Gates of adopting the "master's tools" ("'Who the Cap Fit'" 379) to "gain a voice in the white literary establishment" ("Black Canon" 340), it may make more sense to consider what he was offering deconstruction than what it was offering him.

Arguably, the paramount goal of Gates's critical work in the 1980s was to establish the aesthetic value of the work produced by major black writers. "Black literature and its criticism," he laments, "have been put to uses that were not primarily aesthetic" ("'What's Love?'" 348), insofar as they were treated exclusively as a means of demonstrating what should have been unexceptionable: the humanity of black authors. Although black critics had other ambitions, their objectives nevertheless relegated black literature to a second-class status. "Black criticism, since the early nineteenth century," observes Gates, "seems in retrospect to have thought of itself as essentially just one more front of the race's war against racism. Texts, it seems to me, were generally analyzed almost exclusively in terms of their content" (*Figures* xxii). Gates elaborates, "The tendency toward thematic criticism implies a marked inferiority complex" and a fear "that our literature cannot sustain sophisticated verbal analysis" (41). There are two things to notice in Gates's argument. First, unlike many scholars at the time, he is not allergic to the notion of aesthetic value; rather than the benighted obsession of an outmoded critical project, it is the very prize that must be secured for black literature in order to establish its equality to white literature. Second, his task is explicitly political, a way of furthering the liberal-progressive goal of expanding the canon and thereby challenging a pernicious form of segregation within the literary world. Thus, while the aesthetic represents a retreat from politics for other scholars, it is the opposite for Gates, which may explain why he is able to embrace it so unapologetically.

But to be meaningful and persuasive, claims about black literature's aesthetic value need to be based on criteria embedded within an established critical tradition, and this produces a conundrum for Gates. After all, the most influential school focused on assessing aesthetic value is New Criticism—a methodology Gates is loath to adopt. Fond of quoting black critic Sterling Brown's rejoinder to New Critic Robert Penn Warren's remark, "Nigger, your breed ain't metaphysical," "Cracker, your breed ain't exegetical," Gates resists assimilating New Criticism's principles on more or less inarguable grounds: its practitioners, who were wedded to antebellum southern-agrarian values, "seem not to have cared particularly for, or about, the literature of Afro-Americans" ("'What's Love?'" 349–350). New Criticism's exclusion of black literature from the canon, according to Gates, is predicated on its ascription of universality to values specific to white culture; moreover, its theory of poetic language is unable, as we will see, to account for what Gates finds uniquely compelling about black literature.[32]

The other plausible candidate for a critical tradition that Gates might claim is equally inauspicious. The Black Aesthetic movement of the 1960s and 1970s defends black literature, ironically enough, on anything but aesthetic grounds. Critics such as Stephen Henderson, Addison Gayle Jr., and Houston Baker (in the earlier phase of his career) treat literature exclusively as a vehicle for communicating political ideas, prioritizing its content to the exclusion of its form. "The critical activity altered little," Gates complains, "whether that message was integration or whether it was militant separation. Message was the medium; message reigned supreme; form became a mere convenience or, worse, a contrivance" (*Figures* 31). Moreover, these critics regard "blackness" as a metaphysical entity, a spiritual essence, which black literature is tasked with conveying. Thus they reaffirm what Gates regards as a historically racist conception of African American identity as defined by a set of fixed traits and objectively distinct from other racial identities.[33]

Gates acknowledges that a feeling of excessive familiarity prevented him, in his early studies, from achieving the appropriate degree of critical distance from black literature: "Especially in my painful beginning supervisions, I could only approach black literature by analyzing its content, by analyzing what I thought it was saying to me about the nature of my experiences as a black person living in a historically racist Western culture" (*Figures* xvi). Privileging content and ignoring form, he was, in other words, making the same mistake as those involved in the Black Aesthetic movement. What ultimately helped him to "defamiliarize" the black text, so as to see it "as a structure of literature and not as a one-to-one reflection of [his] life" and thus to attend to its "modes of representation," was in fact theory (xxiv). "Contemporary theoretical innovations," Gates puts it polemically in his debate with Joyce, can help to foreground "that which, in the received tradition of Afro-American criticism, has been most repressed"—namely, "the very language of the black text" ("'What's Love?'" 350–351). While Gates suggests that multiple theoretical frameworks can serve this purpose, including Russian formalism, French structuralism, and even Anglo-American Practical Criticism (that is, New Criticism), he clearly favors deconstructive theory above all others (*Figures* xvi). Indeed, his argument subtly works to exonerate deconstruction of the racism that he attributes to practically every other school of criticism within the European and American tradition.

Wondering whether it is possible to "escape the racism of so many critical theorists from Hume and Kant, through the Southern Agrarians and the Frankfurt School," Gates acknowledges that the resistance to theory among black critics is understandable given the "marriage of logocentrism and ethnocentrism in much of post-Renaissance Western aesthetic discourse" ("'What's Love?'" 350). He seems to side, however, with those scholars who have "attempted to convince critics of black literature that the racism of the Western critical tradition was not a sufficient reason for us to fail to . . . make use of contemporary theoretical innovations" (350). Theory, then, is potentially useful to black critics, even if racist. Later, however, subtly modulating his stance, Gates contends, "We commit intellectual suicide by binding ourselves too tightly to nonblack theory; but we drown just as surely . . . if we pretend that 'theory' is 'white,' or worse—that it is 'antiblack'" (353). While Gates cagily avoids committing to the position that theory is not racist, opting instead for the pragmatic stance that it would be intellectual suicide for black critics to regard it as such, this equivocation is primarily designed to reinforce his status as an outsider to theory and a black critic loyal above all else to his own culture—a status that in turn renders his defense of theory more persuasive. And he uses this rhetorically potent position to single out deconstruction, at least implicitly, as different from all the other theories that might, despite their racism, prove useful to critics of black literature. By contrast with these theories, deconstruction is in fact racism's antithesis, its antidote—a view Gates conveys with his question, "How can the *deconstruction, as it were,* of the forms of racism itself . . . not be political?" (358; emphasis mine), and with his identification of "logocentrism" and "ethnocentrism" as the reasons for black critics' opposition to theory, two tendencies that also happen to be the explicit targets of attack in Derrida's seminal text, *Of Grammatology.*[34]

Especially attractive to Gates is deconstruction's tendency to reveal that phenomena thought to be real, extralinguistic entities, or "transcendent signifieds," are mere tropes, rhetorical constructions. Thus deconstruction is ideally suited not only to turn the critic's attention onto the language of the black text but also to dismantle essentializing conceptions of blackness, exposing what had appeared a biological or metaphysical essence as the product of discourse.[35] And in fact these two functions go hand in hand: the deconstruction of race allows the critic to see black writing as inventing and reinventing the cultural experiences it depicts rather than merely reflecting or expressing a pre-established essence. Deconstruction, in other words, offers a way of attributing agency to the stylistic strategies of black authors.

Theory and especially deconstruction, according to Gates, provide a basis for subjecting the black literary work to "close reading" (*Figures* xix, 38–39). That he uses this phrase repeatedly is significant; it is an indication that deconstruction serves to perpetuate a key New Critical method. One of his most pointed responses to Joyce's accusation that his embrace of theory places him in a servile relationship to white European traditions is to underscore her own implicit indebtedness to New Criticism:

> Is the use of theory to write about Afro-American literature, we might ask rhetorically, merely another form of intellectual indenture, a form of servitude of the mind as pernicious in its intellectual implications as any other form of enslavement? This is the issue raised, for me at least, by the implied presence of the word *integrity* in Joyce Joyce's essay, but also by my own work over the past decade. Does the propensity to theorize about a text or a literary tradition "mar," "violate," "impair," or "corrupt" the "soundness" of a purported "original perfect state" of a black text or of the black tradition? To argue the affirmative is to align one's position with the New Critical position that texts are "wholes" in the first place. ("'What's Love?'" 349–350)

And yet, if the invocation of integrity and wholeness suggests an alignment with New Criticism, Gates is not afraid to deploy these terms, unironically, just a couple of pages later: "We must, above all, respect the integrity, the wholeness, of the black work of art, by bringing to bear upon the explication of its meanings all of the attention to language that we may learn from several developments in contemporary theory" (352). Though he asserts a readiness to employ any critical approach that can serve his purposes, Gates clearly prefers "contemporary theory" to New Criticism. And yet his suggestion is that the former allows for a preservation of both the values—integrity and wholeness—and the practical purpose—cultivating a "sensitivity to language"—fostered by the latter. What contemporary theory seems to offer him, then, is a revamped version of New Criticism, with its close attention to the aesthetic features of the text, but freed of its reactionary baggage.

To be sure, the "integrity" Gates defends may not be exactly the same as that celebrated by the New Critics. He signals the difference in his multiple references to Brown's response to Warren, which claims for black writers an "exegetical" facility and asserts the superiority of this facility to the "metaphysical" thinking championed by Warren. If the New Critics are "metaphysical," it is not only because they like poets such as John Donne and Robert Herrick; it is also because they believe that poetic language reveals a deep truth about the nature of reality. By contrast, Gates indicates, through his quotation of Brown, a preference for exegesis—that is, the interpretation of *texts*—as opposed to an effort to describe or understand an underlying prelinguistic reality. The integrity of the black tradition, as Gates understands it, is a surface or textual integrity, based on an ongoing dialogue between different rhetorical gestures, and not on a fixed, transhistorical black essence: "Ultimately, black literature is a verbal art like other verbal arts. 'Blackness' is not a material object, not an absolute, or an event, but a trope; it does not have an 'essence' as such but is defined by a network of relations that form a particular aesthetic unity. Even the slave narratives offer the text as a world, as a system of signs" (*Figures* 40). Black authors do often seek to represent the "Black Experience," but in all cases, as Gates underscores in his meticulous reading of the black tradition in *The Signifying Monkey*, they fabricate through rhetoric that which they claim to represent. Thus black identity is subject to continuous revision, re-creation, and rhetorical improvisation (*Signifying Monkey* 111). The wholeness of the tradition depends on the tendency of its authors to repeat and resignify the tropes and narrative devices employed by their predecessors; there is continuity, but it exists only at the level of rhetoric. Thus deconstruction, with its attention to language and its critique of metaphysics, is an especially useful tool for interpreting the ontologically groundless but rhetorically robust phenomenon known as "black literature."

Gates's defense renders legible two features of deconstruction that I have sought to underline in this chapter: first, that deconstruction actually preserves the aesthetic values it is often seen as disavowing, and second, that it preserves the aesthetic by facilitating its translation into politics, recasting a sensitivity to linguistic forms as a resource for left and progressive political causes. Consider the consequences of Gates's deconstruction of black identity. In his debate with Joyce, he clearly seeks to demonstrate that his preferred strategy of interpretation can serve a political agenda, supporting black empowerment. But if racial identity is redefined as a rhetorical effect, then securing greater visibility and influence for underrepresented races requires a sensitivity to the discursive strategies through which those races create, perform, and articulate themselves into existence. Celebrating blackness, in other words, means appreciating a certain mode of language. Thus Gates's argument works to establish a position not only for deconstruction but also for its formalist commitments within the identity-based struggles for recognition being waged by critics such as Joyce—struggles that will assume an increasingly central role in political criticism in the decades to come.[36]

But deconstruction, of course, is not the answer to all of Gates's problems. Though willing to use it when necessary, he ultimately argues for the excavation of a specifically black literary theory drawn from African and African American folk traditions—a project he famously carries out in The Signifying Monkey: "I once thought it our most important gesture to master the canon of criticism, to imitate and apply it, but I now believe that we must turn to the black tradition itself to develop theories of criticism indigenous to our literatures" ("Editor's Introduction" 13). He contends even more forcefully, "My position is that for a critic of black literature to borrow European or American theories of literature regardless of 'where they come from' is for that critic to be trapped in a relation of intellectual indenture or colonialism" ("Talkin' That Talk" 406). And yet Gates's construction of a black theoretical framework in The Signifying Monkey, inspired by a challenge issued by Hartman, features multiple references to other deconstructionist figures and a consistent reliance on deconstructionist terminology.[37] Joyce argues, "It is essential when reading The Signifying Monkey to stay alert to the fact that Gates grounds his text in the poststructuralist concept of deconstruction" ("Tinker's Damn" 374). This grounding, she maintains, leads him to emphasize the way trickster figures in Yoruba myths and African American folktales use rhetoric as a means of "destabilization." Thus he "move[s] African-American literary analysis away from its traditional issues of black collectivity and the need for ancestral worship" (378). To be clear, the conclusion to draw from Joyce's argument is not that the tropes Gates identifies do not exist; it is that these particular tropes, and not others, have achieved a privileged status because they both adhere to and serve to validate prevailing aesthetic criteria within the U.S. academic establishment.

Gates, of course, maintains that he, like the black trickster figures he celebrates, is merely signifying on the deconstructive discourse that he borrows, disrupting, perhaps even subverting, its original meaning.[38] It is a compelling posture, one that places him in the tradition of black writers, almost all of whom have had to negotiate cultural forms inherited from white Europeans in order to claim agency. But significantly, it also testifies, both in its rhetorical appropriation and in its theoretical echo, to the mercurial virtue of deconstructive discourse—to the latter's flexibility and mobility, which allow it to be transferred, translated, and resignified without surrendering its identity. To put it another way, *The Signifying Monkey* dramatizes precisely how deconstruction will survive in the decades to come. Though the specific school of criticism denoted by the name will cease to announce itself as a unified framework, though it will fall into disrepute and die multiple deaths, its signature terms and phrases will scatter and spread throughout the discipline, invading all variety of interpretive projects, thus perpetuating a particular set of aesthetic commitments alongside a faith in their subversive political potential.

Johnson's Politics

Published the same year as Miller's *The Ethics of Reading* and Gates's debate with Joyce, Johnson's *A World of Difference* (1987) also seeks to release deconstruction from the prison-house of mere aestheticism by accentuating its worldly character. But Johnson is more willing than Gates to serve openly as a champion of deconstruction and more willing than Miller to embrace left political engagement as a project deconstruction can claim for itself. She asks, "How can the study of suppressed, disseminated, or marginalized messages within texts equip us to intervene against oppression and injustice in the world?" (7). Her challenge is to show how the very tendencies that have led to perceptions of deconstruction as disconnected from real-world political struggles—a focus on abstract linguistic questions, an embrace of ambiguity, a refusal to arrive at categorical certitudes—can paradoxically enable it to play a transformative role within those struggles.

"How," Johnson wonders, "can the plea for slowness, for the suspension of decision, for the questioning of knowledge, ever function as anything other than a refusal to intervene? Nothing could be more convincing than the idea that political radicality requires decisiveness, not indecision; haste, not hesitation" (30). In her view, feminist politics represents a mode of resistance to precisely this imperative:

> The profound political intervention of feminism has indeed been not simply to enact radical politics but to redefine the very nature of what is deemed political—to take politics down from its male incarnation as a change-seeking interest in what is *not* nearest to hand, and to bring it into the daily texture of the relations between the sexes. The *literary* ramifications of this shift involve the discovery of the rhetorical survival skills of the formerly unvoiced. Lies, secrets, silences, and deflections of all sorts are routes taken by voices or messages not granted full legitimacy in order not to be altogether lost. (31)

Johnson is obviously right to insist that rhetorical tactics employed by those denied a voice in the traditional political sphere ought to be treated as political. But it seems telling that, like Miller's deployment of the ethical, Johnson's invocation of the political as a means of valuing certain ways of thinking and writing hinges on a corresponding effort to repress the aesthetic. "It is precisely because the established order leaves no room for unneutralized (i.e., unaestheticized) ambiguity that it seems urgent to meet decisiveness with decisiveness. But for that same reason it also seems urgent not to" (31). To aestheticize, apparently, is to neutralize, to render impotent. Given her sensitivity to the ways that other writers' seemingly random linguistic slips betray them, Johnson's decision to relegate this gesture to a perfunctory parenthesis, one that appears to be offering merely an uncontroversial clarification, is significant. She seems, in other words, to be deliberately deflecting

attention away from her repudiation of the aesthetic, as if afraid that
a too conspicuous denial might actually expose a secret devotion.
After all, like Miller's resignification of the ethical, her unorthodox
understanding of the political involves a refusal of the tendency to
measure certain ways of reading and writing in terms of the practical
effects they can produce. Moreover, she frequently suggests the importance of perceiving language as a purely sensuous object stripped
of any meaning or purpose. The term traditionally used to describe
the kind of noninstrumental value she identifies is of course *aesthetic.*
Thus Johnson's parenthetical aside suggests an anxiety that her assertion of the political may in fact be a means of masking aesthetic
investments.

It is certainly true that the deconstructive rhetorical modes that
Johnson favors are capable of performing a subversive political function within certain contexts, but in order to support that claim, it
would be necessary to identify and describe those contexts. Johnson's
conception of actual political situations, however, is vague at best.
Questioning how deconstructive insights might operate in the real
world, she speculates, "If you tell a member of the Ku Klux Klan that
racism is a repression of self-difference, you are likely to learn a thing
or two about repression" (2–3). Attempting to invoke reality, Johnson
produces pure cinema: this nightmarishly improbable scenario in
which a feminist deconstructionist's conversation with a KKK member
on the origins of racism leads the latter to exact violent retribution is
a caricature of the encounter between theory and the "real world."
Later, explaining how metaphor and metonymy, or resemblance and
contiguity, can become conflated, a tendency encapsulated by the
proverb "Birds of a feather flock together," she observes, "One has only
to think of the applicability of this proverb to the composition of neigh-
borhoods in America to realize that the question of the separability of
similarity from contiguity may have considerable political implications" (157). The intimate relationship between rhetorical figures
(metaphor and metonymy) and politics (the composition of neighbor-
hoods) is in her formulation so obvious, so effortlessly made, that
thinking about one automatically entails thinking about the other. But
this very closeness also licenses her to prioritize the former, rhetoric,
and neglect the latter, politics. Notice: "One has only to think." She

can devote her energy to rhetoric, secure in her belief that her analysis has profound political implications, while leaving the thinking about racial segregation in the United States to someone else.

Johnson imagines that certain rhetorical strategies, including indecision, deflection, silence, ambiguity, the deferral of certainty, and so forth, can play a significant political role within what she calls the "established order" (31) or the "patriarchal order" (133), but the problem with the latter phrases is that they do not designate a specific context. What Johnson does is to construct a pseudo-context, where abstractions—"obscurity and undecidability" (141) on the one hand and "the requirement that everything be assigned a clear meaning" (30–31) or "decisiveness" (30) on the other—come into conflict. But she never quite explains where this supposed obligation to be clear comes from or whose interests it serves. Indeed the conflict she describes bears no resemblance to actual political struggles, traditional or otherwise, in which people or parties vie for power or resources. The struggle that Johnson imagines between rhetorical tropes or between different theories of how language should operate seems like the kind of debate that could happen only within a theoretical text or a seminar. By conflating this fairly limited academic space with the contemporary public sphere as a whole and inventing an enemy with purportedly hegemonic influence that needs to be resisted—that is, the demand for clarity—Johnson is able to turn certain literary devices and interpretive strategies into heroic freedom fighters, assigning them a subversive power as a way of enabling them to retain their importance within the politically oriented academy of the 1980s. And their oppositional power is paradoxically transhistorical; one can imagine an "established order" that demands clarity operating in just about any conceivable context. Ambiguity, as Johnson understands it, brings its enemy everywhere it goes so as to be perceived always and everywhere as a means of furthering radical politics.[39]

The central goal of all literature and interpretation should be, according to Johnson, to produce surprise, a view she defends in uncharacteristically categorical terms:

> The impossible but necessary task of the reader is to set herself up to be surprised.

No methodology can be relied on to generate surprise. On the contrary, it is usually surprise that engenders methodology. Derrida brings to his reader the surprise of a nonbinary, undecidable logic. Yet comfortable undecidability needs to be surprised by its own conservatism. My emphasis on the word *surprise* is designed to counter the idea that a good deconstructor must constantly put his own enterprise in question. This is true, but it is not enough. It can lead to a kind of infinite regress of demystification, in which ever more sophisticated subtleties are elaborated within an unchanging field of questions. (15)

Neither a commitment to a particular methodology nor the pursuit of a particular political vision should determine one's interpretive strategy; the driving force must be the desire to be surprised. But it is almost impossible to remain surprised by anything for very long. Johnson, in other words, prioritizes a particular affective response that is by definition short-lived, one that is almost certain to be confined to the moment of reading. Not only does this sound suspiciously like the celebration of a text's aesthetic power—that is to say, its ability to produce an immediate visceral response—but it also seems entirely inauspicious as a basis for politics. How can something so short-lived sustain the commitment necessary to further a particular ideological vision?

Though she argues that deconstruction can represent a valuable form of political engagement, Johnson, like Miller, is unwilling to consider anything outside, beyond, or after the experience of reading. Her scope prevents her from exploring how deconstruction might exert long-term social influence, subvert particular political arrangements, or help the disempowered groups whose figural representations she analyzes. Thus her criticism functions, despite her own stated intentions, as a mode of aesthetic appreciation, one whose remarkable sophistication allows it to turn political questions into a springboard for the same heady experiences of ambiguity, uncertainty, and paradox that the New Critics had derived from reading metaphysical poetry. The point here is not to join the decades-old chorus of those faulting deconstruction for being insufficiently political. Rather, the point is to recognize how Johnson and other like-minded figures successfully worked to construct an ahistorical, taken-for-granted equation between a particular aesthetic—of obscurity, undecidability, and self-negation—and a posture of radical political opposition, an equation that would persist well after deconstruction fell out of fashion, allowing scholars both to validate and to disguise aesthetic pleasure, while endowing their work with an aura of heroic subversion merely on the basis of its style.

To be sure, the aesthetic experience offered by deconstruction is by no means identical to the one, say, that Brooks celebrates in *The Well-Wrought Urn*; the latter has received a dramatic makeover. Indeed, more lucidly than most other examples, Johnson's book demonstrates how deconstruction serves to perpetuate New Critical formal values by revising them, by not only redeploying them in new contexts but also rethinking both their justification and substance. And surprisingly enough, it is deconstruction's reconception of aesthetics, its answer to the question of what kind of cognitive-affective experience criticism should privilege, rather than any sort of turn to politics, that ends up having the greatest impact on the various ideologically oriented methodologies—most notably New Historicism—that emerge in its wake.

In a fairly obvious sense, deconstruction's strategies for making illegible, tangential, and seemingly nonsensical textual details at the margins of literary works yield unexpected insights obviously provide a model for the analysis of nonliterary materials, including letters, diaries, legal documents, and the like, that comes to prevail within historicist and materialist modes of literary scholarship. But deconstruction is able to render the recalcitrant textual details that it examines readable only by reconceiving the act of interpretation and the goals toward which it is directed. If we consider Johnson's readings, for instance, we notice that any seemingly random detail in the text can become, under her scrutiny, miraculously meaningful, a way of reasserting, complicating, or subverting the preoccupations and arguments that are registered elsewhere in the text. Yet, if every detail is capable of bearing meaning, the text as a whole is blindingly incoherent; Johnson's readings proceed toward maximum complexity; the text becomes a riot of contradictory suggestions, the careful delineation of which puts the reader in a state of total bewilderment—a state that is of course the very aim of deconstruction.

As we have seen, the New Critics recognized that the discovery of heterogeneous particulars and contradictory meanings was a necessary and intellectually satisfying part of the overall experience of reading poetry, but they viewed the latter as a problem that needed to be solved: for an interpretation to qualify as successful, it had to subsume the anarchic semantic impulses that it identified within a unified meaning. Deconstructionists, by contrast, are not satisfied until they confront a problem that cannot be solved; thus they accent the first part of the New Critical interpretive procedure, the discovery of contradictions, in order to exclude or render impossible the second part, the arrival at a coherent interpretation.

While deconstruction has sometimes been read as a departure from the aesthetic orientation central to New Criticism, its embrace of hermeneutic chaos might also be regarded merely as a shift from an aesthetic of the beautiful to an aesthetic of the sublime. The experience of the sublime, unlike that of the beautiful, according to Kant, never results in a synthesis of the heterogeneous particulars into a higher-order state of comprehension: "If something arouses in us, merely in apprehension and without any reasoning on our part, a feeling of the sublime, then it may indeed appear, in its form, contrapurposive for our power of judgment, incommensurate with our power of exhibition, and as it were violent to our imagination" (*Critique of Judgment* 99). There is still aesthetic pleasure, but it does not depend on the discovery of a unified organic form. It is worth noting that many of the political attacks on the aesthetic within academic literary scholarship have actually targeted the aesthetic of the beautiful, equating the latter's privileging of wholeness, unity, and stability with a reactionary attachment to cultural homogeneity and the maintenance of the traditional social order. Emphasizing experiences that might be described as sublime, deconstruction privileges a mode of aesthetic appreciation better able to present itself as a commitment to radical or subversive politics. Moreover, in legitimizing certain sublime aesthetic experiences—of failing to make sense, of remaining perplexed, baffled, thwarted by the text—as a proof of rigor, a sign that one is actually reading, deconstruction in fact prepared the way for New Historicism.

It might seem strange to argue that deconstruction's reformulation of what constitutes a satisfying or fulfilling response to a literary work would enable the emergence of New Historicism, given the latter's purported lack of interest in aesthetic questions. But as I will argue in Chapter 3, New Historicism does in fact continue to privilege certain aesthetic pleasures, certain forms of sensitivity to textual complexity that bear a strong resemblance to those favored by deconstruction. While New Historicists seek to replace formalism with ideological analysis, they nevertheless preserve disciplinary continuity between their work and that of their predecessors; they still seek to produce readings that are recognizable as *literary* scholarship. The way they accomplish this is to make the nontraditional, nonliterary objects that they consider aesthetically compelling in accordance with established criteria. And significantly, it is deconstructive criteria that allow them to achieve this end.

The archival artifacts that the New Historicists interpret are significantly more fragmentary, disorganized, and incoherent than the works of poetry or fiction typically examined by literary scholars. Moreover, the ultimate goal of a New Historicist reading is to offer an analysis of an entire historical situation, one that consists of multiple agents and spheres of activity, and such a situation obviously cannot be read as the expression of a single artistic intention; in most cases the details cannot be made to cohere. Or rather, the imposition of a unified meaning would defeat the impression, central to the New Historicists' agenda, that they are grappling not merely with literary texts but with historical reality in all of its unruly heterogeneity. Deconstructive strategies of interpretation make it possible to preserve this impression without relinquishing aesthetic satisfaction. History may not yield clarity, but it can nevertheless elicit a response akin to that provoked by poetry. When the objective is simply to discover a multitude of resonances and tensions without resolving them into an overarching unity, then New Historicists can treat archival materials the same way they treat literary works. Both can be the basis for the intellectually rewarding, if bewildering, interpretive experience that the deconstructionists had worked to legitimize as the very essence of reading. What deconstruction makes possible, in other words, is not the politicization of criticism but the aestheticization of history.

3

New Historicism and
the Aesthetics of the Archive

ATTEMPTING IN HIS 1986 Modern Language Association presidential address to understand why deconstruction is being assaulted by critics of every possible persuasion, J. H. Miller identifies a quasi-puritanical suspicion of pleasure as a common motive:

> From the left come cries that it is immoral not to be concerned with history, with society, with the real conditions of men and women in society. It is immoral to get lost in the sterile meanderings of language playing with itself. From the right come cries that it is immoral to shift from a thematic concern with literature, a study of the way literature expresses the values of our culture, to a nihilistic and "radically skeptical" concern with language, to get lost in the sterile meanderings of language playing with itself. The word *sterile*, used in attacks from both sides as an epithet defining theory, carries a large sexual freight. The implication is that theory is narcissistic, even self-abusive. ("Presidential Address" 284)

Critics, in other words, disapprove of deconstruction because they regard it as masturbatory. Their metaphor for the alternatives, whether a conservative return to traditional values or a progressive concern for literature's relationship to history and society, is, as Miller wryly observes, "procreation" (284). Pleasure is acceptable, but only insofar as it produces something beyond itself. To appreciate the language of the text for its own sake without regard to the practical ends it might further has become taboo, at least in good company. Seeking aesthetic satisfaction is thus akin to masturbation, an apparently useless solitary ritual that everyone treats as slightly shameful but then eagerly performs when nobody else is looking.

In describing the liberal and left attacks on deconstruction, Miller is of course referring to the variety of methodologies in the 1980s, including New Historicism, Marxism, feminism, African American studies, postcolonialism, cultural studies, and gay and lesbian studies, that reject strictly formalist or aesthetic approaches to literature in the name of greater political engagement. Significantly, while he questions the equation between theory and masturbation, Miller never challenges the axiomatic distrust of aesthetic pleasure evinced by the various kinds of political critics. Although he is concerned that these schools will, in their haste to "make the study of literature count in society" (283), skip over the task of reading carefully, he expresses guarded support for their objectives and ultimately suggests that they form an alliance with deconstruction. "If you oppose theory from the so-called left, I say you should make common cause with those who practice a rhetorical study of literature, that is, with the multiform movement called 'deconstruction,' of which a rhetorical study of literature is one vector of force" (290).

In his desire to defend deconstruction, Miller appears prepared, as we saw in Chapter 2, to cut ties between the methods he has championed and an interest in aesthetic considerations. "Literary theory," he contends, "is the only way to avoid the sequestering of literature within an aestheticism of 'organic form' that deprives the study of literature of any effective purchase on our society" (290). "Organic form" is, of course, the cherished object of that now dreadful specter, New Criticism. But by the mid-1980s, scholars have begun to wonder what exactly distinguishes deconstruction from its predecessor. Notwithstanding his investment in close reading, Miller resists any such association. Recognizing that the aesthetic has become the target of almost universal derision within the academy, Miller dismisses the latter, aligning it with reactionary politics and casting deconstruction as the best possible means of furthering the Left's political agenda.

The urge to "make the study of literature count in society" was obviously the expression of legitimate and commendable political commitments among scholars whose approaches had been shaped by the various social struggles of the 1960s and early 1970s. But it may also be read as a response to growing pressures faced by the humanities from corporate, market-oriented administrators to demonstrate the practical, social, or economic utility of the knowledge they produced and the critical faculties they sought to cultivate. The question this chapter pursues is how the aesthetic modes of inquiry established by earlier schools of interpretation, including both New Criticism and deconstruction, were able to survive within an environment increasingly hostile to the possibility of valuing a particular way of thinking for its own sake and not for the practical consequences it might yield.

In this chapter, I examine the contradictory impulses of one especially influential methodology, New Historicism. Though often accused of banishing aesthetic considerations from the academy, this school of criticism, I want to suggest, in fact did the opposite. Appropriating both New Critical and deconstructive methods, New Historicism found a way to protect formalist analysis and aesthetic satisfaction by transferring them into a new domain, repackaging them as the very means of both understanding and intervening within the political sphere, thus satisfying the instrumental logic that had come to dominate the discipline of English. In this way its project was similar to that of deconstruction's later phase, but with some notable differences. In Chapter 2 we saw how Miller, Henry Louis Gates Jr., and Barbara Johnson served to politicize or instrumentalize aesthetic analysis; in this chapter I will suggest that the New Historicists aestheticized various modes of political and economic inquiry. If the shift from deconstruction to New Historicism was, as some suggested, a shift from unproductive masturbation to productive procreation, it is important to note that the pleasure did not disappear; it persisted, safeguarded precisely by being recast as part of a productive process.

Formal Baggage

Anyone seeking to describe New Historicism confronts difficulties similar to those posed by deconstruction and New Criticism. That is, its practitioners refuse to define their method systematically.[1] Moreover, the category itself is sometimes used to describe the critical projects of a handful of influential scholars, most of whom edited or contributed to the academic journal *Representations*, including Stephen Greenblatt, Louis Montrose, and Catherine Gallagher, and it is sometimes used to indicate a much wider range of scholarly approaches in the 1980s and beyond that sought to situate literary texts within a historical or political framework. In this chapter I examine the work of those most closely identified with New Historicism, but I also treat it as an example of and influence on a broader set of tendencies. Thus I also consider scholarship not typically categorized as New Historicist, in order to identify traces of covert aestheticism across the discipline during the 1980s and 1990s.

To offer a brief preliminary sketch, New Historicists consider literary works in relationship to the material conditions surrounding their production, frequently with a focus on economic structures and marketplace realities. They assert that authors are always shaped by historical and political circumstances, and they contest both the autonomy of literary works and the idea that these works can be measured according to transhistorical criteria of greatness. At the same time, however, they refuse to see literary works as merely the passive symptom of a material base; they invest these works with agency, considering not only how they are influenced by other spheres, such as the marketplace, but also how they influence those spheres in turn. New Historicists reject Marxist grand narratives, which treat all historical phenomena as uniformly and predictably determined by material and economic conditions, offering instead a notion of history as fragmented, heterogeneous, and unpredictable. Power, in their view, does not emanate from a central source such as the state or the ruling class; it is diffuse and omnipresent. Thus they attend to what Gallagher calls the "micro-politics of daily life" ("Marxism" 43). In doing so, they often focus on random or idiosyncratic historical details, subjecting archival materials, including account books, advertisements, personal diaries, newspaper articles, political pamphlets, and the like, to careful scrutiny, discovering unexpected resonances between these and literary works. Even while they reject what they regard as the simplifications of traditional historians, they do not present their version as truer or more accurate; they recognize, in other words, the constructed nature of their own narratives. All knowledge production, they hold, is the result of particular political interests and social pressures, including historical scholarship. Although an understanding of history can help to make sense of literature, there is no direct or neutral access to what actually happened. New Historicists are dedicated, as Montrose puts it, to underscoring both "the historicity of texts and the textuality of history" ("Professing the Renaissance" 20).[2]

While New Historicism was a response to all the varieties of formalism that had predominated in previous decades, its proponents defined themselves most frequently in opposition to New Criticism, perhaps because the latter was already so universally spurned that it represented an easy target.[3] On the first page of *Learning to Curse*, Greenblatt offers the most devastating takedown while describing his early graduate training at Yale. After a day of vainly wrestling with arch New Critic William K. Wimsatt's notion of poetry as a "concrete universal," he would visit the all-male Elizabethan Club, where he would encounter a "black servant in a starched white jacket," before listening to Wimsatt "hold forth like Dr. Johnson on poetry and aesthetics" while eating cucumber sandwiches (*Learning* 1). Though he avoids explicit accusations, what Greenblatt is suggesting is fairly obvious: the New Critics were sexist and racist. Or, as Graham Harman puts it, this passage "makes the familiar implication that all 'formalism' tends towards sociopolitical blindness—an aestheticism exploiting the marginal servitude of subaltern actors" ("Well-Wrought Broken Hammer" 191).

Eventually Greenblatt would figure out how to defeat his old masters; the title *Learning to Curse*, a reference to William Shakespeare's Caliban, tacitly posits the New Historicist as the hip rebel, heroically fighting back against stifling conventions upheld by stodgy authorities such as Wimsatt. The hostility directed against New Criticism is curious, however, given the already much maligned status of the latter. Greenblatt and his compatriots seem, in other words, to exert extraordinary effort to assault an already mortally wounded foe.[4] Indeed, as numerous observers, including Carolyn Porter and Judith Lowder Newton, have pointed out, deconstructionists, feminists, Marxists, and race theorists had been issuing cogent critiques of New Criticism, steadily eroding its power in English departments, for quite some time.[5] Thus it is worth considering whether the New Historicists' excessive, belated interest in New Criticism suggests a relationship more complicated than mere opposition. Greenblatt has no qualms about confessing his own ambivalence: "There are days when I long to recover the close-grained formalism of my own literary training" (*Shakespearean* 3). The primary argument of this chapter is that the New Historicists did, in a strange way, recover the formalist modes of interpretation that Greenblatt found so intimidating during his graduate years at Yale. Confronting an academic culture already invested in the project of political interpretation as a result of the left, feminist, and antiracist scholarship inspired by the protest movements of the late 1960s and early 1970s, the New Historicists were able to reactivate aesthetic and formal analysis by lending them a viable role within political interpretation.

Both Greenblatt and Gallagher present New Historicism as a methodology capable of accommodating aesthetic appreciation. Distinguishing themselves from orthodox Marxists, they underscore the need to recognize the specificity of literature as a mode of writing distinct from other social practices. Insisting that literature reproduces prevailing ideologies, Gallagher nevertheless declares, "I assume there is normally some sort of tension between ideology and literary forms," and she argues that "literary forms often disrupt the tidy formulations and reveal the inherent paradoxes of their ostensible ideologies" (*Industrial Reformation* xiii). Greenblatt goes further, attacking Fredric Jameson's position that any assertion of autonomy for the aesthetic realm is "a malignant symptom of 'privatization'" ("Toward a Poetics" 2). "Would we really find it less alienating," Greenblatt wonders, "to have no distinction at all between the political and the poetic—the situation, let us say, during China's Cultural Revolution?" ("Toward a Poetics" 3). "Great art," Greenblatt asserts, sounding more like his New Critical forebears than he might realize, "is an extraordinarily sensitive register of the complex struggles and harmonies of culture"

(*Renaissance Self-Fashioning* 5). In his famous essay "Resonance and Wonder," he goes on to argue that moments of aesthetic appreciation, in which the viewer gazes in admiration at a work of art, are a contingent product of institutional and economic forces, but also "one of the distinctive achievements of our culture" and thus "worth cherishing and enhancing" (*Learning* 180).

And yet, despite such attempts to pay their respects, when they describe aesthetic appreciation, New Historicists tend to drain it of any vitality or complexity. Montrose, for instance, defines formalism as a commitment to an "autonomous aesthetic order that transcends the shifting pressure and particularity of material needs and interests" ("Renaissance Literary Studies" 8). Echoing this characterization, Greenblatt observes, "The island in *The Tempest* seems to be an image of the place of pure fantasy, set apart from surrounding discourses; and it seems to be an image of the place of power, the place in which all individual discourses are organized by the half-invisible ruler. By extension art is a well-demarcated, marginal private sphere, the realm of insight, pleasure and isolation; and art is a capacious, central, public sphere, the realm of proper political order made possible through mind control, coercion, discipline, anxiety, and pardon" (*Shakespearean* 158–159). *The Tempest*'s setting represents art as either a source of aesthetic experience or a site of political negotiation. While the first option seems to involve a fair amount of pleasure and serenity, it is difficult to imagine anyone remaining very long on the remote island of aesthetic satisfaction that Greenblatt envisions without getting bored. Whether deliberately or not, his account makes aesthetic contemplation seem not only "marginal" but tedious, unworthy of scholarly attention, as does Montrose's image of a static order, unresponsive to the vicissitudes of actual life. Though it involves "discipline" and "coercion," the "capacious public sphere," with its ups and downs, its moments of "anxiety" and "pardon," its material needs and interests, seems far more exciting. For Greenblatt and Montrose, the aesthetic is only ever a pristine alternative to the gritty material struggles, erotic negotiations, and cunning political machinations that capture the majority of their interest.

It might seem, then, that sifting through New Historicist scholarship in search of insights about aesthetics would be a futile effort.

Though Greenblatt acknowledges the value of traditional aesthetic contemplation, the New Historicists never present it as exciting or capable of yielding interesting ideas. They categorically refuse to consider works of literature in isolation from broader historical conditions. They are not interested in developing an explicit definition of great art or poetic language. Unlike their predecessors, they avoid offering a specific set of aesthetic criteria or challenging those put forward by other critics. Beyond a few token acknowledgments, the New Historicists do not, in other words, appear to uphold any particular aesthetic principles. And yet it would be an error to conclude on the basis of their silence that the New Historicists' work does not depend on aesthetic commitments. Rather, they tend to betray these commitments precisely when they are *not* addressing aesthetic questions, when they are focusing instead on the subjects that capture the majority of their interest: ideology, politics, and social struggle. Although they are unconcerned with traditional modes of aesthetic response that isolate literary works from broader historical contexts, they translate history itself into an aesthetically compelling object of contemplation, and they do so in accordance with criteria inherited from both the deconstructionists and the New Critics.

Aestheticizing History

Reflecting on their scholarly tendencies in *Practicing New Historicism*, Greenblatt and Gallagher observe, "We mine what are sometimes called counterhistories that make apparent the slippages, cracks, fault lines, and surprising absences in the monumental structures that dominated a more traditional historicism" (17). From the beginning, the New Historicists sought to distinguish their methodology from the old historicism that had dominated literary scholarship before New Criticism.[6] Old historicism, according to Greenblatt, presented history as a "stable background" to literary works, a repository of knowable, objective facts that could be brought together into a coherent, objectively valid narrative and used to make sense of the text's various allusions and eliminate its ambiguities (*Shakespearean* 95). According to Marjorie Levinson, "[Older modes of literary history] recovered contexts of reference and reception considered external to the artwork and useful in clarifying its aesthetic values, its position within larger cultural narratives, and also within genre study. New historicism challenged this model's a priori distinction between internal and external domains, pressing for an integral and also a generative relationship between text and context, and between form and content, in this way grafting a core thesis of the formalist paradigm onto traditional historical scholarship" ("Reflections" 357). Rejecting the "distinction between internal and external domains," the New Historicists treat history the same way scholars treat literary works. To argue for the "textuality of history," as Montrose does, is to recognize that history is no more stable, unified, or knowable than the works that are embedded in it. It too is a mysterious and complex object in need of interpretation.

To make history worthy of the attention of literary scholars, the New Historicists cast it as a very specific kind of text, one that consists of slippages, fissures, contingencies, disruptions, radical uncertainties, shifting grounds, fragmented multiple identities, and unsettled, contradictory positions. Their rhetoric sometimes makes it sound as if they are attempting to explore an immense cavern in the middle of an earthquake.[7] Significantly, the terminology they use to describe history is remarkably similar to that used by the deconstructionists to describe the formal features of literary works. Though their emphasis has shifted, their vocabulary still presupposes a particular set of assumptions about what constitutes an interesting object of scrutiny and what makes for a worthwhile interpretive experience. Their approach is shaped by an aesthetic of the rough, the fragmented, the myriad, the unpredictable, and the opaque; the intellectual responses they favor include ambivalence, skepticism, uncertainty, an openness to multiple contradictory meanings, and a refusal to impose sweeping narratives onto the apparently multifarious historical landscape that they are examining.[8] The New Historicists' most consistent commitment, according to Greenblatt and Gallagher, is to "particularity," and this too is an inheritance from their formalist forebears (*Practicing* 19). A devotion to particularity motivated the New Critical investment in the local textures of poetry. However much he misses the "close-grained formalism" of his graduate years, Greenblatt and his allies discover, it would seem, an equally satisfying fine grain within the historical archive.[9]

Numerous scholars have in fact accused the New Historicists of being covert aesthetes. Hayden White, Vincent P. Pecora, and Alan Liu all ascribe a residual "formalism" to their work.[10] Brook Thomas observes, "In fact, Greenblatt's mode of analysis owes more to his formalist training than his attack on it would indicate" (*New Historicism* 42). Sonja Laden contends that one of their main functions has been to revive the "category of the aesthetic" ("Recuperating" 2). And in an especially cogent and sustained critique, Porter observes, "This [New Historical] operation, in effect, retextualizes the extraliterary as literary. I would call it Colonialist Formalism, not new historicism" ("Are We?" [1990] 58). Moreover, she notes that the New Historical method seems to consist of subjecting archival materials to strategies of close reading inherited from the New Critics: "In literary studies [a principle of "arbitrary connectedness"] serves to legitimate an equally suspect formalism, which seems to treat the social text in much the way it has been accustomed to treating the literary one. As if you could say, in response to the question of how you relate text to reality, reality *is* a text, and then proceed to read it, like a New Critic, for its paradoxes, tensions, and ambiguities" ("Are We?" [1988] 780). Examples of New Historicists using the New Critical technique of close reading in order to discover "paradoxes, tensions, and ambiguities" within the historical archive are too numerous to count. One representative early instance is Gallagher's analysis, in *The Industrial Reformation of English Fiction*, of the polemics that constituted the Condition of England debate during the industrial era. In that book, Gallagher identifies all variety of ironies and paradoxes within nonliterary political discourse, which in her view actually inspired commensurate forms of complexity in the novels that were produced at the same time.[11] Another is Greenblatt's examination of Thomas Harriot's narrative *A Brief and True Report of the New Found Land of Virginia* (1598) in *Shakespearean Negotiations* (21–47). There Greenblatt finds the same intricate dialectic between registering subversion and supporting dominant power structures that he finds in *Henry IV, Part I*.

In *Practicing New Historicism*, Greenblatt and Gallagher are happy to acknowledge that their analysis sometimes serves to aestheticize the objects they examine: "Major works of art remain centrally important, but they are jostled now by an array of other texts and images. . . . The conjunction can produce almost surrealist wonder at the revelation of an unanticipated aesthetic dimension in objects without pretensions to the aesthetic" (9–10). Yet, while they present this state of wonder, this aesthetic experience of the archive, as if it were a felicitous accident, it might be more accurately read as a structural feature, even a central goal, of their scholarship. A particular methodological premise, which Walter Benn Michaels has identified, would seem to guarantee the translation of archival materials into a springboard for aesthetic pleasure. Though at one time aligned with New Historicism, Michaels finds fault with the agenda voiced by Greenblatt in his memorable opening to *Shakespearean Negotiations:* "I began with the desire to speak with the dead" (1). The traditional historical project, according to Michaels, is to turn the past into an object of knowledge. But Greenblatt wants something else; he yearns to have a direct *experience* of the past, the same way the deconstructionists, through their interest in performative language, strive to experience rather than understand the literary work. In both cases, Michaels suggests, a perceptual affective response becomes the priority ("'You Who Never'").[12]

To say that New Historicists textualize or recast history necessarily raises the question of what exactly it is they are recasting. The term *history* is ambiguous; it can refer to actual events, things that happened, particular actions, or situations; it can also refer to various texts and other artifacts found within the archive; and it can refer to the narratives created by historians to explain the past or scholarly interpretations of the archive. Generally unconcerned with precise definitions, the New Historicists use the term to refer to all three phenomena at different moments. While their most common strategy is to focus carefully on a particular archival artifact, their goal is to produce readings of larger situations that extend beyond the boundaries of a single document or text, in search of symbols, ambiguities, and paradoxes. In analyzing these situations, it is important to note, the New Historicists are generally not hoping to find some unifying meaning, the way a New Critic might in interpreting a poem. They recognize, in other words, that the realities they are considering have not been shaped in accordance with a coherent artistic intention, and they usually seek to magnify the complexities, contradictions, and competing meanings of whatever phenomenon they are considering to such a point that it refuses any overarching sense of comprehension. Such an aim obviously bears the mark of deconstruction's influence, and it suggests the same commitment to an aesthetic of the sublime. The New Historicists, as Greenblatt puts it, "have been more interested in unresolved conflict and contradiction than in integration" (*Learning* 168). Indeed, as I suggested in Chapter 2, deconstruction's success in making hermeneutic bewilderment, the sense of complexities multiplying beyond one's comprehension, the very goal and measure of serious interpretive work allowed a much wider range of objects beyond the strictly literary to be viewed as worthy of close reading. They opened the door, in other words, for New Historicists to aestheticize all variety of confusing, fragmented, ungainly, or otherwise opaque materials that would never be able to yield the kind of synthetic, unifying interpretation favored by the New Critics.

But, if the New Historicists do not present the historical details they consider as the expression of a particular artistic intention or as the means of conveying a coherent meaning, then in what sense are they aestheticizing these details? How is their presentation of history any different from that of other historians—all of whom organize, select, and embellish their materials in various ways so as to produce an interesting narrative? The distinguishing tendency of the New Historicists is the way they curate the objects that they uncover—the images, gestures, artifacts, and episodes—framing them so that they arrest the reader's attention, awakening a sensitivity to their particularity in the same way a New Critical or deconstructive reading lends peculiar vividness to the individual elements of a poem. In *Learning to Curse*, Greenblatt announces, "I am committed to the project of making strange what has become familiar" (8). He has, in other words, appropriated for his scholarship the role first attributed to poetic language by the Russian formalists. Employing what Greenblatt and Gallagher call, quoting Ezra Pound, "the method of the Luminous Detail" (*Practicing* 15), New Historicists trace the resonances between a given historical particular and all the other contextual details that surround it. Thus they treat it like a literary motif, but in a work too chaotic to yield a unified meaning, cataloging, like deconstructionists, a dizzying multiplicity of echoes, antimonies, symmetries, ironies, and homologies, which, failing to resolve into a clear or coherent picture of the historical period, simply reflect back on the object itself, lending it mysterious significance, making it glow, as it were, in the darkness of its obscure connections with everything around it. The effect is a quickening of the reader's perceptual responsiveness that does not lead to comprehension—an almost textbook example, in other words, of the sublime as Immanuel Kant understood it.

The rhetorical strategy for which the New Historicists are most famous is, of course, the anecdote. Establishing a formula still in vogue across the field of literary scholarship, they invariably begin their arguments by narrating an obscure historical episode culled from the archive, generally circumscribed enough in scope to conform to the Aristotelian unities, before using the episode to illuminate a broader set of historical issues. In many essays, they interrupt their interpretations mid-argument to introduce new anecdotes that complicate whatever claim they are making. Greenblatt in particular enjoys pausing to tell stories apparently irrelevant to the subject at hand—whether about an entirely different historical moment or his own life—before revealing an unlikely resonance, one designed to startle readers into a deeper state of comprehension. H. Aram Veeser contends that the purpose of these anecdotes is to reveal "the behavioral codes, logics, and motive forces controlling a whole society" (introduction xi), and while anecdotes do often perform this synecdochal function, the New Historicists also embrace them for their power to resist broad generalizations about a given social context. Underlining the anecdote's "strangeness or opacity," Greenblatt and Gallagher argue that it "functions then to subvert a programmatic analytical response" (*Practicing* 22–23). "The anecdote binds structures and what exceeds them, history and counterhistory, into a knot of conflicted interdependence" (68). Insofar as it defies theoretical abstractions and foregrounds particular incidents, the anecdote seems to allow scholars, as Joel Fineman puts it, "pointed, referential access to the real" ("History" 56).

For the purposes of exposing the New Historicists' aesthetic investments, it is worth emphasizing the resemblance between their understanding of the anecdote and the New Critics' reading of the poetic detail or local texture. "The texture of a poem," according to John Crowe Ransom, "is the heterogeneous character of its detail, which either fills in the logical outline very densely or else overflows it a little" (*New Criticism* 163). What makes a poem difficult to paraphrase, according to the New Critics, are the particular images, metaphors, rhythms, and paradoxes, which both convey and subvert the poem's larger structure and meaning. "Poetical discourse," observes Ransom, "does not deny its logical structure as a whole, but it continually takes little departures from it by virtue of the logical impurity of its terms" (*New Criticism* 42). It is this "incessant particularity," in fact, that allows poetry to escape the abstractions of science and gain a purchase on the real in all of its concreteness and heterogeneity (25).

For the New Critics, then, the poetic detail performs the same ontological function that the anecdote performs for the New Historicists. In both cases, the stylistic strategy being used defies the general abstractions that it also supports, seeking to disrupt, through a particular use of language, the very barrier that linguistic forms generally create between the observer and reality. There is, however, one significant difference. The devices to which Ransom and Cleanth Brooks turn their attention operate mostly within poetry. What Ransom underscores is the way meter, rhyme, and other poetic patterns require unusual verbal choices that would not be necessitated in prose writing motivated solely by the urge to convey a predetermined meaning; thus any particular image or word, dictated by conflicting imperatives, exists in a tension with the meaning it communicates. Employing a close reading method predicated on this theory, the New Critics were far more adept at interpreting poetry than narrative forms. The reverse is true for the New Historicists, whose approach has never worked especially well with poetry, and whose privileged stylistic device, the anecdote, functions only as part of a larger narrative.[13] While the New Historicists are usually credited with ushering in a transfer of attention from the isolated literary work to the broader historical context, their intervention might also be read as a transfer of attention from one genre to another. By establishing the significance of the anecdote, in other words, the New Historicists found a way to produce a mode of aesthetic response roughly equivalent to the one favored by the New Critics but applicable to the genres that were, in the 1980s, quickly coming to supplant poetry as the center of scholarly attention—namely, drama and, far more importantly, the novel.[14]

The New Historicists use anecdotes in order to make not only fictional works but also their own nonfictional historical narratives capable of inspiring aesthetic satisfaction. Insofar as the anecdotes they privilege are the "outlandish and irregular ones," as Greenblatt and Gallagher put it, the process of selecting materials obviously plays an important role. Although the New Historicists sometimes seem able to invest any phenomenon, however mundane, with a degree of complexity to rival the most intricate literary work, as Gallagher's tour de force reading of the potato in nineteenth-century England demonstrates, that essay is more the exception (*Practicing* 110–135). Typically, the New Historicists make history richly fascinating by considering phenomena that are relatively amenable to their interpretive exercises. Fineman wryly describes New Historicism's "characteristic air of reporting, haplessly, the discoveries it happened serendipitously to stumble upon in the course of the undirected, idle rambles through the historical archives" ("History" 52). As Maurice Lee suggests, these discoveries are never entirely random. The ability to identify surprising resonances between idiosyncratic materials necessitates a kind of preliminary aesthetic discrimination that precedes and makes possible the subsequent analysis. Comparing New Historicists' method of selecting their materials to the narrator's engagement with the Custom House archive in *The Scarlet Letter*, Lee remarks, "Because such judgments, if we can call them such, are so devilishly hard to justify logically, they often seem like intuitions, a phenomenon that leads Hawthorne and his contemporaries to vindicate the role of aesthetic judgment in archival reading practices" ("Searching" 756).

New Historicists tend to fixate on eccentric individuals, acts of unspeakable cruelty, scenes of illicit transgression, and—as per their continuous deployment of metaphors of "circulation"—financial transactions, the incessant movement of money through different milieus and across various borders.[15] Notwithstanding their interest in making the suppressed or the forgotten visible, they sometimes appear to ignore what Fernand Braudel calls the "humble level of material life" that exists outside the dramas of high finance and the politics of the court or the capital (*Capitalism* xiii). To suggest that the New Historicists emphasize certain phenomena and disregard others is not, of course, to discredit their arguments. But it is worth recognizing that certain criteria regarding what will produce strange and interesting anecdotes and what situations will be most likely to yield rewardingly complex modes of interpretation are at work in shaping the historical narratives they construct.

Subversive Particulars

To be clear, it is not merely that the New Historicists aestheticize history; history serves as the very means of smuggling back in the aesthetic values that the turn to history was purportedly designed to banish. Indeed, one might argue that the New Historicists' ability to use history in this way, as a springboard for heightened aesthetic experiences, is a key reason they succeed at garnering more widespread allegiance and exerting greater influence than other schools of political criticism that are agitating for change in the same moment. And this dominant position allows New Historicism to determine interpretive protocols and intellectual criteria across the discipline, even among its competitors, for decades to come. Few observers have recognized the unlikely basis for New Historicism's institutional strength, given that no schools of criticism at the time of its ascendancy claim to take aesthetic pleasure seriously. But the unacknowledged reasons for its appeal become legible, strangely enough, in the various critical responses it provokes.

Consider Wai-Chee Dimock's "Feminism, New Historicism, and the Reader" (1991), an essay that attempts to resolve the "acrimony" between feminists and New Historicists (601). Contending that the latter find the feminist "celebration of women's difference" to be "misguided," while the former find the New Historicist tendency to disregard that difference to be "nothing short of reactionary," Dimock proceeds to offer a New Historicist and a feminist reading of Charlotte Perkins Gilman's short story "The Yellow Wallpaper," before proposing a way of reconciling the two. Her New Historicist interpretation describes the text as the product of an ideology of "professionalism" in the late nineteenth-century United States: even while it critiques the husband-doctor whose rest cure drives his wife to insanity, it requires the reader to diagnose the various disorders and delusions of the characters and thus to occupy a position of "rational authority, expert knowledge, and interpretive competence" (609). Her feminist reading, by contrast, treats the text, in line with Gilman's own explanation, as an appeal to a specifically female reader aimed at encouraging her to defy the institutions, including the medical profession, that would confine her to a life of dull, psychologically debilitating domesticity (612–613). The difference between these readings, Dimock admits, is stark: the New Historicist regards "subjectivity as the determinate effect of discursive formations whose structural totality generates, saturates, and circumscribes all individual practices" (611), whereas the feminist treats the story as a source of potential agency in opposition to patriarchal power structures. But what happens, Dimock asks, when the two interpretations are combined? What if we view the text as addressing an imagined reader who is both a professional authority and a woman, thus positing a subject position that hardly existed, outside of a few exceptional cases, during the time period when Gilman published the story?

Read in light of this synthesis of two opposing interpretations, Gilman's "Yellow Wallpaper" defies the ideological coordinates of its historical moment, gesturing toward a future social order within which the categories of woman and professional have ceased to be mutually exclusive (613–614). One can interpret the text this way, Dimock contends, without denying that it is "conditioned by history"; what is necessary is not a turn away from history but a more complex notion of history than the one typically offered by the New Historicists. "'History' must itself be seen not as a field of synchronized unity but as a field of uneven development" (614). The New Historicists, she argues, tend to isolate the historical moment under consideration from what comes before and after, assuming that any given phenomenon can be understood entirely through an analysis of its structural relationships to other contemporaneous phenomena. To address the inadequacies of this framework, Dimock proposes a more diachronic account, one that regards history as a "precarious conjunction of the 'has been' and the 'not yet,' the 'already' and the 'probably,' a conjunction brought into play by the very passage of time, by the uneven velocities and shifting densities of social change" (615).

Dimock's essay appears to expose the limitations of both feminist and New Historicist criticism in an even-handed fashion, identifying what each can teach the other. And yet the two critiques she offers betray a subtle bias. What is needed to problematize the static and essentializing gender categories employed within early feminist criticism—of the kind practiced by Annette Kolodny, for instance—is a sense of history: "What makes the female reader the locus of 'not yet'—what suspends her between the 'not' and the 'yet' and preserves her as an indeterminate and therefore untotalized quantum—is not the agency of gender but the agency of history" (620). Later feminist critics such as Eve Sedgwick, Alice Jardine, and Mary Poovey produce more compelling interpretations, according to Dimock, precisely insofar as they historicize gender (618–619). Seeking to preserve the symmetry of her analysis, Dimock then proceeds to suggest that New Historicism needs to take gender into consideration, but she offers an unorthodox definition of gender, treating it primarily as a figure for instability, contingency, and change. It is, she contends, "a principle productive of uneven textures, productive of the discrepancy between the dominant and the emergent" (621). But this, of course, could be read as yet another way of describing history. What is necessary, in other words, to complicate New Historicism is also more history, or, as Dimock puts it, "The problem, I submit, is not that [New Historicism] is too historical but that it is not historical enough" (621). Though she insists that she is not privileging one methodology over another, denying a moment earlier that gender gets "subsumed by history," her need to issue this denial is telling (620). After all, the criteria of judgment that she employs, the ultimate measure of a given interpretive framework's rigor and persuasiveness, is whether it is sufficiently historical. In this regard, of course, Dimock's argument represents a pervasive tendency. To this day, there is hardly anything more damning than to claim that a particular argument is ahistorical. It is worth noting, however, that even in challenging the New Historicists, Dimock employs the standards they developed and championed.

But what exactly does Dimock mean by "historical"? She observes, "This, at least to my mind, is one way to understand that well-known phrase 'the textuality of history.' By this phrase we usually refer to the idea that the past is transmitted by texts, that it can never be recovered or apprehended as a lived totality. Here I want to use the phrase in a somewhat different sense, focusing not on the process of textual transmission but on the dynamics of historical development, on its sedimented, non-uniform, and therefore untotalizable *texture*" (615). Significantly, Dimock borrows her concept of history from New Historicist Louis Montrose, and her gloss on it accentuates how this concept, by accenting history's *texture*, can translate it into an aesthetic object. Dimock's characterization here renders history palpable and pleasing to the senses; *texture* is also the word used by the New Critics, most famously Ransom, to articulate the defining feature of poetry.[16] Made of "uneven velocities and shifting densities," history becomes exhilarating to behold ("Feminism" 615). Like the poetic works that it is now being called on to frame, it is deeply paradoxical, in tension with itself, every moment of its development containing traces of that which it has negated and hints of that which will negate it. And the language through which Dimock articulates this viscerally stimulating, cognitively demanding image of history is, despite her critical stance, entirely resonant with the discourse of New Historicism. After all, her desire to locate dynamic gestures capable of defying the logic of the historical grid is entirely commensurate with the New Historicists' motive for concentrating on the historical anecdote as a way of narrating "what exceeds [structures]" (Greenblatt and Gallagher 68). Dimock, in other words, is offering not so much a correction as a further intensification of their mode of analysis.

Early feminist criticism is, in Dimock's account, governed by "tactical wisdom" ("Feminism" 618). It offers, in short, a powerful basis for action. Its flaw is that it is too simple, a term, notwithstanding its apparent harshness, that she uses more than once, maintaining that early feminist critics treat gender "simply as a category of *difference*—simply as the ground of distinction between two discrete terms," and, a paragraph later, she states that they treat it "simply as a category of identity" (618). Significantly, feminism's rival in the competition staged by her article, New Historicism, is anything but simple; its virtue is its capacity to describe forms of historical complexity that all but forestall action. Though Dimock wants both—the agency of feminism and the contemplative richness of New Historicism—she implicitly judges the latter to be aesthetically superior. It is not a surprising verdict; early feminist critics such as Kolodny actively repudiated precisely the New Critical aesthetic standards that the New Historicists and Dimock, with her celebration of texture, tacitly reaffirm.[17] Moreover, this verdict about aesthetic value, though never outwardly stated, appears to be the one that counts most for Dimock. This is why New Historicism subtly wins out in her analysis over feminism, and why its key term, *history*, gets to serve as the subject of her final two sentences, a repository of richness, achieving there a quasi-infinite magnitude. Meanwhile, feminism's key term *gender* is a mere qualifier—one of two, actually—and just a pun embedded inside a larger, more ambiguously suggestive word: "History, thus engendered and thus decentered, is anything but a totalizing category. In fact, it is not even over and done with, but a realm of unexhausted and inexhaustible possibility" (622).

In another critique of New Historicism, "Are We Being Historical Yet?," Porter also faults the latter for being insufficiently historical, and in doing so she pinpoints even more explicitly than Dimock the source of New Historicism's appeal, though she underestimates the degree to which this appeal is a reflection of broader imperatives within the discipline. Porter finds a glaring omission in Greenblatt's influential essay "Invisible Bullets": his analysis of the conflict between English colonists and Native Americans does not include any Native American voices ("Are We?"). In fact he elides history altogether by failing to provide a description of actual material or political struggles between the two groups, offering instead a close reading of one document, Harriot's *Brief and True Report of the New Found Land of Virginia*. In his argument, Greenblatt makes a move that typifies the New Historical understanding of power, finding a moment of apparent resistance and then showing how it is ultimately co-opted by the dominant power structure. Harriot's narrative entertains the Native American explanation of a disease brought to North America by the Europeans, which threatens to challenge the British account, but this threat is ultimately contained, as Harriot's representation turns the Native American perspective into an object of British knowledge in order to exert control over it. "The recording of alien voices, their preservation in Harriot's text," Greenblatt contends, "is part of the process whereby Indian culture is constituted as a culture and thus brought into the light for study, discipline, correction, transformation" (*Shakespearean* 37). And later he argues that "the subversive voices are produced by and within the affirmations of order" (52). The problem with this analysis, according to Porter, is that the conclusion is guaranteed, tautologically, by the very methodological strategy that Greenblatt employs ("Are We?" [1990] 40). Of course he never discovers any authentic resistance to British hegemony, because he considers only the texts produced by the British. Any hint of subversion will, by definition, turn out to be contained within the dominant discourse because it was a part of that discourse in the first place. "Quite obviously, if the subversive is displaced from the realm of the subordinate culture—whether that of the Italian peasantry or the Algonkians—to the orthodox texts authorized by the dominant culture, the orthodox discourse *necessarily* produces the subversion it contains" (47). Had Greenblatt tried to represent the actual views or voices of the Native Americans, and not simply their perspective as registered by the texts of the British colonists, then he might have arrived at a different result.

Whatever Greenblatt's reasons for occluding the perspective of the Native Americans, his choices reveal certain foundational assumptions about what will make for an interesting historical argument and what will constitute a satisfying interpretation. Porter observes, "For if some of us have found it necessary to go 'after' the new historicism, it is partly because this movement has generated forms of critical practice that continue to exhibit the force of a formalist legacy whose subtle denials of history—as the scene of heterogeneity, difference, contradiction, at least—persist" ("History" 253). But Porter stops short of recognizing the extent of this formalist legacy in supplying criteria for determining what constitutes good literary scholarship not just for the New Historicists but across the entire discipline—even for those who claim to have left formalism behind. To be truly historical, Porter maintains, Greenblatt would need to register authentic evidence of Native American resistance so as to describe an actual political conflict between two equally represented parties. But if Greenblatt chooses instead to analyze a single text at war with itself, a text that produces and then contains its own subversion, this is because his scholarly aim is always to discover a certain kind of complexity, one defined by internal contradiction or paradox. However useful or historically accurate it might be to describe a clash between two worldviews, there is in such a situation no paradox, no irony to be dissected. Like many scholars invested in the project of historicizing literary works, Greenblatt is still wedded to New Critical and deconstructive premises about what sort of problems literary interpretation must address and what kind of analysis it must produce.

Especially striking is the resemblance between Greenblatt's understanding of subversion and the New Critical concept of irony. Describing the poetry favored by I. A. Richards, Brooks remarks, "Richards' poetry of synthesis, on the other hand, is impervious to irony for the very reason that it carries within its own structure the destructive elements—the poet has reconciled it to them" (*Modern Poetry* 44). Irony is the poem's strategy for defending itself against rebuttal by incorporating opposing viewpoints into its own meaning. John Donne's poems, according to Brooks, cannot be undermined by mockery because they have already mocked themselves. The power structures that register resistance in order to contain it in Greenblatt's reading of history operate exactly like the New Critical poem.

Greenblatt's interest in identifying and exploring certain ironies and paradoxes within the historical archive is not, then, merely an idiosyncrasy; rather, it signals the persistent power of New Critical criteria in shaping what kinds of arguments qualify as legitimate and sophisticated forms of academic literary interpretation, what kinds of complexity must emerge in order for those arguments to *count* as literary scholarship. It is true that not all political criticism yields the paradoxes privileged by the New Historicists. But the comparative success of the latter in reorienting the discipline—the fact that they are the ones that everyone feels the need to "go 'after,'" as Porter puts it—has been premised, ironically, on their capacity to engage history while tacitly satisfying New Critical aesthetic criteria. The knotty paradoxes that Greenblatt illuminates function to legitimize his work, making it clear that, while he is examining history, he is not jeopardizing the specificity of his own discipline. He is in effect saying, Have no fear; I may be dealing with nonliterary subjects, raising political questions, and denying any autonomy to art, but my analysis will nevertheless produce the requisite experience of complexity, the negotiation with irony, ambiguity, and paradox, that you have come to expect from literary scholars. Indeed, it is this aesthetic experience, more than any particular texts, that continues to define academic literary studies, while allowing it to venture into new territories. Ironically, when Porter faults the "formalist legacy" for interfering with efforts to understand history as "the scene of heterogeneity, differ-ence, contradiction," her investment in this particular scene, her de-sire, in other words, to present history as a theatrical spectacle of complexity, bears the influence of the same formalist criteria that, in her view, entraps New Historicism, demonstrating the tenacity of the criteria that she is hoping to repudiate ("History" 253).

Greenblatt's analysis of Harriot is, of course, just one prominent in-stance of a much broader tendency. The dialectic between subversion and containment that he identifies is ubiquitous not only within New Historicism but within almost all academic literary study of the 1980s, 1990s, and beyond.[18] Reproduced in countless monographs, articles, and conference papers and used to understand postcolonial power dy-namics, class resentment, and the parodic repetition of heteronorma-tive gender roles, it may well represent the central problem of political criticism, as scholar after scholar wonders whether a given text or gesture represents resistance to a particular power structure or whether that resistance gets co-opted by the structure that it appears to oppose. To treat these various analyses of power relations as a source of aes-thetic satisfaction is, of course, to read them against the grain of their own stated intentions. After all, the scholars who consider the ambig-uous relationship between subversion and containment generally hold that the function of their work is to understand power, not to produce aesthetic pleasure. And yet it is important to note that this particular dynamic—power that produces its own subversion—is an abstract form, an ahistorical pattern, rather than a description of a particular situation or political dilemma, as demonstrated by scholars' readiness to apply it to any and all historical moments.[19] As Caroline Levine has noted, "the ruptures themselves follow an insistent pattern: contain-ment and subversion, law and transgression, and boundaries and boundary-crossing, all of these sharing a repetitive, organizing struc-ture" (Forms 55). Moreover, the idea that acts of apparent resistance are often props supporting an existing social order is perfectly designed to produce political quiescence.[20]

Consider the prototypical example of this mode of analysis, Michel Foucault's Discipline and Punish—a touchstone for practically all New Historicist scholarship. His fatalistic, clinical tone, employed to catalog one historical atrocity after the other, seems to warn against the belief that efforts to bring about improvements or promote justice will do anything other than serve the interests of power. However valid Foucault's paranoid readings of history happen to be, his hypersophisticated, tortuous account puts readers into a position of well-nigh abject passivity. History, under Foucault's gaze, is thoroughly aestheticized; his understanding of politics makes any kind of intervention seem futile, any hope for the future naïve. All we can do is behold, in a state of appalled fascination, the various spectacles of sublime suffering and injustice that we are called on to witness. The only consolation is the perverse pleasure we experience in being put into this passive position, which allows us to enjoy the extraordinary complexity of his analysis for its own sake—a complexity exactly equal in degree to the feeling of powerlessness that it imposes on us.

The Aesthetics of Solace

To be sure, many politically engaged scholars eschew the posture of dispassionate scrutiny that serves, in Foucault's work, to aestheticize the cruel workings of power. Indeed, political critics often claim that they are deploying insights about the past in order to critique or challenge the present social order—an agenda particularly pronounced among those arguing on behalf of various socially marginalized groups. Such endeavors, particularly when rooted in an examination of discrimination based on race, class, religion, gender, or sexual identity, would seem antithetical to the project of promoting aesthetic appreciation. And yet the reality of brutal political oppression does not in all contexts necessitate the wholesale erasure of the aesthetic; nor must it preclude the assertion of aesthetic commitments among those considering such contexts. To illuminate the role that the aesthetic can play in scholarship focused on situations that would seem categorically inhospitable to it, I turn now to Saidiya V. Hartman's analysis in *Scenes of Subjection* (1997) of the modes of coercion under slavery and during Reconstruction that masqueraded as acts of benevolence or rituals of pleasure. Hartman is not generally grouped with the New Historicists, but for this reason she represents a useful example: her work demonstrates just how ubiquitous the assumptions and procedures employed by the New Historicists are within literary studies by the 1990s, how central they are to a variety of fields adjacent to New Historicism, including both cultural and African American studies. Moreover, on the surface at least, Hartman appears to take New Historicism's ostensible rejection of formalism even further, and thus she provides a good test case for determining whether this rejection serves to conceal covert aesthetic commitments even within modes of political criticism more radical than New Historicism.

Although Hartman is a literary scholar by training, *Scenes of Subjection* does not consider many actual literary works, focusing instead on situations, spectacles, habits, laws, instruction manuals, and other nonliterary texts. She examines various instances of theatricality, but she places the forms of pleasure that these scenes elicit under suspicion, treating them as inevitably complicit with the subjugation of others. Overall her book seems to disregard questions about the aesthetic value of the performances and gestures that she considers in favor of political questions focused on how these performances either support or challenge racist ideologies. And yet her rationale for condemning certain social practices and praising others relies on strongly held, if unacknowledged, aesthetic principles—rooted in both New Critical and deconstructive assumptions. Moreover, far from bracketing or banishing aesthetic considerations, her analysis actually entails a necessary and productive way of understanding the category of aesthetic: not as a realm that exists outside or beyond political forces but rather as a form of experience whose very meaning and value depends on its precarious position within significant political constraints.

It is worth noting first of all the resemblances between Hartman's approach and the New Historicists'. She contends that history is the product of fictions as much as facts. She rejects sweeping grand narratives. She regularly produces anecdotes, and uses one, in New Historicist fashion, to open her first chapter. Like Greenblatt, she claims to be engaged in the project of "defamiliarizing the familiar" (*Scenes of Subjection* 4). Perhaps most importantly of all, she reproduces the dialectic of subversion and containment so often analyzed within New Historicism. Her book relentlessly demonstrates how scenes of apparent emancipation, resistance, celebration, and self-cultivation among African Americans before, during, and after the Civil War actually serve to reinforce white domination. At the same time, she considers how various forms of submission to slave owners' demands may, in certain circumstances, entail authentic subversion or disruption.

To argue, on the basis of these similarities between Hartman and the New Historicists, that Hartman, like the latter, is seeking to aestheticize her subject matter is obviously to invite controversy. While some of the figures she considers do try to extract aesthetic satisfaction from the suffering of slaves, she clearly finds such efforts morally repugnant. Although Hartman seeks to uncover hidden complexities within mundane situations, she does not aim to heighten readers' perceptions of the world's beauty or elicit wonder in the face of the historical materials that she presents. Her work is too preoccupied with the responsibilities that engaging with the history of slavery places on readers to encourage the kind of disinterested aesthetic satisfaction aroused by Foucault's descriptions of state power. She certainly does not seek to elicit readerly pleasure; for pleasure is, in her analysis, "inseparable from subjection" (33), and to enjoy is, according to *Black's Law Dictionary*, "to have, possess, and use with satisfaction; to occupy or have the benefit of" (23)—that is, it is to be complicit with the logic of slavery.

And yet, while Hartman calls the experience of pleasure into question, she does not reject aesthetic values per se; rather, she simply rejects one set of aesthetic criteria in favor of another. In considering strategies for representing the experience of slavery by slave owners, abolitionists, or slaves themselves, she condemns any gestures aimed at promoting emotional connections with or feelings of compassion for the slaves, which in her view represent yet another means of turning slaves into property, making them serve the emotional purposes of the observer. "Thus the desire to don, occupy, or possess blackness or the black body as a sentimental resource and/or locus of excess enjoyment is both founded upon and enabled by the material relations of chattel slavery" (21). But she embraces any gestures that obscure reality, confuse observers, or estrange them emotionally from the scenes they are witnessing. Identifying a hint of subversion in certain slaves' modes of submission to their masters, Hartman observes, "In addition, these performances constituted acts of defiance conducted under the cover of nonsense, indirection, and seeming acquiescence" (8). Considering the spirituals that the slaves sing, she observes approvingly, "The opacity of these sorrowful and half-articulate songs perplexes and baffles those within and without the circle of slavery" (48). Profoundly disturbed by the feelings of pleasure that observers, particularly white observers, might extract from slave performances, Hartman celebrates an aesthetic of the obscure, the ambiguous, the unassimilable, and the unenjoyable.

One could argue that aesthetic criteria have nothing to do with Hartman's judgments, since she seems motivated entirely by political principles. It is worth pointing out, however, that her preferences align closely with twentieth-century modernist aesthetic criteria, which also favor difficult, alienating, or inscrutable gestures and reject sentimental literature aimed at promoting sympathy and identification. The New Critics use the same criteria in deciding what constitutes great poetry, and deconstruction obviously tends to embrace the difficult, the ambiguous, and the refractory. Hartman explicitly betrays her attachment to the latter when she remarks that a female slave's suggestion, during an inspection, that a trader look under her dress to see whether she has any teeth down there "merits being called a deconstructive performance" (41).

Hartman would likely claim that she is endorsing these strategies on the basis not of their intrinsic aesthetic value but of their political efficacy, insofar as they thwart the efforts of white people to take full possession of black subjects. Yet, compared to other scholars of nineteenth-century sentimental literature such as Jane Tompkins, she is relatively uninterested in the actual political consequences of the scenes and gestures that she considers.[21] Examining an abolitionist's effort to imagine what it is like to be a slave by putting himself in the latter's position, she comments, "Does this not reinforce the 'thingly' quality of the captive by reducing the body to evidence in the very effort to establish the humanity of the enslaved? . . . So, in fact, Rankin [the white abolitionist] becomes a proxy and the other's pain is acknowledged to the degree that it can be imagined, yet by virtue of this substitution the object of identification threatens to disappear" (19). Notice: the violence she identifies exists "in the very effort" to feel the slave's pain. The slave gets "disappeared," as it were, but only figuratively, in the imaginative response of the abolitionist. The morally questionable character of identification depends entirely on what happens in the moment of its operation, not on the practical results it produces. It does not matter whether Rankin's account lends support for abolitionism. It is in itself a means of enjoying the slave's body and thus intrinsically pernicious. To put it another way, Hartman is far more concerned with noticing immediate meta-phorical resonances—between emotional identification and enslave-ment or between inscrutability and revolt—than with understanding the instrumental efficacy of the scenes she examines. Insofar as she assesses the intrinsic value of performances, texts, and modes of re-ception, favoring opacity over sentimentality, without regard to their utility within broader social struggles, her judgments seem to be based more on aesthetic than political criteria. This is not, however, to invalidate her conclusions; on the contrary, despite Hartman's tendency to cast her argument in political terms, her analysis demon-strates that aesthetic judgments have an important role to play in under-standing and evaluating various historical gestures and actions.

To be sure, Hartman's aesthetic preferences are context specific; she does not suggest that opacity is always valuable and sentimentality al-ways blameworthy. She is focused specifically on slavery and Recon-struction, and as such she does not presuppose universally applicable aesthetic criteria. Nevertheless, her argument does suggest a way of recognizing the validity of aesthetic practices and aesthetic judgments as situated within and shaped by specific political contexts. That is to say, her analysis entails the possibility of valuing certain forms of expression and the emotional or intellectual responses they elicit for their own sake within a socially constituted, politically determined moment without regard to the longer-term or broader political conse-quences they might produce.

Hartman envisions this possibility most concretely in her reading of everyday slave practices, including dances, songs, storytelling rit-uals, and other forms of recreation described by one participant as "having a good time among our own color" (58). While she relentlessly underscores that these moments of apparent enjoyment were perfor-mances demanded by the slave owners and a means of reinforcing the latter's power, she also recognizes their importance for the slaves, and thus she struggles to find a set of terms that can register their value.

Wondering whether it makes sense to treat the slaves as political actors, she acknowledges that their everyday practices were, by virtue of their severely subjugated status, incapable of mounting any real challenge to the systems in which they operated. The most they could do, she suggests, was to "offer a small measure of relief from the debasements constitutive of one's condition" (61). Seeking an appropriate characterization, Hartman considers James Scott's "infrapolitics of the dominated" and Paul Gilroy's "politics of a lower frequency" (62). Both phrases suggest a recognition that the practices to which they refer, though significant, may not quite qualify as political according to its conventional definition. As Hartman later observes, "All of this is not a preamble to an argument about the 'prepolitical' consciousness of the enslaved but an attempt to point to the limits of the political and the difficulty of translating or interpreting the practices of the enslaved within that framework" (65). In a gesture similar to Lauren Berlant's invocation of the "juxtapolitical," which we encountered in the introduction, Hartman seems to acknowledge the need for an entirely different category, perhaps even a nonpolitical means of evaluating the slaves' rituals. Her urge to characterize these rituals as low-frequency politics—that is, as *sort of political*—her inability, in other words, to articulate their value in any other terms, suggests the role the political has come to assume within academic literary studies as the ultimate measure of a given gesture's value or importance.

Ironically, it is only a situation characterized by extreme oppression, in which meaningful political action or resistance is well-nigh impossible, that allows Hartman to recognize the need for a different kind of measure. The slaves' activities do not transform the broader political system or the horrible material conditions that this system sustains. But they are fulfilling and emotionally resonant in themselves and thus profoundly important. They represent a way, as Hartman puts it, of "cultivating pleasure as a limited response to need" (52). They are, in short, *aesthetically* valuable. Though she does not use the word, she does hint at this possibility by describing the slaves' activities as a kind of "play," a "playing with and against the terms of dispossession" (69). She recognizes the risk that such a term may obscure the hardships slaves confronted: "The use of the term 'play' is not intended to make light of the profound dislocations and divisions experienced by the enslaved or to imply that these tentative negotiations of one's status or condition were not pained or wrenching" (69). Typically, play and other kinds of aesthetic practices are regarded as a sign of absolute freedom, autonomy, or even frivolousness. Here the reverse is true: the slaves resort to play because they have no other options. The aesthetic in this situation signifies not freedom but rather radical conscription: an intense focus on the particular moment and the value that can be extracted from it because nothing beyond that moment is guaranteed. Lacking any real political power, slaves turn to the aesthetic as the only sphere in which they can experience any satisfaction or agency. Remarkably enough, the existence of excessive political constraints does not, as many political critics assume, negate the significance of the aesthetic. On the contrary, in this situation, it is the very thing that enables the aesthetic to achieve visibility, though given the category's disreputable status within the academy, Hartman is not willing to name it as such.

A Market for Close Reading

While the disavowal of the aesthetic was obviously the result of an increased interest among academics in both producing political insights and participating in political struggles, it can also be understood as a response to new institutional challenges that the humanities confronted during the last few decades of the twentieth century. This was, after all, the time when scholars in the humanities first began to view their discipline as in crisis. Enrollments in liberal arts programs plummeted. According to Donogue, between 1970 and 2001, BAs in English fell from 7.6 percent of the student population to 4 percent; foreign languages from 2.4 percent to 1 percent; math from 3 percent to 1 percent; and social science and history from 18.4 percent to 10 percent (*Last Professors* 91). Severe cuts in public funding to higher education, initiated during the 1970s, continued unabated. And the job market collapsed, producing a huge surplus of PhDs with no stable or reliable form of employment, many of whom would join the growing ranks of adjunct professors, allowing university administrations to fill more and more of their teaching positions with inexpensive contingent labor in the name of economic efficiency, thereby eroding tenure and increasing their own power relative to the faculty.[22]

In the face of potential budget cuts, departments found themselves under significantly greater pressure to demonstrate the value of the knowledge that they produced and disseminated, generally in terms of its practical utility or marketability. This pressure, which often came from increasingly dictatorial university administrations, also reflected student demands. A much greater percentage of the population enrolled in universities and colleges during the latter half of the twentieth century than ever before, and the primary goal of many of these first-generation students was economic advancement.[23] They were less interested, in other words, in knowledge for its own sake than in technical skills that would help them succeed financially. Thus programs with a vocational orientation, such as computer science, engineering, and business administration, grew considerably (Donogue 91).

At the same time, the hard sciences experienced extraordinary growth, at first through massive government funding aimed at fostering technological innovations necessary to compete with the Soviet Union, and later through donations from the private sector. A crucial spur to corporate funding was the passage of the Bayh-Dole Act of 1980, which made it easier for universities to patent scientific innovations. This allowed laboratories to raise funds by transferring these lucrative patents to corporations in exchange for contributions. The upshot was that the sciences, particularly biology and chemistry, increasingly privileged research that might yield profitable discoveries.[24] Meanwhile, humanities departments, which brought in relatively little outside financial support, were increasingly viewed as a burden by university administrations.

The crisis in the humanities, as many observers have noted, coincided with the ascendance of neoliberalism.[25] The 1970s marked the beginning of the collapse of the Keynesian welfare state, a process that would accelerate under the conservative governments that took power in the United States and England in the 1980s. In addition to reduced state investment in social services and in higher education, this period witnessed the deregulation and privatization of numerous sectors of the economy, the decline of organized labor, the emergence of economic precarity for millions of workers, and the growth of global free trade—all driven by the myth that unfettered free markets, rather than rational planning, represented the best solution to all variety of problems. This free-market mentality clearly influenced universities, which increasingly viewed education as a product and students as consumers, with disciplines measured on the basis of the popular demand for their classes and the marketability of the skills they disseminated. According to Bill Readings, it was during this period that universities finally relinquished the task of cultivating values and ideological commitments central to the maintenance and identity of the nation-state and turned their focus to training students to succeed within a globalized economy, thus supporting the needs of multinational corporations (*University in Ruins*).

A key early incubator for debates about the role of the university in a contemporary capitalist society was Berkeley, the very school where Greenblatt first developed his theories about the relationship between literature and history. He arrived there in 1969, just five years after students famously shut down large portions of the campus as part of the free speech movement.[26] While their initial grievance was the administration's attempt to restrict student political activity just outside campus boundaries, they also strongly objected to the University of California president Clark Kerr's vision of higher education, which he had outlined in a series of lectures published under the title *The Uses of the University*. In those lectures, Kerr suggested that the university, a relatively unified institution organized around the mission of fostering traditional humanistic values, was being supplanted by the multiversity, which consisted of multiple competing structures and agendas, one of which was to serve as an engine for technological development and economic growth. The multiversity, according to Kerr, was coming to "merge its activities with industry as never before" (65) as it "became a port of entry into the new economy, which placed heightened priority on 'human capital' in its many forms" (202). Though Kerr claimed to be offering a neutral description, many at Berkeley saw it as an endorsement, indeed as a road map for the University of California system. "The salient characteristic of the multiversity," lamented student leader Bradford Cleaveland, "is massive production of specialized excellence. The multiversity is actually not an educational center but a highly efficient industry engaged in producing skilled individuals to meet the immediate needs of business or government" ("Education" 89).

As Greenblatt remembers it, Berkeley was still "in turmoil" when he first started teaching there in 1969: "Everything was in an uproar; all routines were disrupted; nothing could be taken for granted. Classes still met, at least sporadically, but the lecture platform would often be appropriated, with or without the professor's permission, by protesters, and seminar discussions would veer wildly from, say, Ben Johnson's metrics to the undeclared air war over Cambodia" (*Learning* 4). New Historicism was in part an answer to the desire, among faculty and students, to connect academic questions about literature to the political controversies of the day. It can also be read, however, as a response to institutional developments within the university, most notably the greater emphasis of higher education on technical skills and marketable forms of knowledge. New Historicism's left political stance functioned to critique the capitalist, corporate orientation that was shaping the decisions of university administrations. As several observers have noted, the interest of Greenblatt, Gallagher, Montrose, and others in discovering pockets of either real or imagined resistance within larger social structures may reveal as much about the predicament of the humanities scholar within the late twentieth-century university as it does about the historical situations they examine in their research.[27] At the same time, their efforts to highlight connections between literary texts and social, economic, and political realities were intended to challenge perceptions of English departments as insulated from real-world problems. In a university culture obsessed with demonstrating the practical utility of the knowledge that it produced, New Historicists were in effect arguing that studying literature could be useful as well; its function was not to promote the kinds of masturbatory formalist exercises that J. H. Miller sought to disavow in his MLA presidential address but rather to foster political critique and inspire concrete social engagement.

By drawing connections between literature and its social contexts, New Historicism was implicitly drawing connections between English departments and *their* social context, thus seeking to establish the relevance of what they taught to other political and economic spheres. If this meant embracing left or progressive political positions, it also helped to present the study of literature as a good form of preparation for various kinds of remunerative work, thus serving the multiversity's corporate vision.[28] Though one could argue that English has always offered marketable job skills, including the ability to communicate effectively and think critically, New Historicist scholarship is especially well designed to encourage the deployment of traditional modes of textual interpretation within other spheres, requiring students to make connections between ostensibly unlike phenomena, navigate archives, and interpret a diverse set of nonliterary materials. Considering the role of late twentieth-century English studies as a form of job training, Michael Bérubé observes, "Degrees in English may still be convertible into gainful employment—*not* because they mark their recipients as literate, well-rounded young men and women who can allude to Shakespeare in business memos, but because they mark their recipients as people who can potentially negotiate a wide range of intellectual tasks and handle (in various ways) disparate kinds of 'textual' material, from memos, legal briefs, and white papers to ad campaigns, databases, and electronic newsmagazines" (*Employment* 22–23).

Significantly, New Historicism actually performs, in its very interpretive exercises, precisely the reapplication of the methods associated with the discipline of literary studies to other, more practical or worldly contexts, yielding important insights not just about literature but also about economics, politics, and society. What makes New Historicism such a persuasive advocate for English studies is its ability to apply and reapply the technique of close reading to a seemingly limitless range of situations and materials. A central priority of the corporate-oriented university, especially given the rapidly changing, unstable job market, with whole bodies of technical knowledge becoming obsolete every few years and the likelihood that graduates will end up working in a variety of fields increasing, is, as Bérubé notes, transferable skills—ways of thinking that can be translated into multiple spheres and repackaged to fit the needs of various sectors of the economy. Given this demand, New Historicism represents a perfect advertisement for the usefulness of English, revealing just how widely applicable close reading can be, demonstrating how it can be used to interpret all variety of documents, objects, and contexts. Unlike more technical forms of training that provide specific skills relevant to a specialized field, close reading can be effective within practically any sphere, and New Historicist scholarship represents a tour de force demonstration of this extraordinary versatility.

As I have sought to demonstrate in this chapter, however, New Historicists do not single-mindedly focus on encouraging interpretive strategies that can prove practical or useful. Indeed, New Historicism's residual attachment to aesthetic values may, in light of the particular institutional pressures that English departments face, acquire a new significance. If at times Greenblatt, Gallagher, and Hartman view certain objects, images, and gestures aesthetically—that is, as valuable in themselves, and not merely for the uses they might serve—then these moments may represent a refusal of the university's market-driven technocratic agenda. Those who regard aesthetic concerns as aligned with conservatism may be right, but within this particular context, the New Historicists' covert conservatism represents an effort to insulate at least some part of their thinking and teaching from the corporatization of the university.[29] To be sure, such gestures are more pragmatic than subversive: New Historicism functions as a defense of the discipline of English by underscoring precisely how it can support the university's larger, market-driven mission. What New Historicists accomplish is to protect the defining activity of academic literary studies, close reading, by demonstrating its utility when deployed in nonliterary contexts. But this allows them paradoxically to perpetuate a mode of aesthetic criticism committed to valuing particular forms of linguistic and sociohistorical complexity for their own sake. They are able, in other words, to preserve certain intellectually and emotionally satisfying experiences—states of wonder, exhilaration, fascination, and even bafflement—by casting them as the serendipitous by-products of socially useful critical procedures, thus providing a safe place, if not an explicit justification, for aesthetic pleasure within an institution committed to assessing all knowledge in terms of its instrumental value.

4

Lolita and the Stakes of Form

W<small>HEN THE NARRATOR</small> of Vladimir Nabokov's *Lolita* (1958), Humbert Humbert, imagines that his memoir will be read "in the first years of 2000 A.D." (*Annotated Lolita* 301), the accuracy of his prediction might seem to justify his pathological arrogance. At least in this instance, however, Humbert actually stops short of guessing the true staying power of his narrative. He requests that it be published only upon Lolita's death, which he projects fifty years into the future. He is, in other words, anticipating the first moment of its publication, not its longevity. But Lolita, for all her pluck, dies young, whereas the novel about her has managed to thrive despite its controversial subject matter, enduring five decades of critical and cultural vicissitudes in order to reach twenty-first-century readers, an uncontested literary classic. In this chapter, I consider its success within one particular interpretive community, the academy, which has dedicated two separate literary journals and innumerable conference papers, articles, and monographs to its author. *Lolita*'s ability to command attention over this period testifies in part to its versatility; its dense, rhetorically mercurial prose, the multiplicity of its cultural allusions, and the sheer crowdedness of the American landscape that it depicts lend purchase to all variety of methodological approaches. Indeed, organized chronologically, the academic readings of the book perfectly track the succession of critical fashions—from

New Criticism to deconstruction to New Historicism—that have pre-vailed over the past several decades.[1] And yet the most salient feature of this half-century-long conversation is a surprising continuity, based on a sense of ambivalence regarding the novel's commitment to what Nabokov terms "aesthetic bliss"—an ambivalence shared by its early formalist readers and its later politically and ethically oriented readers (*Annotated Lolita* 316). One explanation for its persistent appeal within the academy, as I will attempt to demonstrate in this chapter, is that it provides some especially potent strategies for exploring and resolving that ambivalence by aligning the aesthetic with broader ethical and po-litical concerns.

Lolita appears while New Criticism is still the dominant fashion, in the mid-1950s, and undoubtedly benefits initially from the preva-lence of formalist interpretive strategies. The novel's generous supply of puns, ironies, puzzles, ambiguities, and recurring motifs invites critics such as Carl Proffer, Page Stegner, William Rowe, and Alfred Appel to decipher it as they might a metaphysical poem. Even more importantly, this fixation on form yields a crucial alibi for Nabokov, allowing readers to conclude that the book is not, despite its meticulous descriptions of a middle-aged man's lust for a twelve-year-old girl, ac-tually *about* pedophilia but is rather about language, or the romance genre, or the act of artistic creation itself.[2] Such defenses discover new weapons with the rise of deconstruction, as scholars contend that *Lo-lita* is pure metafiction, its chains of signifiers radically severed from any knowable material or social reality.[3] By the time feminists and other politically minded critics turn their attention to the suffering of Lolita, the cruelty of her tormenter, and the morality of a book that appears at times to eclipse the former and glorify the latter, it is too late: *Lolita* has become an obscene fixture within the academy.[4] It cannot be dislodged; it can only be problematized.

And yet skepticism regarding formalism as a framework for under-standing *Lolita* appears not only in the work of later naysayers but also in a majority of earlier readings that would qualify, by virtue of their focus on stylistic or textual questions, as formalist. This thread of doubt, which connects scholars of *Lolita* across a variety of method-ological boundaries, complicates the conventional narrative that pre-sumes a hegemony of benighted formalist complacency in the 1950s and 1960s in need of assault by more socially responsible critics. Formalism presents itself in the responses to *Lolita* as already embarrassed, irrepressibly prone to self-criticism. To be sure, these tendencies may simply reflect *Lolita*'s particular capacity to raise uncomfortable moral questions. But I would suggest that this may be exactly why scholars are drawn to it in the first place—because it provides a platform for confronting and wrestling with preexisting anxieties about the dangers of aestheticism. Paradoxically, *Lolita* has earned significant academic attention in part because it creates trouble for the very aesthetic criteria through which its value has been asserted.

"Verbal Hocus-Pocus"

In his 1956 *Partisan Review* piece, "The Perilous Magic of Nymphets," John Hollander anticipates what will be the central debate about *Lolita:* "One thinks of Thurber's mad fixation on the linguistic games with which he avoids social confrontations. But in *Lolita,* the word-play leads back to love-play always; it is a little like an extended trope on the pathetic fallacy, in which verbal hocus-pocus makes the obsessive object light up, in intellectual neon, everywhere" (559). "Word-play" and "verbal hocus-pocus" can be strategies for evading "social confrontations." What saves *Lolita,* Hollander implies, from irrelevance is that its verbal games are not played merely for their own sake; they serve a purpose and reference a reality beyond themselves, illuminating the obsessive character of Humbert's love. Echoing Hollander, Andrew Field observes, "Important as the stylistic figurations are in the novel, however, *Lolita* depends primarily upon a vivid realistic portrayal of the major characters" (*Nabokov* 327). And Stegner, who intends the title of his study *Escape into Aesthetics* (1966) as a compliment, nevertheless avers, "[Humbert] has aesthetic vision but his moral vision is very seldom operative. Ultimately, distinctions have to be made, if one is to function in this world, between aesthetics and morality—between art and life. Humbert loses the ability effectively to distinguish the reality of his imagination from the reality of his physical life, and in so doing removes himself from the combined reality that is the source of art" (115). Art, Stegner's thorny formulation implies, can neither be merged with nor entirely divorced from reality—and the latter category includes both imagination and the material world. Moreover, the correlation Stegner draws between a concern for morality and a concern for life suggests that art, in order to draw energy from its true source— that is, reality—must engage with moral questions.[5]

Similar statements asserting the need to treat Nabokov's brilliant verbal games as related to some actual, extralinguistic material context or to some serious social or ethical imperative recur in almost all of the academic criticism of *Lolita,* becoming especially forceful in later decades. Summing up the problem that the novel seems invariably to raise, Leland de la Durantaye remarks in his 2007 study, "What has remained enigmatic in [*Lolita*] is nothing less than its nature: whether it is a sterile exercise in linguistic virtuosity or a deeply human account of love and loss, whether it is an incitement to vice or an encouragement to virtue, whether it is art for nothing but its own sake, or a work of rare moral force" (*Style Is Matter* 4). While critics have been tempted to insulate *Lolita* from controversy by insisting that its style is more important than its content, or that its self-conscious artifice severs the world it imagines from the so-called real world, they have also worried that doing so might serve to evacuate the novel of seriousness, rendering it lifeless or "sterile."

The desire to read the book as referencing reality does not, of course, require one to downplay its aesthetic power. Moreover, to argue, as many have, that *Lolita* should be read not merely as a language game but as a truthful reflection of some external reality—whether it be postwar suburban America, the ennui of the expatriate European exile, or the sexual anxieties of adolescent girls—is not necessarily to ascribe to it an ethical or ideological agenda. The early critics and scholars of *Lolita* do not, in other words, categorically repudiate formalist readings or make ethical or political questions their primary focus—as later scholars will. Nevertheless, the extravagance of Nabokov's style makes them uneasy, particularly when used to describe such unpalatable yearnings. What they find both troublesome and compelling about *Lolita* is that it dramatizes the hazards of an overcommitment to form, thereby suggesting the need to pay careful attention to the purposes, moral or otherwise, served by a "fancy prose style" (to use Humbert's

famous description) (*Annotated Lolita* 11). In doing so, the novel ultimately leads purported formalists to betray uncertainty about their
own interpretive principles.

Such misgivings are perhaps most pronounced in Appel, the editor
of *The Annotated Lolita* (1970), whose obsessive tracking of the extended patterns of images that make up the novel's textual surface
has earned him the reputation as one of the closest readers of Nabokov's formal exercises. And yet, while Appel asserts that Nabokov's
fiction is "artifice or nothing," he also regards it as an assault on formalism: "Readers trained on the tenets of formalist criticism have
simply not known what to make of works which resist the search for
ordered mythic and symbolic 'levels of meaning' and depart completely
from post-Jamesian requisites for the 'realistic' or 'impressionistic'
novel—that a fiction be the impersonal product of a pure aesthetic impulse, a self-contained illusion of reality rendered from a consistently
held point of view and through a central intelligence from which all
authorial comment has been exorcised." Moreover, he goes on to argue
that "Nabokov's present eminence signals a radical shift in opinions
about the novel and the novelist's ethical responsibilities" (introduction xviii).

"Levels of meaning" is Appel's pejorative term for the New Critical emphasis on ambiguity; one motive for repudiating the latter's formalism is to protect his own equally formalist approach from being
perceived as commensurately stodgy or outdated.[6] The melodrama of
the revolt that he describes bears all the marks of an internecine conflict: this is formalism protecting itself by casting off its own aging
progenitors. Appel's reading of *Lolita* betrays at once a frustration
with and an excessive investment in form—a desire to escape from
formalism's apparent sterility through an even more thoroughgoing
formalism. Style, rhetoric, and artifice must, in order to escape triviality, be put in relation to something—must be *about* something. In
order to satisfy this imperative without placing Nabokov's writing in
a position of subservience to some external phenomenon, Appel emphasizes how that writing is ultimately *about* itself. What gives Nabokov's textual devices life for Appel is not their ability to take hold of
anything beyond the text but just the opposite: their capacity to twist
elastically back on themselves and expose their own operations before

the reader's eyes, a trick he admiringly dubs "involution" (introduction xxii–xxvii).

It is possible to read Appel's desire to rebrand formalist criticism so as to underscore its radical potential as merely a sign of the times: in 1968, the year he completes his introduction, students are occupying universities; the *nouveau roman* and its American metafictional counterpart are vying with the realist novel over the future of literature; and deconstruction is beginning its invasion of the American academy. But, as we have seen, Appel's comments echo concerns about the limitations of formalism and the "pure aesthetic impulse" present at least implicitly in almost all of the critical responses to *Lolita* since its publication. Though the social turmoil of the late 1960s may have lent them urgency, such concerns can be read as an expression of more longstanding anxiety about the apparent triviality of aesthetic concerns within an American social landscape dominated by a utilitarian worldview—a worldview responsible, as I have argued, for the postwar university's emphasis on marketable forms of knowledge. It is their fear of this instrumental mind-set that leads the New Critics to imagine themselves as endlessly embattled; and it is the same fear that leads all variety of formalist and aesthetic criticisms, like Appel's, to doubt their own significance and to try to outrun such doubts by disavowing the very legacy they are covertly seeking to continue.

"Poets Never Kill"

What makes *Lolita* so compelling for critics worried about the precarious position of aesthetic criticism in the United States is that it directly addresses their concerns, not only through its ostentatious style but also through its subject matter. Consider Humbert. Costumed impeccably like a fin de siècle decadent—in velvet and silk—professing his "wonderful taste in textures and perfumes" (*Annotated Lolita* 52), he is a caricature of a traditional aesthete. Moreover, before he dedicates himself full-time to pedophilia, he is also a scholar of French and American literature—a fact that has received so little critical attention, as Frederick Whiting notes, that it seems to have been the subject of systematic repression ("'Strange Particularity'" 855).[7] And no wonder: Humbert's primary significance for aesthetically inclined academic critics of *Lolita* may well be that he offers them a painfully unflattering image of themselves.

Probably the most important feature of Humbert's character in this regard—one generally obscured by both his sexual predilections and his muscular rhetoric—is his weakness, his inability, for much of the novel, to produce any significant impact on the world around him, a feature he tends to underscore particularly when addressing his scholarly and artistic endeavors.[8] "I published tortuous essays in obscure journals," Humbert admits, adding, "A paper of mine entitled 'The Proustian theme in a letter from Keats to Benjamin Bailey' was chuckled over by the six or seven scholars who read it" (*Annotated Lolita* 18). Unable to support himself through such work, Humbert lives off a moderate inheritance and the sinecure from a wealthy uncle perfume maker, before accepting a room in Charlotte Haze's suburban house for an "absurdly, and ominously, low price" (40), where he suspects he will become a kept man. There, he sits around all day in his purple dressing gown, tracking the random movements of Charlotte's daughter Dolores (aka Lolita) through the house, perusing her *Young People's Encyclopedia*, masturbating, and drinking gin and pineapple juice before Charlotte, upon marrying him, forbids that particular indulgence (42–99). During their penultimate marital spat after she proposes a sojourn to England, Humbert blames Charlotte for dragging him daily to Hourglass Lake and thus interfering with the scholarly research he never considers doing when left alone (93). Unemployed, haughty, snobbish, endlessly distracted, filled with self-loathing but prepared to blame anyone and anything for his lack of productivity, Humbert is a portrait of the frustrated academic as a middle-aged man.

Humbert experiences his feelings of powerlessness as a kind of emasculation, one the novel presents as a defining characteristic of the postwar scholar-aesthete. His angry reaction to Charlotte's travel plans suggests not only his anxiety about being separated from Lolita but also his resentment upon finding his life fully under the control of a woman—a position he treats as a threat to his masculinity, most graphically registered by his intermittent sexual impotence. Moreover, Charlotte is "one of those women whose polished words may reflect a book club or bridge club, or any other deadly conventionality" (39)— that is, a proud member of the rapidly expanding class of postwar

American middlebrow readers invariably coded as feminine, who, according to numerous intellectuals, including Nabokov, are unable to recognize the true value of serious literature and thereby imperil its survival in the United States.[9] Charlotte not only circumscribes Humbert's agency in her personal relations with him; she also represents the category of female consumers responsible for marginalizing the work he hopes to perform as a literary scholar.

If Humbert instantiates that peculiar combination of egotism and abjection, of cultural capital and vague disrepute, that often attends those in the postwar United States who try to make aesthetic appreciation into a career—that is, academic literary critics—he does so most memorably by conflating his carefully cultivated artistic sensibility with pedophilia. Humbert characterizes what he famously calls "nympholepsy" as a rare faculty akin to that possessed by those few individuals sensitive enough to appreciate great art or literature. "We who are in the know," Humbert contends, can tell a true nymphet from a typical girl (18). "You have to be an artist and a madman, a creature of infinite melancholy, with a bubble of hot poison in your loins and a super-voluptuous flame permanently aglow in your subtle spine" (19)—the spine being the organ that, according to Nabokov, allows one to experience aesthetic satisfaction.[10] Later, Humbert laments that Lolita avoids him after crying: "I regretted keenly her mistake about my private aesthetics, for I simply love that tinge of Botticellian pink, that raw rose about the lips" (66). Describing Lolita's friend, Humbert remarks, "Eva Rosen, a displaced little person from France, was on the other hand a good example of a not strikingly beautiful child revealing to the perspicacious amateur some of the basic elements of nymphet charm" (192), thus suggesting the possibility, one Humbert himself has apparently realized, of becoming a *professional* pedophile. That he views his sexual obsession in this way suggests that it has filled the void left by his failure to turn his scholarship into an actual career, while also hinting at a disconcerting parallel between the two, between scholarly work and nympholepsy. Unable to appreciate literature for a living, Humbert chooses to appreciate young girls. Though the former might, unlike the latter, provide a salary, Humbert's joke subtly includes both: it is laughable to think of either as a useful profession.

What makes Humbert's pedophilic desire a particularly appropriate figure for his aesthetic cultivation is that, at least until he finally sleeps with Lolita, it seems to impose on him a condition of almost total passivity: "Oh, how you have to cringe and hide!" (19). In documenting his early urges, Humbert is very concerned to impress on his readers that his fantasies have had no impact on the objects of his lust. He even presents his orgasm, achieved with Lolita fidgeting, unwittingly as far as he can tell, in his lap, as an innocent pleasure. Indeed, at least in his de facto rationalization, his ability to enjoy it depends on his belief in its innocence: "Lolita had been safely solipsized" (62)—that is, converted into a fictional character constructed by his imagination so as to protect the safety of the actual Dolores. "Absolutely no harm done" (64), he gloats afterward. His sexual experience, according to his own account, preserves Lolita's autonomy. Moreover, his pleasure, he suggests, is derived not from any consideration of how he might possess, influence, or use her; it is derived merely from the act of passively perceiving her, or indeed perceiving his own perception of her. As such, it appears to represent a quintessential instance of Kantian aesthetic appreciation, one rendered in duly lofty terms: "What had begun as a delicious distension of my innermost roots became a glowing tingle which *now* had reached that state of absolute security, confidence and reliance not found elsewhere in conscious life" (62).

But Humbert's defenses are of course invariably disingenuous, often flamboyantly so, and his rendition of this moment is no exception. Lolita retreats from his lap the moment after he climaxes: "(As if we had been struggling and now my grip had eased) . . . she stood and blinked, cheeks aflame, hair awry" (63). Just how unaware she has been and how free to resist his desires remains disturbingly ambiguous. Furthermore, Humbert is obviously not at this moment, or ever in his relations with Lolita, a mere disinterested spectator. He continually plots to take possession of her, by murdering her mother if necessary, throughout his stay in their house. Thus Humbert's claim to an innocent, wholly aesthetic appreciation of Lolita functions mostly as a false alibi. But crucially, by presenting this posture as an alibi that fails, Nabokov's novel, as we will see, supports a paradoxical conception of the aesthetic, central to its functioning in the postwar period, that enables it to assume contradictory guises and perform contradictory functions.

Consider first why asserting an aesthetic motive might seem to Humbert a compelling self-defense. To argue for his controversial claim that he did not violate Lolita in this instance, he seeks common ground with his readers, some uncontroversial assumption to which they will lend their assent without much protest. What he offers is the belief that artistic endeavors are essentially passive, confined to the imagination, devoid of consequence within the actual world. If, in other words, he can cast his pedophilia as poetic, he can prove that it is harmless. Humbert observes,

> Ladies and gentlemen of the jury, the majority of sex offenders that hanker for some throbbing, sweet-moaning, physical but not necessarily coital, relation with a girl-child, are innocuous, inadequate, passive, timid strangers who merely ask the community to allow them to pursue their practically harmless, so-called aberrant behavior, their little hot wet private acts of sexual deviation without the police and society cracking down upon them. We are not sex fiends! We do not rape as good soldiers do. We are unhappy mild, dog-eyed gentlemen, sufficiently well integrated to control our urge in the presence of adults, but ready to give years and years of life for one chance to touch a nymphet. Emphatically, no killers are we. Poets never kill. (89–90)

The final statement is shocking not because of the false claim it makes for poets but because of the way it uses that claim as an alibi for pedophiles, whose identity with poets it ludicrously asserts. Insofar as his acts are poetic, Humbert suggests, they cannot be criminal—they probably do not even qualify as acts. He echoes this characterization a few episodes later, describing his first night in a hotel bed with Lolita: "I insist upon proving that I am not, and never was, and never could have been, a brutal scoundrel. The gentle and dreamy regions through which I crept were the patrimonies of poets—*not* crime's prowling ground. Had I reached my goal, my ecstasy would have been all softness, a case of internal combustion of which she would hardly have felt the heat" (133). Poetry is a mere dreamworld; the pleasure it yields (for either those who produce or those who read it) can never be pernicious, since the experience is one of "internal combustion"—it expires in the very moment of its emergence, without producing any perceivable impact beyond itself.

At this point, careful readers of Humbert's terminology may protest: the argument offered here has treated his defenses as mobilizing certain widespread views of aestheticism and aesthetic criticism, and yet the category he applies to himself in these moments is "poet," not "aesthete." Surely the two refer to distinct characters and distinct kinds of activities. But it is worth noting first of all that Nabokov treats *poetic* and *aesthetic* as practically synonymous, insofar as the defining goal of poetic language is, in his view, to produce aesthetic pleasure.[11] Moreover, Humbert imagines himself in certain moments as an aesthete, one who merely appreciates Lolita's beauty, and at other moments as a poet, using his imagination to construct a poetic version of Lolita. Given the vagueness of Humbert's self-definition, it is reasonable to conclude that the term *poet* is designed to capture a broadly conceived ensemble of activities dedicated to imagining, creating, or appreciating beauty. While Nabokov believes that stressing poetry's capacity to promote aesthetic pleasure is the only way to capture its particular significance, Humbert's invocation of the same function seems unwittingly to denigrate poetry's value. It is, in his formulation, merely an internal-combustion engine without influence or consequence—the province of the weak, the timid, and the socially marginalized.

Yet, despite his claim to passivity, Humbert does of course act; he does have sex with Lolita; he does assume power over her life after her mother's death and coerce her into obeying his whims. Indeed, he takes his revenge on the middle-class culture responsible for his sense of emasculation by raping a young girl, asserting his power within a world that has thus far seemed wholly impervious to his brilliance. And this, according to critics, is where he goes wrong. Humbert constructs a particular vision of beauty, which involves a number of romantic fantasies: escaping time, recovering innocence, uniting with a supernatural or demonic being, attaining the unattainable, and so forth. Though perversely predicated on the bodies of pubescent girls, this vision is not, numerous critics have argued, morally objectionable as long as it remains confined entirely to his imagination.[12] Humbert's crime is his attempt to translate his aesthetic vision into an embodied reality, to seek a real-life version of his perfect image and to take possession of it. While the moral of the story seems fairly obvious—Nabokov's glib version of it is "Do not hurt children" (interview by Anne Guérin 26)—

Humbert's narrative assumes a broader allegorical significance, representing the dangers of the unrestricted romantic imagination. The effort to create or pursue the beautiful ought to be confined to the sphere of fantasy or art. As Lucy Maddox puts it, summarizing the scholarly consensus, "The source of Humbert's despair is his inability to recognize that the kingdom by the sea which is the true home of his nymphets is a country of the mind, and that sanity, morality, and even love require a clear distinction between the ideal and the actual, between art and life" (*Nabokov's Novels* 75–76). For the many critics who share this view, Humbert does have an important piece of wisdom to offer, even though his self-exoneration fails. Perversely enough, his false alibi acquires validity as a prescription: poets should not act; aesthetic appreciation should remain a passive experience; the desire for the beautiful can be satisfied only within works of art, not in the actual world; aesthetic urges, in other words, must be circumscribed.[13]

Thus far, it is not clear why anyone would turn to *Lolita* in order to defend aestheticism. At best, aesthetic appreciation comes across as a useless pastime with minimal social significance akin to masturbation for those, like Humbert, with nothing more important to do. At worst, it can become a dangerous obsession, one that produces all variety of misanthropic behaviors. Moreover, the poetic language that Humbert employs, so beautifully designed to arouse admiration and awe, seems to dignify, if not justify, his cruelty while converting Dolores into a symbol, thus masking her suffering and eliciting sympathy for her victimizer. If aesthetically powerful language is not itself evil, Nabokov seems to insinuate, it is fully equipped to serve as evil's accomplice. Notwithstanding his own stated commitment to "aesthetic bliss" (*Annotated Lolita* 316), Nabokov has produced a novel that endows aestheticism with an odor of corruption, implying insidious associations between it and far more odious perversions. A number of critics, most famously Richard Rorty, have extracted this message, treating *Lolita* as a morality tale, one that dramatizes the dangers of an excessive focus on aesthetic satisfaction.[14] Strangely enough, however, *Lolita* has attracted far more attention from scholars at least residually invested in formalist or aesthetic modes of interpretation than from those categorically committed to repudiating or demonizing such modes. Thus it is worth considering what function the novel performs precisely for the scholar-aesthetes whom it seems so brutally to satirize.

Power to the Aesthetes

One way of accounting for *Lolita*'s appeal among formalist critics is to recognize how it works to alleviate or resolve the anxieties that it arouses. If at first Nabokov seems to reaffirm various negative stereotypes about postwar academic literary critics—presenting them as passive, vain, ineffectual figures whose work is devoid of consequence— he eventually dismantles these stereotypes by offering a portrait of a scholar-aesthete who *acts*, who translates his vision of beauty into a reality—one that has serious consequences for those around him. Although most *Lolita* scholars read this as Humbert's tragic mistake, it is also the one that makes him a source of critical interest. Arguably, the sympathy and admiration that Humbert has managed to elicit among academics, despite his egotism, cruelty, perversity, and criminality, depend in part on his efforts to make his vision of beauty socially significant, first by taking possession of Lolita and later by writing about what he has done, thus offering an allegory of aesthetic empowerment.[15] To be sure, Humbert is also a source of great repugnance; and feminist critics in particular have been less willing than others to identify with him, particularly given how his feelings of both powerlessness and triumph are bound up with virulently misogynistic attitudes.[16] And yet the reason the novel's strategies for magnifying the significance of aesthetics have proved effective even among those most inclined to resist Humbert's rhetoric is that these strategies do not depend on an ability to present his actions as justifiable or comprehensible. Quite the contrary: precisely insofar as his quest elicits emphatic condemnation, it demonstrates that aesthetic commitments matter.

Nabokov accentuates the importance of aesthetics by placing it in direct relationship with ethics.[17] He does so most obviously by explicitly offering two apparently opposed ways of reading the book, the first, the ethical approach, in the foreword by fictional editor John Ray Jr., who insists that Humbert's narrative achieves a "moral apotheosis" (7), and the second, the aesthetic approach, endorsed by Nabokov in his 1956 afterword (appended to all editions of the novel starting in 1958), where he claims that "a work of fiction exists only insofar as it affords me what I shall bluntly call aesthetic bliss" (316). While it might seem possible to treat the two as entirely independent modes of interpretation without any bearing on each other, Nabokov clearly envisions a competition between them, inviting the conclusion that one acquires legitimacy only at the expense of the other. His aim is to assert the categorical superiority of aesthetic over ethical interpretation, but by staging this competition he places the two in an intimate relationship, one best articulated by Humbert in the couplet he falsely attributes to "an old poet": "The moral sense in mortals is the duty / We have to pay on mortal sense of beauty" (285). A majority of critics have read the relationship between ethics and aesthetics suggested by *Lolita* as an entanglement, concluding that it is nearly impossible to dissociate judgments about the one from judgments about the other.[18]

What *Lolita* does fundamentally is to weigh aesthetics down with moral baggage. It is almost impossible to disregard the ethical problems raised by Humbert's behavior in order to allow for a simple appreciation of the beauty of his language, because Humbert's search for beauty and the style he uses to dramatize that search are entirely complicit with his ethical misdeeds. Moreover, not only does the novel dramatize through Humbert the moral hazards of focusing too exclusively on beauty or aesthetic power; it places readers in an analogously fraught dilemma. If we enjoy Humbert's rhetoric too thoroughly, reading the novel only for aesthetic pleasure, then we are committing an error similar to the one that leads Humbert to disregard the suffering of others. The very way we experience the novel thus seems freighted with ethical significance, so that it is possible to be good or bad readers in a moral sense, to err or succeed ethically simply by virtue of how we feel while reading *Lolita*.

While a sense of the interdependence of the two domains appears explicitly in statements like Harriet Hustis's that "ethics and aesthetics are ultimately (and, for many, problematically) interconnected in Nabokov's complex novel" ("Time Will Tell" 106), one can find the same sense of conflation even in those critics who favor one approach over the other. Formalist Julia Bader cleverly interprets John Ray Jr.'s moralistic warning about dangerous social trends as an argument about literary form: "Without knowing it, John Ray is telling the truth: that

Lolita 'warns us of dangerous trends,' except that the warning is not moral or social, but rather aesthetic and literary. 'The wayward child, the egoistic mother, the panting maniac' are, from an artistic point of view, not social evils, but the evils of hackneyed characterization and theme in contemporary novels" (*Crystal Land* 65). Notice that even as she attempts to distinguish carefully between the ethical and the aesthetic so as to underscore Nabokov's exclusive interest in the latter, Bader appropriates Ray's rhetoric, relying on a moral vocabulary to establish the importance of aesthetic discrimination. Hackneyed characterization is an "evil." On the other side of the debate, feminist critic Colleen Kennedy notes the gender politics of the text's rhetorical modes of address: "This sharing [of disdain for "the culture Lolita represents"], however, requires what Fetterley calls an 'immasculated' reader, and according to Kappeler, exposes the 'disinterested' aesthetic as a power play" ("White Man's Guest" 51). The effect both of Humbert's stylistic dexterity and of the mandate issued by Nabokov to treat the book exclusively as a source of aesthetic satisfaction is, according to Kennedy, to efface Lolita's pain and to silence the ethical concerns of those women readers unable or unwilling to place themselves in the position of white male privilege necessary to interpret the book in the way that Nabokov demands. Thus, *Lolita* serves to "cancel out" women's voices (53). Kennedy's critique is compelling, but it is important to recognize how, in reading the aesthetic as a "power play," she endows it with great moral significance, serving, if anything, to inflate its social importance.

One reason, then, that the mutual contamination enacted by *Lolita* is so attractive to literary scholars is that it lends social consequence to certain priorities, values, and agendas—centered on style, form, and beauty—that are frequently posited as *merely* aesthetic concerns. Eager to rebut this apparent trivialization, the majority of scholarly readings use *Lolita* to yoke the aesthetic to the ethical, thereby instrumentalizing aesthetic choices, treating them as means to either greater societal well-being or harm. Such gestures betray a recognition on the part of academics about the limited capacity of aesthetic questions to capture interest on their own, while simultaneously serving to ensure the centrality of these questions in future discussions of literature. In a sense, the scholarly response to *Lolita* perfectly exemplifies the means by which a commitment to the aesthetic has survived in the past several decades, by attaching itself to other registers—social, moral, and political—thus concealing the desire to value certain experiences of beauty, formal complexity, and stylistic felicity for their own sake by placing them in the service of other, more socially responsible ends.

Critics of *Lolita* frequently warn readers against extracting too much pleasure from the novel.[19] In so doing, they interpret *Lolita* as an indictment of Humbert's aestheticism, one that presents it as complicit with callousness, cruelty, smugness, arrogance, misogyny, and the like, thus casting doubt on the larger project of postwar aesthetic criticism, for which he stands as an unattractive representative. And yet it is important to notice how these critiques invariably rely on a subtle magnification of the aesthetic's significance. Reiterating the most popular interpretation of the novel, Ellen Pifer contends, "Some of Nabokov's most talented and proud artists—Axel Rex, Humbert Humbert, and Van Veen—are exposed, in their cruelty, for seeking to extend their sovereign power beyond the domain of art. Unlike their author, they do not perceive a distinction between the natural condition of human freedom and the inhuman privileges of art. Such failure of insight constitutes, for this celebrated champion of aesthetic bliss, the most lethal form of vulgarity" (*Nabokov* 171). "Sovereign," a synonym for supreme, analogizes the power of the artist with that of a political ruler. Presumably she means over the "domain of art" only. Yet in underscoring the "lethal" hazards that may follow from any overstepping of the boundaries that constitute this domain, she suggests that the godlike powers of the artist's inhuman imagination can translate into a commensurate degree of potency when applied to the human world. De la Durantaye's rhetoric is higher pitched:

> This moral duty is nothing other than vigilance—vigilance as regards the danger of art, the threat that in its single-minded pursuit of its goal, in its heat and hurry it might trample the tenderness that the artist, more than any other, should know to prize and protect. In his *Defense of Poetry*, Shelley claimed that "the greatest instrument of moral good is the imagination" (Shelley, 488). Nabokov may have felt similarly, but he found the matter far from simple as, for him, the imagination and the senses that fire it must be reined in, must learn

to limit themselves to the artistic sphere so that they may remain
an instrument of widening and deepening perception, not of pain and
loss. (*Style Is Matter* 187)

Like other critics, de la Durantaye reads *Lolita* as a cautionary tale
about the dangers attendant on the obsessive pursuit of beauty. Yet, as
with Pifer, the argument in favor of restraint presupposes a belief in
art's awesome potential, in this case likened to that of a wild herd of
stallions capable, when unreined, of trampling on whatever tender beings cross their path, spreading "pain and loss" wherever they go.

A series of revealing ambiguities emerge in these and similar responses to *Lolita*. First of all, it is worth noting how the apparent critique of aestheticism, predicated on an awareness of the immorality
that it seems to license, easily slides into a reassertion of aestheticism's
core principle—that is, that artistic works should constitute a world
of uncorrupted beauty separate from everyday life. And yet such statements are prescriptions, not declarations: art *ought* to confine itself to
its own proper sphere. The need to repeat this demonstrates a belief
that it does not always do so, that it can and does intervene in society,
often with major repercussions. The concern voiced in these readings
is not merely that certain figures like Humbert take it as their prerogative as artists to mistreat the people around them, but that art itself
can operate in an analogous fashion when it oversteps its boundaries
and attempts to exert influence on the world. As Pifer puts it, "Only
in unique, independent, and essentially nonutilitarian forms, then,
does art embody the true of nature of man, who may not justifiably be
subverted to serve any individual or collective will. Only by art's
freedom from function will it truly 'serve' us" (*Nabokov* 169). Moreover, Pifer, de la Durantaye, and others attribute the potential to exert
extraordinary power over society not just to literature or art broadly
speaking but more specifically to those features of art most likely to
earn the designation "beautiful"—the stylish, the verbally brilliant,
the formally harmonious—in short, to all those features designed to
arouse aesthetic satisfaction that figure so largely in Nabokov's fiction.
They are not, in other words, addressing those relatively unadorned
genres—like the naturalist novel, for instance—whose social engagement is obvious. Pifer's invocation of the "inhuman" and de la Duran-

taye's emphasis on the imagination make it clear that they are describing works that glory in their own difference from reality, that foreground their own peculiar form. Yet these critics are paradoxically endowing precisely this seemingly hermetic artistry with terrifying worldly power, recasting the effort to preserve the autonomy of art as a socially responsible act aimed at shielding society from beauty's destructive power.

It is worth remembering, of course, that the aesthetic only ever represents an inadequate term for describing Humbert's ways of appreciating Lolita. Nabokov, as we have seen, dispenses frequent hints that his protagonist's pursuits are never truly disinterested. The fraudulence of Humbert's self-characterization is worth underlining since it ought, at least in theory, to undermine *Lolita*'s power to ascribe social significance to the aesthetic. After all, thus far the claim that Humbert offers a model of a consequential, if harmful, aestheticism and the related argument that *Lolita* lends moral weight to aesthetic commitments have assumed the premise that Humbert's relationship to Lolita exemplifies a viable expression of the aesthetic. And yet it is possible to argue that insofar as Humbert actually goes beyond disinterested appreciation, he transgresses the boundaries of the aesthetic and thus fails to demonstrate anything about the latter's significance. But a majority of scholars have not reached this conclusion. It seems, then, that *Lolita* has accomplished a remarkable sleight of hand: persuading readers to accept at face value Humbert's claim that his sins do in fact fall within the domain of art, thereby reassigning the guilt that ought to belong solely to his own personal misdeeds to the aesthetic as such. And thus gestures that willfully surpass the aesthetic's purview serve to expand its very scope, making its potential to exceed the boundaries of its own definition a structural property of its essence, so as to magnify its perceived potency, whether as a force for evil or good. Yet at the same time, by offering such perversions of the aesthetic as object lessons within a morality tale—as examples to be avoided—it simultaneously appeals to those who regard the aesthetic as a realm of pure, disinterested contemplation, even if it offers the latter as a regulative ideal rather than a fact: something to strive for, something, indeed, that Nabokov's prose, in its more forgivably lyrical moments, occasionally fosters.

By offering such a paradoxical conception of the aesthetic, *Lolita* appeals to both formalist and political critics, and the purposes that the two camps have made it serve reveal an assumption shared by both. Despite their differences, both formalist and ideological interpretations of the novel participate in a rhetoric pervasive within literary studies across methodological divisions that assigns enormous social significance to the aesthetic. Political modes of interpretation, which unmask aesthetic devices as ideological mechanisms, presuppose first and foremost that aesthetics actually matter enough to support particular political arrangements. What they are fundamentally challenging is not aestheticism but the opposite: the view, ubiquitous outside academia, that aesthetics and, more broadly, the arts and the humanities make no difference whatsoever. Because *Lolita*'s formalist interpreters are not, despite their ambivalence, as prepared to disavow the aesthetic bliss championed by Nabokov, their response to the novel reveals somewhat more openly than other discourses how the critique of the aesthetic can serve as its tacit defense.

Moreover, it is possible, apparently, to critique aestheticism without denying or avoiding its pleasures. As critics ranging from Lionel Trilling to Wayne Booth to Leona Toker have argued, *Lolita* actively solicits the reader's identification with Humbert.[20] In order to grasp the true threat that Humbert poses, we must come to recognize the persuasive power of his lyrical rhetoric and the allure of the pleasures that he imagines. To escape his particular mode of aestheticism, numerous scholars contend, readers must first experience it fully. As James Phelan puts it, "Through these signals, Nabokov clearly communicates his ethical disapproval of Humbert and invites the authorial audience to share in it. Yet Nabokov's technique also means that before we can stand with Nabokov and away from his character, we have to stand with Humbert and share his perspective. It's a very uncomfortable ethical position because it allows Nabokov to have his cake and eat it, too: to indulge in pedophilic fantasies through his creation and then to say, 'But of course we right-thinking people condemn such fantasies'" ("Dual Focalization" 135). This pattern of response is a common strategy among both formalist and political scholars for negotiating the aesthetic pleasures of reading: indulging them in order to reject or restrain them, enjoying them, indeed, in the form of a principled disavowal.

Ecstasy and Ethics

If *Lolita* works to alleviate the anxieties that it provokes, offering a drama in which aesthetic commitments come to appear anything but trivial, marginal, or socially insignificant, many critical accounts nevertheless struggle to find within the novel a basis for assigning these commitments a positive or socially productive role. The aesthetic is important in *Lolita*, it would seem, only because it is dangerous. Indeed, the one virtuous function the aesthetic resources of the novel perform, according to many interpretations, is to dramatize their own hazards, to offer an object lesson in what horrible suffering the pursuit of beauty can unleash or what dangerous modes of complicity and callousness a fancy prose style can elicit.[21] The aesthetic gains social power, in other words, only by negating itself. Many scholars, of course, are unsatisfied with these conclusions. After all, even those who read *Lolita* as asserting the need to confine the aesthetic within a carefully circumscribed domain find the book to be compelling only because of the transgressions that it both depicts and enacts. It is, in other words, only because Humbert refuses to restrict his fantasies to writing or his mind that he can serve as a protagonist within a socially significant drama; it is only because Nabokov's narrative, in poeticizing Humbert's perversions, uses aesthetic techniques for arguably morally dubious ends that it becomes worthy of critical attention. Refusing to be merely or innocuously beautiful, the novel itself is the product of an urge to violate the very prescription that it apparently makes. And this urge, some critics maintain, need not be in all cases vicious. The narrative of aesthetic potency that Nabokov offers, in other words, seems to hold out the promise of directing that potency at more socially useful or redemptive ends than the ones that Humbert chooses.

The use that a majority of *Lolita*'s critics want its aesthetic strategies to serve is ethical. To say that the novel delivers a particular moral, however, is to risk treating its stylistic strategies as a mere vehicle, a trivial packaging used to deliver a preestablished message, in effect subordinating the aesthetic to the ethical—a worry voiced by Nabokov in the afterword.[22] Thus several scholars contend that the rhetorical strategies *Lolita* employs serve not merely to communicate but rather to rethink or recast ethical truths, presenting the novel's specifically literary elements as a substantive contribution to the question of how to live—a contribution synonymous with its formal means of expression and as such untranslatable into another mode of discourse. One can find a suggestion of this in Appel's refusal of "didacticism" in favor of "moral resonance" as a description of what the novel offers—the latter suggesting that its moral value depends on its musicality ("Springboard" 225). Michael Wood arrives at a similar conclusion, claiming that *Lolita* offers no "general lesson" but instead provides "practice for the moral imagination" ("*Lolita* Revisited" 18), positing a hybrid cognitive faculty, one that makes moral action possible but depends on a kind of habitual cultivation that only imaginative works can offer. For Peter Levine, the ethics of the book assume the form of narrative, which can grapple with the complex moral problems raised by particular situations in a way that Platonic principles or Kantian imperatives cannot ("*Lolita*").

In order to present aesthetic cultivation as the very basis for ethical awareness, numerous scholars have argued that the central lesson of *Lolita* is not the need to reject aesthetics in favor of ethics but rather the need to reject one aesthetic in favor of another, to reject Humbert's aesthetic in favor of Nabokov's.[23] Those committed to this possibility tend to underline the peculiar definition of aesthetic bliss that Nabokov provides in his afterword: "a sense of being somehow, somewhere, connected with other states of being where art (curiosity, tenderness, kindness, ecstasy) is the norm" (*Annotated Lolita* 316–317). Indeed, the contrast between this and Humbert's masturbatory pleasure—"that state of absolute security, confidence, and reliance" (62)—could not be greater. Whereas Humbert's notion of aesthetic bliss emphasizes self-containment, solitude, and control, Nabokov's emphasizes vulnerability, an openness to surprise, and a concern for others.

The lesson of the novel, according to numerous critics, is to recognize the limitations of Humbert's perspective not in order to invalidate the project of cultivating aesthetic sensitivity but to embrace an entirely different kind of aesthetic sensitivity, one that can serve as the very foundation for a complex sense of moral responsibility. Seeking the right kind of aesthetic bliss, in other words, will make you a better, kinder person.[24] It is a message, significantly, well equipped to rationalize academic literary studies. Thus it is perhaps no coincidence that the one figure to cast serious doubt on this interpretation, Rorty, is affiliated with philosophy and not literature. "If curiosity and tenderness are the marks of the artist," Rorty remarks dubiously, "if both are inseparable from ecstasy—so that where they are absent no bliss is possible—then there is, after all, no distinction between the aesthetic and the moral. The dilemma of the liberal aesthete is resolved" (*Contingency* 158–159). But is it not possible, Rorty conjectures, that the opposite is true? Perhaps, in other words, a deep commitment to aesthetic pleasure will, as Humbert's example suggests, invariably produce a corresponding decrease of moral virtue.

While Rorty's critique is forceful, *Lolita*'s readiness to entertain the possibility he raises, its refusal to resolve questions about the moral consequences of aesthetic commitments, is arguably central to the act of valorization that it performs for literary scholars. Precisely by wrestling with this problem, scholars are able to reaffirm both the theoretical sophistication and the ethical rigor of their interpretive work. By placing aestheticism under doubt, in other words, *Lolita* allows critics to enjoy the textual pleasures it offers in a sufficiently self-critical fashion so as to stave off accusations of hedonism or self-indulgence. In a way similar to deconstruction in its later varieties, the response to *Lolita* recasts radical ambiguity as a heroic test of the reader's capacity for virtue.[25]

The Pleasures of Suspicion

It is worth nothing that *Lolita* raises difficult questions not only for formalists but also for political critics. Thus far, I have argued that Humbert represents a satirical caricature of a quintessential postwar aesthete. He is also, however, a textbook example of a paranoid reader; and *Lolita* highlights certain surprising continuities between the two—between aestheticism and the hermeneutics of suspicion.[26] All throughout the narrative and with greater intensity as it progresses, Humbert views seemingly random occurrences as the result of a conspiracy on the part either of an impersonal cosmic force, which he dubs "McFate," or of an actual human agent—first Detective Trapp, then Clare Quilty—designed to torment him. By the end, after Lolita escapes him, his semi-delusions of persecution motivate him to read, literally, for clues regarding the identity of his nemesis in hotel registries across the United States. Significantly, Humbert's paranoia is a constitutive element of his nympholepsy, and though it often seems a source of pain, it plays a central role in fostering aesthetic satisfaction. It enables Humbert to convert people and things into motifs within a grand plot; it isolates him within his own private space of heightened sensation; and it imposes a coherence onto the world as he perceives it, making its parts resonate, albeit obscurely and sometimes cruelly.

Moreover, Humbert's paranoia also seems to produce a fair amount of aesthetic satisfaction for readers. The subplot that is both the cause and outgrowth of his suspicion, centered on Quilty, the figure who eventually steals Lolita from Humbert, has garnered attention primarily from scholars committed to interpreting *Lolita* in formalist or aesthetic terms. Such critics revel in the search for clues as to Quilty's identity in the form of puns, anagrams, and cryptic allusions to his dramatic oeuvre, treating the verbal surface of the novel as an intricate, endlessly rewarding puzzle. Attention to Quilty's ludicrously elaborate plot tends to coincide with a focus on the plotting of the novel in general—the array of coincidences, motifs, and ironies that appear to lend credence to Humbert's paranoia while also reminding readers that his account is a pure fiction.[27] At the same time, an emphasis on the novel's artifice tends to entail reduced concern for Lolita's suffering parallel to Humbert's own disregard, as critics turn her into an allegorical figure or pawn in the symbolic struggle between Humbert and Quilty over authorship of the narrative.

The hermeneutics of suspicion is generally thought to enable political critique by working to decipher ostensibly trivial or unrelated gestures, signs, and events as symptomatic expressions of political power or ideological inscription. What *Lolita* dramatizes is the way in which this interpretive habit produces aesthetic pleasure. To be sure, Humbert's paranoia is not without connection to politics—and certain historicist critics, such as Adam Piette, have read it as a response to

Cold War anxieties. But *Lolita* also demonstrates how paranoia can intensify perceptions and the way they get articulated so as to arrest and gratify the reader's attention. The more suspicious Humbert becomes, after all, the more meticulously he observes his surroundings in search of confirmation, making the everyday American landscape on which he gazes radiate with portentous, if unknown, meaning. As Rita Felski puts it in her characterization of suspicious reading, "The device of the clue has the effect of coating mundane or irrelevant details with a sheen of supercharged significance" (*Limits of Critique* 99).[28] To be clear, the purpose of identifying Humbert's sensibility with a particular academic trend is not to demonize the hermeneutics of suspicion any more than it is to demonize aestheticism. To view paranoia as an aesthetic device is not to assign it a fixed ethical or ideological meaning but just the opposite: to delink it from any particular social or political program so as to accentuate its variability, to reveal the multiple purposes it can be enlisted to serve. In some situations it can enable excessive abstraction and callousness; in others, acuteness and radical intervention.

A common tendency among academics is to speculate about the distant future as a means of justifying suspicion: the critique it mobilizes will purportedly contribute to political struggles that will one day overturn a deeply unjust system. Humbert too rationalizes his interpretive habits with reference to the distant future. He aims his paranoia at his posthumous readers, whose judgment he fears but whose fascination he hopes his narrative will arouse, not just fifty years hence but for generations, lending him and Lolita immortality. Humbert's posture thus bears comparison to that of another paranoid reader, whom we encountered in the introduction: that other taboo breaker, childhood destroyer, and compulsive pun maker, queer theorist Lee Edelman, who is, despite his protests, no less obsessed with the future than Humbert—so much so that he ends his polemic *No Future* with a fantastical apocalyptic scenario borrowed from Hitchcock, in which an unstoppable flock of queer birds, in response to a future gay hate crime, "keep[s] on coming" (154).

Edelman's main argument, as we saw, is that our culture's hyperconcern for the safety and innocence of the child represents a symbolic investment in the future that shores up our faith in the current social order, masking the meaninglessness and misery of the present by embedding it in a narrative of progress. His theory serves to illuminate why the taboo on pedophilia is so fiercely enforced, why Humbert's desires continue to be so scandalous, but in doing so *No Future* also offers a useful way of approaching other questions central to this chapter. I suggested in the introduction that Edelman's commitment to present enjoyment over and against futurist ideals might be read as a mode of aestheticism. But alongside Humbert, he also exemplifies a contradiction at the heart of the aesthetic between a single-minded concentration on the present—the beautiful or sublime moment that is complete and sufficient unto itself—and a concern for the future legacy of that moment. One does not need to be a psychoanalyst to deduce that Edelman's obsessive denial of the future may mask an unspoken attachment. What, after all, is he seeking to accomplish by articulating the anarchic, self-consuming, future-defying moments of *jouissance* that, according to his own theory, require no rationalization, no subsequent reflection or evaluation, other than to endow them with a fixed, academically legitimized form? Humbert's ambitions render the paradox more legible. His relentless pursuit of momentary pleasures with Lolita, which destroys both her childhood and her future, compels him to produce as compensation an aestheticized version of her, by writing his memoir for posterity, so that she can persist into the far-off future. "I am thinking of aurochs and angels, the secret of durable pigments, prophetic sonnets, the refuge of art. And this is the only immortality you and I may share, my Lolita" (*Annotated Lolita* 311). Humbert's treatment of Lolita thus reveals a dual focus split between the visceral intensity of the present and the prospect of immortal fame.

One urge entails the other. Aesthetic appreciation consists of enjoying the moment in which a particular object is perceived for its own sake, designating that object worthy of attention on the basis only of how it shapes the moment of perception, not on the basis of future uses it might serve or consequences it might produce. And yet, while this orientation appears to be entirely fixated on the present, it is also a way of ensuring durability by defending the moment of aesthetic appreciation against future contingency, against subsequent moments that might instigate a revision of the original judgment. The New Critics were so obsessed with asserting the immemorial status of the poetry they preferred that they refused even to consider the effect its pristine organic form might have on readers as a way of measuring its value.[29] The claim that the significance of either the work of art or the aesthetic experience it promotes does not depend on the subsequent consequences it produces is a way of allowing that work or that experience to survive intact, in all of its integrity, into the distant future.

But if aesthetic criticism turns out, despite its purported attachment to ephemeral pleasures, to be inescapably future oriented, then the future-obsessed outlook of political criticism also nurtures an aesthetic function well equipped to foster pleasurable experiences in the present. This function is especially pronounced, ironically enough, in those most radical and paranoid forms of criticism, often Marxist or Foucauldian, that claim to reject the viability of any form of immediate comfort, solace, or promise within the current political order in their effort to underline the latter's total coerciveness and cruelty and thus the need to work toward the creation of an entirely different system. Notwithstanding his apparent refusal of futurism, Edelman's contempt for near-term, reformist measures shares this paranoid logic, and in fact his celebration of queer counterpractices seems at times to betray fantasies of a world remaking apocalyptic scenario. What such a hermeneutic does, in all of its manifestations, is to promote a joint fixation on the present—its contradictions, its sublimely unmappable structures of power, its oppressive inescapability—and the far-distant future, which will emerge out of and miraculously resolve the problems of the present. It is an approach that interlocks the two in a mirroring embrace and thereby excludes the quotidian immediacies and urgencies of tomorrow or the next day.

Such paranoia is tempting and at times necessary, and scholarship over the past forty years has exhaustively demonstrated its many virtues. It is a way of refusing to be duped by false lures and inadequate temporary fixes, thus insulating one's ideals and one's critical intelligence against the corrosive effects of compromise, preventing any truce with a status quo that is manifestly inadequate. It can lend legibility to disappointments and frustrations that would otherwise seem merely arbitrary; recasting them as the coordinated expression of a system—one that takes each individual's life seriously, even if only as an object of manipulation. Imagining a utopian alternative can also throw into re-lief structural injustices that might otherwise have remained invis-ible or appeared unalterable, thus opening up new avenues of critique and resistance.[30] But it is also worth noting, as Humbert demonstrates, that a key motive for suspicious reading, given the great uncertainty that inevitably enshrouds the far-off future toward which it beckons, is the intense, at times masochistic, pleasure it affords in the moment of its operation.

5

Why Is *Beloved* So Universally Beloved?

IT IS OBVIOUSLY no coincidence that Toni Morrison's rapid entry into the canon occurred at precisely the same moment as the rise of political criticism in the academy. Just as scholars sought to foreground how literary works engaged various social, ideological, and racial issues, Morrison provided a series of novels in which such engagements were explicit and unapologetic. And just as academics wondered how literature and their responses to it might either further or thwart the possibility of justice, Morrison gave them books whose unflinching portrayals of racism, sexism, and other forms of oppression made reading itself feel like a socially responsible act. Yet even while a good portion of Morrison scholarship endorsed her texts on the basis, ultimately, of the strenuous political work they perform, it was impossible for anyone to ignore the dazzling salience of Morrison's style. And thus I want to make the counterintuitive claim that the decision of the newly politicized antiformalist scholars who achieved prominence in the 1980s and 1990s to embrace such an undeniably *stylish* author may also have been no coincidence.

While those calling for a return to formalism have characterized the last several decades as a period when scholars systematically disregarded aesthetic considerations, a careful analysis of the academic reception of Morrison's most celebrated novel, *Beloved* (1987), yields a

167

slightly different picture. Confronting this massive archive of scholarly work, one discovers not merely that plenty of critics directly consider questions of form, style, and narrative structure in Morrison's fiction but also something more important, if less obvious.[1] Namely, even those readers who appear to focus on *Beloved*'s political function continue to privilege specific aesthetic experiences, predicated on implicit stylistic criteria, even when they seek to valorize those experiences in political terms. Thus, like *Lolita*, *Beloved* has offered scholars an opportunity to rethink the relationship between the novel's aesthetic power and its social responsibilities, to imagine new ways in which these functions might be allied, even while they have tended to place the aesthetic in the position of subservient or silent partner.

If *Beloved* is a source of aesthetic satisfaction, how can one account for the fulfillment that it yields? Dramatizing the tragic effects of slavery, Morrison's novel seems designed to deny readers any experience of catharsis. It focuses on the haunting of the protagonist, Sethe, and her family by the ghost of the baby she murdered, which culminates in the inexplicable appearance of a grown woman named Beloved with a childlike mind and supernatural physical strength, but no coherent memories, who comes to reside in Sethe's house and demand, as a newborn might, every last bit of her host's attention and energy. But whether this woman is truly Sethe's murdered child returned from the grave, whether she is real or a delusion, whether she is successfully exorcised at the end of the narrative, whether she will subsequently return in a new form, and whether Sethe will remain in the near-catatonic state into which she falls in the final scenes or whether she will recover—all of this remains totally unclear, and thus the book ends without offering any sense of closure. Indeed, if readers find themselves vexed, this likely means that *Beloved* has produced its intended effect: it is named after a ghost that harasses people, terrifies them, angers them, and forces them to confront things they would rather forget.[2] Morrison herself claims that she believed *Beloved* would be a commercial failure, "the least read of all the books I'd written because it is about something that the characters don't want to remember, black people don't want to remember, white people don't want to remember" ("Pain of Being Black" 257).

Critics often treat *Beloved* not as a novel that arouses spontaneous affection but as a novel, like the ghost, that imposes impossible ethical obligations on us. And yet it is important to remember what it is that Beloved, the ghost, fundamentally demands: love above all else and, in some moments, desire—responses that she successfully elicits, even as she torments Sethe and her family. Obviously *Beloved*, the book, operates in a similar fashion. Although Morrison sometimes appears bent on torturing readers, the same devices that produce this effect also paradoxically offer aesthetic satisfaction. Thus in this chapter I want to consider several political responses to the novel, to uncover evidence of this satisfaction, to bring out, as it were, the love that *Beloved* so desperately seeks and that critics so stubbornly refuse to acknowledge.

Oppositional Aesthetics

Before we turn to the scholarship on *Beloved*, it is worth noting that the aesthetic is a central subject of concern within the novel. All of the major characters seek out experiences of beauty as a respite from their daily hardships: Sethe with her "fistful of salsify" designed to "take the ugly out of" the slavemaster's kitchen (27); Baby Suggs with her obsessive interest in colors (4); Denver with her secret ring of boxwood bushes (34–35); Paul D. with his love of trees (25); and Amy with her quest for velvet (40–41). To be sure, Morrison's portrayal of these attachments is thoroughly unsentimental. She notes, for instance, the inadequacy of Sethe's efforts to transform her workplace: "As though a handful of myrtle stuck in the handle of a pressing iron propped against the door in a whitewoman's kitchen could make it hers. As though mint sprig in the mouth changed the breath as well as its odor. A bigger fool never lived" (28). Moreover, she presents Baby Suggs's interest in "pondering color," abstracted from any context, as pathological, a sign that she has surrendered her volition. Thus the novel seems to indict aestheticism as a refusal not only of responsibility but of life itself.

And yet, even while Morrison underscores the limitations of the aesthetic as a response to political oppression, she refuses to deny its value insofar as the capacity to be fulfilled aesthetically—the ability to enjoy or value a particular experience for its own sake—is something that the slave system has systematically endeavored to strip from African Americans. As Denver puts it, "Slaves not supposed to have pleasurable feelings on their own; their bodies not supposed to be like that, but they have to have as many children as they can to please whoever owned them" (247). For African Americans, every act, every experience, including the one most often linked to pleasure—sex—has been instrumentalized, converted into a means of production, valued only insofar as it can serve the needs of the slave system.

Before she succumbs to despair, Baby Suggs actively defies this logic, inviting her fellow former slaves into the Clearing, where she urges them to love their own bodies: "Yonder they do not love your flesh. They despise it. They don't love your eyes; they'd just as soon pick em out. No more do they love the skin on your back. Yonder they flay it. And O my people they do not love your hands. Those they only use, tie, bind, chop off and leave empty. Love your hands! Love them. Raise them up and kiss them. Touch others with them, pat them together, stroke them on your face 'cause they don't love that either. *You got to love it, you!*" (103–104). The collective act of self-care that Baby Suggs choreographs is exactly like the slave rituals described by Saidiya V. Hartman in *Scenes of Subjection*, which we encountered in Chapter 3—rituals that "offer a small measure of relief" but do not represent effective political resistance (Hartman 61). Baby Suggs describes the brutality of white people but does not encourage her followers to challenge or try to destroy the system on which that brutality is based. The advice she gives to her daughter-in-law affirms her commitment to avoiding direct political engagement: "Lay em down, Sethe. Sword and shield. Down. Down. Both of em down. Down by the riverside. Sword and shield. Don't study war no more. Lay all that mess down" (101). Paradoxically, Baby Suggs's gatherings represent a powerful response to conditions of unbearable political oppression, indeed a rejoinder to a vicious ideology, but insofar as she insists on finding satisfaction in the flesh here and now, their value for their participants is more aesthetic than political. This is another instance, then, of the aesthetic operating within conditions of extreme political constraint.

The lesson Baby Suggs hopes to impart to her community is one that Sethe, her daughter-in-law, has particular difficulty learning. When her partner, Paul D., suggests that they have a baby together, Sethe's first reaction is to consider "how good the sex would be if that is what he wanted" (155). On the one hand, she seems to assert the importance of her own bodily pleasure; on the other hand, what heightens this imagined pleasure is its procreative power. Sethe continues to conceive of herself, in other words, as primarily a producer of children. Unable to escape the slave owner's ideology, she cannot imagine her life or experiences as valuable for their own sake, which is why she responds with such profound disbelief to Paul D.'s final statement in the novel: "You your best thing, Sethe. You are" (321). Although Morrison frequently underscores their incapacity to mount a substantive challenge to the political conditions within which they arise, nonproductive forms of pleasure—that is, aesthetic modes of fulfillment—function as one of the key signs that characters have escaped (even if just briefly) the demand for absolute submission demanded by slavery. Admittedly all of the pleasurable outlets the characters discover prove to be precarious, endangered by a world that works to deny their right to any such satisfaction. A terrifying sign of the refusal of white people to allow African Americans to indulge even the slightest self-beautifying urge, for instance, is the red hair ribbon that former Underground Railroad worker Stamp Paid finds "knotted around a curl of wet woolly hair, clinging still to its bit of scalp"—an image that reminds him of Baby Suggs's fixation on color (213). Thus Morrison makes it clear that producing a world within which aesthetic practices will not be jeopardized by the possibility of deadly retribution requires concrete political change. Nevertheless, her lyrical prose confers a kind of absolute validity on the furtive efforts of her characters to secure moments of pleasure and beauty even within conditions of subjugation—moments whose value as refusals of slavery's logic depends precisely on their failure to produce any practical benefit beyond themselves.

Scholars of *Beloved* have, as I have indicated, recognized the importance of the novel's aesthetic techniques, but they have almost always treated these techniques as a means to serve other ends. Among those who focus on Morrison's formal devices, some have noted that her fiction borrows tropes from African and African American folk culture, including her use of a call-and-response structure, which deliberately leaves gaps for the reader to fill; her reliance on cyclical notions of time; her deployment of supernatural elements; and her efforts to give her language an improvisational quality characteristic of jazz.[3] Other critics have positioned her work within the postmodern, experimental school of fiction, noting its antilinear, antirealistic narratives; its refusal to offer fully rounded characters; and its tendency to thwart single, closed interpretations.[4] While these two camps have frequently argued over how to categorize Morrison, both treat her aesthetic strategies as important insofar as they serve a radical political purpose, and both regard these strategies as a counterpractice in opposition to the standards upheld by the literary and academic establishment.

A statement Morrison made in her contribution to the 1984 essay collection *Black Women Writers* would seem to lend support for such approaches: "You ought to be able to make [art] unquestionably political and irrevocably beautiful at the same time" ("Rootedness" 345). Formal beauty and political engagement, in her view, are not mutually exclusive; indeed, the two are at their most effective when paired together. But the problem with much of the Morrison scholarship is that it does not in fact acknowledge the independent value of each. Even those critical works that attend to both aesthetics and politics frequently privilege the latter over the former. The claim that the two cannot be clearly disentangled in many cases produces a lopsided equation, one that renders them inseparable but unequal, favoring politics as the ultimate measure of the work's importance. Morrison's assertion that a novel can be political and beautiful "at the same time" is provocative because it demands that two *distinct* functions be harnessed together; far from conflating aesthetics and politics, it acknowledges the unique character and absolute importance of each.

It is also important to recognize that Morrison issued this statement at a moment when, to her mind, "the political" was seen as a "pejorative term in critical circles" ("Rootedness" 344). While one might argue that political criticism had already begun to reshape academic scholarship by the time she published her essay, Morrison was responding to the residual influence in the 1980s of various formalisms, New Critical and deconstructive, as well as to the conservative backlash against the militantly political Black Aesthetic movement, and thus she presented her position as a necessary corrective. Needless to say, three decades later, "the political" is no longer a pejorative term, at least within academic critical circles. If, in what follows, I give the aesthetic disproportionate attention, seeking to tease it out as a motive underwriting the purportedly political interpretations of Morrison's *Beloved*, I do so not in order to invalidate political interpretations of the book but simply in order to show how these approaches have served to obscure the specificity of their own aesthetic commitments.

The enlistment of Morrison's aesthetic strategies within a broader political project of contesting dominant social values also makes it somewhat difficult to account for her extraordinary success as a novelist. It is possible, of course, that *Beloved*'s status as not merely canonical but in fact the recipient of more accolades than any other work in recent history is the product of its audaciously transgressive character.[5] This, however, gives a fair amount of credit to readers for embracing that which challenges their most fundamental beliefs, and a far more plausible conclusion would be that *Beloved* has achieved success because it has given us exactly what we wanted in the first place. How many academic essays and monographs, one might speculate, need to be published, celebrating *Beloved* for its subversive force, before people concede that the book may not be all that subversive at all, and the reason that it has been so well received is that it conforms brilliantly to established aesthetic standards? The refusal among scholars to acknowledge any basis for aesthetic appreciation other than the capacity to challenge accepted criteria is obviously rooted in a belief that there cannot and ought not to be any universal standards of literary greatness. And yet most scholars today do presuppose certain conceptions of what makes for strong writing and what constitutes a powerful aesthetic experience.

James Berger's "Ghosts of Liberalism: Morrison's *Beloved* and the Moynihan Report," for instance, seems as far removed from aesthetic concerns as one could fathom. Berger reads *Beloved* as an intervention into an argument that liberals, conservatives, and radicals have been having since the 1960s about the position of African Americans in the United States. In one telling moment, however, Berger seems to acknowledge that his political reading depends on an exclusion of other considerations:

> Morrison introduces historical trauma into the narrative primarily through the figure of the returning and embodied ghost. There is not space here to discuss in the necessary detail the ghost's status as symptom of the traumas suppressed in the debates I have outlined—how Beloved's return, how her existence in a physical body, her ambivalent, often destructive, connections to symbolic and social structures conflate all the social, personal, and familial traumas of American race relations, which persist to this day. Instead I turn to the end of the novel, to Beloved's exorcism and the novel's puzzling final chapter, and attempt again to evaluate *Beloved* in terms of American discourses on race. (415)

If Beloved, the ghost, embodies precisely the historical tensions he is seeking to investigate, what leads Berger to bracket this figure's metaphorical significance? Beloved scares many people in the book, but what makes her frightening here is her function as a condensation of multiple ideas and connotations and her demand for lengthy interpretation. One could argue that this has served, at least since New Criticism, as the defining feature of literature: the ambiguous symbol, in which a field of competing meanings gets concentrated. The ghost, then, seems to represent the very thing that Berger's argument needs to banish: the literary as a distinct phenomenon and mode of experience.

Berger never returns to Beloved, except to consider the scene of her exorcism—an exorcism his own reading uncannily repeats, as though a longer engagement with this figure would take up the "space" needed for his political analysis. But Berger's exorcism, like the one in the novel, is only partially successful. Having described the positions on race in America taken by three different political camps, liberal, conservative, and radical, Berger explains how the novel responds to this debate: "*Beloved* is a challenge to all American racial discourse of the 1980s—to Reaganist conservatism and to New Left and black nationalism" (414). It rejects the conservative view that racism is no longer a problem in America; it rejects the black nationalist view that African American communities are free of serious dysfunction; it accepts the liberal view that the African American family continues to be a site of pathological trauma, but then it critiques this perspective for its hypocrisy, condescension, and failure to attribute agency to African Americans. What distinguishes *Beloved* from the discourses produced by the various ideological camps, then, is its power of negation, its ability to forward a particular position only in order to subvert it.

The article's conclusion centers on Bodwin, the abolitionist in *Beloved* whom Berger reads as a stand-in for the white post–World War II liberal. That Sethe, the protagonist, attempts to murder this man near the end of the novel has provided evidence for some critics that she has escaped the pathologies produced by slavery and thus no longer directs her violence at her own children, but at the true enemy: the white man.[6] *But*, Berger insists in his effort to defend white liberalism, Bodwin is on Sethe's side: "Bodwin is a lifelong and active abolitionist, not an owner of slaves" (416). *And yet*, he acknowledges a paragraph later, Bodwin does hold a stereotypical view of black people, and his motives for becoming an abolitionist seem to have been "the feelings of moral elevation and political excitement he derived from the movement personally." Sethe's attack, then, "rejects white liberalism as hypocritical" (417). *Still*, it is important to remember that "for Morrison, however, these aspects of Bodwin, and of liberalism are not the whole story." Although Bodwin has his own "history and concerns which are not congruent with those of African Americans," he "provides jobs and housing for the African American community, exactly what civil rights activists have demanded." Therefore, "Sethe's attack on him is delusional." *But* even this reading is inadequate: "This analysis has suggested a kind of detachment for Bodwin. He helps with jobs and housing but remains absorbed in his own concerns. Morrison's portrayal does not allow us to grant Bodwin this detachment" (417–418). In fact, the day Sethe attempts to murder him, Bodwin is visiting the house where she lives, but also where he was born, partially in the hopes of recovering a box of tin soldiers he buried there as a child; thus his interests intersect with Sethe's, though his personal motive for the visit might also be read as proof of his "self-absorption." Indeed, this final defense of Bodwin sounds more like an indictment—exemplifying the kind of thinking that *Beloved*, in Berger's reading of it, demands, whereby each affirmation leads inevitably to its own negation.

While he obviously wants to situate *Beloved* as a participant within ongoing political debates, Berger believes that the novel offers a way of responding to race that is more appealing than all of the available ideological positions. But what makes it superior to these other positions is that it does not offer a position at all. What it offers instead, in Berger's description, is something more like an aesthetic experience: one that consists of entertaining, revising, qualifying, and rejecting a series of competing views, each of which ultimately proves insufficiently complicated to handle the heterogeneous realities represented by the text. Significantly, while this experience seems to represent a refusal of the programmatic positions required by political debate, it does not operate independently of politics. In fact it seems to be aligned or at least contingently correlated with a particular ideology, the one Berger favors. The negative capability that *Beloved* encourages, that is to say, exemplifies what one might call the aesthetics of contemporary liberalism—featuring the mode of thinking that liberal intellectuals privilege as proof of open-mindedness, a capacity to entertain contradictory points of view valuable for its own sake, independent of the concrete political ends it might serve.

A similar dialectical approach structures Madhu Dubey's "Politics of Genre in *Beloved*," an essay that foregrounds the question of whether Morrison's novel embraces its status as literature or rejects it in favor of African oral folklore traditions. Unsurprisingly, Dubey finds the text to be unresolved, at first seeming to condemn both Western literature and the very ideal of literacy, but then adhering to the conventions of the realist novel in its ending and banishing folkloric elements. But of course the negation of these elements is not definitive, not impervious to yet another negation. Or, as Dubey puts it, "But although the form of the realist novel does in some respects win out in the end, displacing the oral and magical elements embodied in Beloved, this is not the end of the story. If Denver's literacy and entry into the public sphere represent the promise of the future, at the same time the novel also enacts a strong counter-impulse, investing hopes of communal redemption in the forms of oral expression that are presented in stark opposition to the literate modern sphere" (199). These forms, though effaced by the book, continue to exist as "absent contents of the modern novel" (200).

Throughout her essay, Dubey carefully tracks Morrison's logical os-cillations, suggesting, as Berger does, an endless semantic instability motivated by an urge to subvert whatever provisional postures the novel briefly assumes. If Berger's analysis requires a generous use of terms such as *but* and *however*, Dubey's crowds such terms together with phrases such as "but although" (199) and "but despite" (200), sug-gesting that the rebuttal to whatever straightforward assertion she has made must itself assume a more paradoxical form, a form that includes as a part of its very content and as a condition of its intellectual power the very tension between it and the converse statement that has ani-mated it into being. No less telling are the similar figures of speech that the two critics use to denote this power, with Berger insisting that a particular reading is "not the whole story" and Dubey remarking that her own interpretation "is not the end of the story" (199), sig-naling that this capacity to resist categorical certitudes defines the aesthetic domain.

Ironically, the only axiom that Dubey is prepared to affirm cate-gorically is that the aesthetic on its own is devoid of value, when she describes the claim (made by Dick Hebdige) that theories of the sub-lime "evacuate the aesthetic of any political intents or effects" as a "biting critique" (201)—as if the aesthetic can acquire value only in-sofar as it serves a political function. And yet Dubey favors Morrison's extravagant irresolution at least in part on the basis of its aesthetic power, especially given that it is not likely to produce decisive action. That is, irresolution is not a rhetorical strategy that can be easily aligned with well-defined "political intents or effects."[7] To be clear, I am not suggesting that Berger and Dubey are not invested in the po-litical problems they foreground; nor am I suggesting that they are wrong to foreground these problems. What I am suggesting is that their analyses rely on certain unacknowledged aesthetic criteria, which they uncritically reaffirm.

"The Tradition of Both-And"

Though neither Berger nor Dubey pays much attention to the stylistic features of Morrison's work, her writing obviously caters to a wide-spread preference for undecidability, ambiguity, and paradox, even at the scale of the sentence. Consider, as but one brief example, a moment shortly after Sethe comes to believe that the strange woman she has been housing is in fact her murdered child Beloved:

> When Sawyer [her boss] warned [Sethe] about being late again, she barely heard him. He used to be a sweet man. Patient, tender in his dealings with his help. But each year, following the death of his son in the War, he grew more and more crotchety. As though Sethe's dark face was to blame.
>
> "Uh huh," she said, wondering how she could hurry time along and get to the no-time waiting for her.
>
> She needn't have worried. Wrapped tight, hunched forward, as she started home her mind was busy with the things she could forget.
>
> Thank God I don't have to rememory or say a thing because you know it. All. You know I never would a left you. Never. It was all I could think of to do. When the train came I had to be ready. School-teacher was teaching us things we couldn't learn. I didn't care nothing about the measuring string. We all laughed about that—except Sixo. He didn't laugh at nothing. But I didn't care. Schoolteacher'd wrap that string all over my head, 'cross my nose, round my behind. Number my teeth. I thought he was a fool. And the questions he asked was the biggest foolishness of all. (*Beloved* 225–226)

Her boss, Sethe conjectures, blames the death of his son on her face. A violently pared-down register of how each black person's body is made to signify not only his or her entire race but also the traumatic historical conflicts produced by the enslavement of that race, Sethe's phrase also represents the first of several instances of rhetorical confusion surrounding personhood, in which the latter designation, absent any self-evident referential logic, gets arbitrarily assigned to various objects and detached from others. If it seems odd to accuse a face of murder, it seems odder still to imagine that an entity not merely inhuman but antihuman in its defiance of comprehension, such as "no-time," could engage in that most pedestrian human activity "waiting." The paradox, of course, thickens if one considers that waiting means nothing more or less than consciously experiencing the passage of time.

In the next paragraph an interruption, which momentarily leaves the modifiers dangling, conceals the strangeness of what is being said. "As she started home," is merely a temporal designation, which thus denies "wrapped tight" and "hunched forward" a home, until "her mind" appears as the true subject of the sentence, except that it is objectified. In an inversion of the ascription of ethical agency to Sethe's face, her mind is now treated like a body part, one that can be wrapped tight and hunched forward. The reminder a moment later that "Schoolteacher'd *wrap* that string all over my head" confirms that this is no mere syntactical blunder; Sethe's mind, as she anticipates the "no-time" she will spend with Beloved, is becoming more like a thing, in a traumatic repetition of the dehumanizing experiments she suffered at the hands of Schoolteacher, the terrifying slavemaster on the plantation from which Sethe has escaped. But even within this pair of physical attributes another contradiction emerges: if "wrapped tight" suggests the womb-like state of deathly nonbeing that has tempted Sethe's mind throughout the novel, "hunched forward" suggests the urge to escape the past and continue living. But here the two are paired, reinforcing the novel's relentless insistence that striving to move forward can be paralyzing, while digging deeper into the mind's grave may be the only way out. Which of the two applies to Sethe as she rushes home to be with the ghost of her dead child is anyone's guess.

What follows is a monologue delivered to Beloved before Sethe reaches her. It is a peculiar rhetorical structure, similar to the examples of poetic apostrophe examined by Barbara Johnson, in which a female speaker addresses her aborted baby in an effort to animate the latter back to life—an address that destabilizes the distinction between self and other, thus compromising the very subjectivity that the mother is seeking to confer on the addressee.[8] Though she says "you," Sethe is not actually speaking to Beloved, since she is walking home alone; moreover, she indicates that Beloved does not need to hear what she is saying: "I don't have to rememory or say a thing because you know it" (*Beloved* 226). Thus Beloved represents an imagined listener for thoughts that Sethe can entertain only by pretending she is directing them at someone other than herself. But she needs the figure of Beloved in order to claim as true what seems, in its incomplete, conditional form, barely to pass as something one could "know": that she "never would a left you [Beloved]." It is an infant's inarticulate certainty, based on the inconceivability of the mother's abandonment, that Sethe yearns to possess as her own, as proof of her love. But her language betrays her. Not only does "would," particularly in the past tense, invite a question of what *did* happen, Sethe's subsequent assertion that handing her baby over to someone else, when she gave her to the Underground Railroad worker, was *"all* [she] could think of to do" lends specificity to the "all" that Beloved purportedly knows. The "all" that Beloved knows, the only thing she knows, in other words, is that Sethe did leave her, twice: when she sent her and her siblings away to the North, and then when she killed her to prevent her from being returned to the South.

And yet, if all Beloved knows is that her mother abandoned her, this "all" is still preferable to the "nothing" that Schoolteacher sought to impose on them—the "nothing" that Sethe refused to care about and that her fellow slave Sixo refused to laugh at. "Schoolteacher was teaching us things we couldn't learn." What Schoolteacher was trying to teach them, in other words, was the very fact that they could not learn because they were black and thus deprived, in his view, of one of the faculties that defines personhood. But it was, of course, paradoxically this very inability to learn that they could not, owing to their fierce claim to personhood, learn. Not then at least, but perhaps now, as Sethe approaches the "no-time" of thinghood, a "wrapped tight" state impervious to further discovery, Schoolteacher's lessons are finally sinking in. Sethe's apostrophe seeks, of course, to defy this death sentence by endowing, as Johnson would have it, her dead child with life. But as in the abortion poems, the apostrophe betrays the knowledge that Sethe is seeking to disprove: it presupposes that Beloved is absent, gone, dependent for her continued existence, her continued personhood, on Sethe's address. Moreover, by speaking to the dead Beloved in her head, Sethe may be aiming not to bring her daughter back to life but rather to join her in her death. Thus her apostrophe represents an especially poignant example of the power rhetoric assumes throughout the passage to assign or deny personhood arbitrarily, the same rhetoric Schoolteacher deploys in his effort to dehumanize the slaves, now appropriated by Sethe.

Perhaps rhetoric has this power; or perhaps it does not. Perhaps what will save Sethe is her failure, despite her efforts, to "get to the no-time." "She needn't have worried," the narrator insists. Why not? Because "her mind was busy with the things she could forget." Before trying to understand the elusive logic of these sentences, it is worth pausing to remember what Sethe's struggle represents. Beloved, as critic after critic has insisted, symbolizes black history, including the Middle Passage and slavery, and thus her haunting of Sethe's family raises the question of whether it is healthy to remain focused on that history, whether it ought to serve as the basis for black identity.[9] The passage under consideration seems to represent an intimacy with Beloved as a pathological attachment, one that entails psychic death. And yet being with Beloved, Sethe hopes, will not mean dwelling in the past but quite the opposite: now "she could forget"; now she no longer needs to "rememory." This might mean a psychotic delusion of full reentry into the past so visceral that it obviates the need to remember what appears to be fully present. Or it might mean a full and cathartic confrontation with the always repressed but never absent memories of the past, which allows one to forget and move on. Unless, that is, forgetting rather than remembering is the real threat to Sethe's subjectivity, the process that will empty her mind, reduce it to a thing, and finally accomplish Schoolteacher's fantasy of depersonification. This seems to be what Sethe hopes will happen. But the text suggests otherwise. "She needn't have worried." What she intends, in other words, does not matter. Aiming to forget is precisely what keeps her thinking, keeps her mind busy with things of the past and prompts the long narrative explanation of her decision to flee from slavery. Complicating the question of whether remembering or forgetting slavery is the key to black agency, then, is the book's suggestion that it may not be possible to distinguish the two or make a meaningful choice: trying to do one, Sethe ends up doing the other.

The tendency to view such paradoxes as central to *Beloved*'s importance—whether that importance is cast primarily in political, ethical, or artistic terms—testifies to the persistent influence of New Critical and deconstructionist aesthetic criteria over contemporary interpretive strategies. Consider Cleanth Brooks's conceptualization of wit:

> The poet attempts to fuse the conflicting elements in a harmonious whole. And here one may suggest a definition of wit. Wit is not merely an acute perception of analogies; it is a lively awareness of the fact that the obvious attitude toward a given situation is not the only

possible attitude. Because wit, for us, is still associated with levity, it may be well to state it in its most serious terms. The witty poet's glancing at other attitudes is not necessarily merely "play"—an attempt to puzzle us or to show off his acuteness of perception; it is possible to describe it as merely his refusal to blind himself to a multiplicity which exists. (*Modern Poetry* 37–38)

What makes a work aesthetically powerful according to this formulation is its capacity to unite contradictory ideas or impulses. "We are disciplined," notes Brooks, "in the tradition of either-or, and lack the mental agility—to say nothing of the maturity of attitude—which would allow us to indulge in the finer distinctions and more subtle reservations permitted by the tradition of both-and" (*Well-Wrought Urn* 81). It is arguably just this kind of agility that *Beloved* displays and that critics such as Berger and Dubey celebrate and reenact in their readings of *Beloved*.

To suggest that a New Critical aesthetic paradigm undergirds the methodologically diverse efforts in the academy to describe *Beloved*'s importance is, admittedly, to risk exacerbating a politically suspect critical tendency, against which Barbara Christian warned in 1993. Scholars who evaluate Morrison's novel by means of prevailing academic frameworks serve, she argues, to blunt the sense of it as a "specifically African American text" ("Fixing Methodologies" 6). Thus she seeks in her essay to understand *Beloved* as an exploration of traditionally African religious beliefs and philosophical premises. Curiously, however, Christian defends her own intervention in terms entirely commensurate with New Critical aesthetic values. Seeking to reassure her potential interlocutors, she remarks, "I have no argument with psychoanalytic, Marxist, or formalist interpretations of *Beloved*. Although at times I can be testy about any one of these approaches to particular texts, because of its richness of texture, *Beloved* does and should generate many and various, even contending, interpretations" (7). *Texture*, as we have seen, was John Crowe Ransom's term for the distinguishing feature of poetry.[10] What Christian applauds here, and what opens *Beloved* up to "contending interpretations," including her own approach, is its ambiguity, its ability to accommodate contradictory meanings— the very quality that, according to the New Critics, defines serious literature.

But ambiguity does not merely render a novel such as *Beloved* amenable to multiple interpretive frameworks; it also recasts each of the approaches whose plurality it enables. As the implicit marker of aesthetic sophistication, ambiguity becomes, in other words, the quality that scholars must locate within whatever specific thematic area they are foregrounding, whether that subject is racial politics in the case of Berger, genre in the case of Dubey, or African religious traditions in the case of Christian. "Many contemporary forms of Afrocentrism," Christian contends, "undercut the very concept they intended to propose—that there are different interpretations of history and different narratives, depending on where one is positioned, in terms of power relations as well as distinctive cultures and that there are, given the various cultures of our world, multiple philosophical approaches to understanding life" (7). Though Christian is more sensitive to the role played by power and politics, her insistence on the world's openness to "multiple philosophical approaches" bears an uncanny resemblance to Brooks's argument about multiplicity. Even what Christian regards as the very sign of *Beloved*'s Africanness, its representation of a "plane of in-betweenness" (14) that defies the categories of being and nonbeing, conforms to Brooks's preference for the tradition of "bothand" over that of "either-or." Demonstrably, *Beloved* does make use of traditional African cultural sources and is critically illuminated by them. But just as Henry Louis Gates Jr.'s celebration of African and African American folk traditions was, as we saw in Chapter 2, predicated on deconstructive intellectual criteria, Christian's reading of *Beloved* suggests that in order to establish their status as intellectually legitimate areas of inquiry and thereby achieve visibility within the discipline of English, literary works, interpretive modes, and even purportedly alternative philosophical traditions must satisfy certain still-dominant New Critical aesthetic criteria centered on ambiguity, irony, and an openness to multiplicity.

To be sure, a majority of the readings of *Beloved* have resisted the New Critical imperative to make the book cohere. Deploying strategies of reading more obviously inflected by deconstruction, many scholars have argued that *Beloved* does not fully master the chaotic elements that it handles and thus refuses thematic closure.[11] And yet a different interpretive urge—namely, the desire to treat the book as a source of moral guidance—has tempered the deconstructive tendency to revel in fragmentation and undecidability. Ethical readings generally find in *Beloved* an unequivocal condemnation of slavery and racism and a recipe for justice or psychic healing.[12] The psychoanalytic strain of Morrison criticism has offered the most influential version of this argument. *Beloved*, in its account, unearths the repressed racial traumas embedded in American history, symbolized by the murdered baby; stages the ongoing project of mourning that these traumas have necessitated; and seeks to move our society beyond mourning by initiating or fully enacting a healing process.[13] Admittedly, this approach, no less than deconstruction, represents a departure from New Criticism insofar as it attributes a social utility to literature. Strangely enough, however, when the two, deconstruction and ethical criticism, are brought together— as they often are—they end up reproducing precisely the mode of response to literature that the New Critics sought to encourage: one that celebrates uncertainty but nevertheless discovers in the work a unified purpose.[14] Indeed, the experience in reading *Beloved*, described by scholar after scholar, of unresolved interpretive play and unequivocal moral indignation instantiates the paradoxical combination of semantic ambiguity and tonal coherence that, according to the New Critics, represents the total aesthetic effect of all great literary works.

If *Beloved* represents a coupling of deconstruction and absolutism, then it answers a desire evident in a good deal of academic scholarship today for works that can bridge the postmodern and the postsecular.[15] And in this odd couple, which *Beloved* apparently exemplifies, we can find a basis for the diametrically opposed reactions to the book by two formidable theorists, Slavoj Žižek and Walter Benn Michaels. I turn now to their readings, in order to uncover the aesthetic basis for the former's endorsement and the latter's condemnation of Morrison's novel.

Žižek versus Michaels

What Žižek finds most admirable in *Beloved* is Sethe's decision to murder her own children rather than permit them to return to slavery. In *The Fragile Absolute*, he categorizes this, alongside several gestures in the movies *Speed*, *Ransom*, and *The Usual Suspects*, as a model for subverting the current political order. In all of these moments, some figure threatens to destroy that which the hero cherishes above all else, and the latter responds by preemptively attacking the very object under threat (150). Systems of power, Žižek argues, control subjects by granting them a mode of autonomy that appears to exist outside the political sphere altogether. Typically such spaces appear to represent a limit or check to the power of the political order. But Žižek contends that systems grant individuals the freedom to devote themselves to a particular object precisely in order to police them more completely. Wedded to this beloved object, they will do whatever is necessary to protect it, including whatever the political order demands of them. Destroy the "cause-thing" with which you identify your hope, your freedom, and your life, and you undermine the means by which power paradoxically subjugates you. "This act, far from amounting to a case of impotent aggressivity turned against oneself, rather changes the co-ordinates of the situation in which the subject finds himself: by cutting himself loose from the precious object through whose possession the enemy kept him in check, the subject gains the space of free action" (150).

Žižek's analysis betrays a noteworthy indifference to the content of the enemy's goals or the hero's attachments in each scene. What he finds compelling is not a particular political or ethical vision but instead the stunning formal logic, the dialectical movement, dramatized by these moments. Sethe's affirmation of her children and their right to live entails her decision to negate them in an act of murder, but this negation, a self-negation, subverts the very basis of the slave system's power and thus becomes a self-affirmation, thwarting the intentions of the slave master. Affirmation becomes negation becomes affirmation. This scene features the same pattern of continuous semantic reversal that Berger and Dubey identify in their readings of the book. But as a radical Marxist, Žižek is less sympathetic to such oscillations than other political critics. He is eager to escape what he calls the "vicious cycle of interpretation" (140), wherein "the truth is never fully established; there are always pros and cons; for each argument there are counter-arguments; there is 'another side' to every point; every statement can be negated; undecidability is all-encompassing"

(139), and he reads Sethe's dialectical strategy as a neo-Hegelian means of founding a new absolute truth and utopian order. Especially commendable about her murder is "the way she refuses to 'relativize' it, to shed her responsibility for it, to concede that she acted in an unforgivable fit of despair or madness—instead of compromising her desire by assuming a distance toward her act, qualifying it as something 'pathological' (in the Kantian sense of the term), she insists on the radically ethical status of her monstrous deed" (156).

Does Žižek believe that *Beloved* offers a viable recipe for revolution and the establishment of ethical absolutes? At the very least, Sethe succeeds in preventing the slave owner from reclaiming her and her surviving children, but here it is important to remember precisely what Žižek disregards: her status as a fictional character. The actual woman on whom Sethe was based, Margaret Garner, accomplished nothing by murdering her child; she and her remaining baby were sent back into slavery. The tragic difference between fiction and reality is important, especially since Žižek is intent on distinguishing his formula for political subversion from the conventional utopian fantasies that he reads as props for the current political order. "When we abandon the fantasmatic Otherness which makes life in constrained social reality bearable, we catch a glimpse of Another Space which can no longer be dismissed as a fantasmatic supplement to social reality" (158). And then: "It should thus be clear how the standard notion of artistic beauty as a utopian false escape from the constraints of reality falls short: one should distinguish between ordinary escapism and this dimension of Otherness, this magic moment when *the Absolute appears* in all its fragility" (159). Žižek's painstaking attempt to uphold a difference between his revolutionary vision and the "utopian false escape" suggests a fear that there is no difference—or that Sethe's extraordinary decision entails revolutionary possibilities only within a work of fiction. Indeed, Žižek uses the same term to denote both the typical pedestrian fantasies of escape from the current political order and his recipe for radical action: "Otherness"—thus unwittingly equating the two.

Or perhaps Žižek is up to something more devious. In order to subvert the political order, the true radical is prepared to sacrifice the very "cause-thing" that he most cherishes. On the final page of *The Fragile Absolute*, Žižek identifies what *he* most cherishes: "the brief apparition of a future utopian Otherness to which every authentic revolutionary stance should cling" (160). If this beloved apparition is Žižek's "cause-thing," then his own logic would dictate that clinging to it is a means not of challenging but in fact of succumbing to prevailing power structures. Žižek's apparition, in other words, becomes precisely what he fears: the "utopian false escape" that upholds the system. But by implicitly equating the two, Žižek actually sacrifices his cherished utopian ideal, reducing it to a mere fantasy. In a fairly dizzying paradox, this gesture seems both to annihilate his revolutionary hopes and to reinstall them in an act of radical sacrifice, akin to Sethe's murder of her own baby. Whether this seems like a compelling way of furthering radical politics, Žižek's self-negating logic implies an identification between his "apparition of a future utopian Otherness" and the "standard notion of artistic beauty as a utopian false escape," or, in other words, the aesthetic. And insofar as these two are identical, then "artistic beauty" or aesthetic satisfaction, strangely enough, comes to represent the very *cause-thing* to which Žižek secretly clings, as demonstrated by his fascination with the formal, dialectical logic at play in *Beloved*— a logic he abstracts from any concrete political goals. This secret attachment would explain why he must, in essay after essay, ritualistically sacrifice the notion of "artistic beauty" as a bourgeois ideal or ideological delusion. Moreover, given Žižek's status as the foremost celebrity theorist within literary studies, one might say that he exemplifies the predicament of the entire discipline: compelled by a guilty conscience to sacrifice the very thing it secretly cherishes, aesthetic pleasure, in the service of an impossible fantasy of revolutionary political efficacy.

If Žižek hopes to move from deconstruction to a quasi-religious ethical absolutism, Michaels rejects both in favor of a return to Enlightenment rationality. In *The Shape of the Signifier*, Michaels launches a wholesale attack on what he views as the dominant worldview in contemporary American society, epitomized by *Beloved*: one that is identarian, anti-ideological, and pluralistic. Deconstruction, the first example that Michaels examines, shifts focus from the author's intention to the reader's experience of the text. It replaces the rational effort to arrive at the correct interpretation of the literary work with the belief that there are no correct or incorrect interpretations; there are only different subjective responses. The same premises are also at work, Michaels contends, in multiculturalism and liberal pragmatism—both of which categorically reject any attempt to decide whether one philosophical position is rationally superior to another. In all cases, diversity of experience, of perspective, of culture has become an object of celebration. The problem with this state of affairs, according to Michaels, is that it forestalls political debate, making it impossible to offer arguments in favor of a particular social formation. And thus two cultures that come into conflict, because they cannot decide which is superior through rational debate, are required to resolve their differences through war. Multiculturalism, in Michaels's account, entails neoconservatism. At the same time, the current paradigm rationalizes inequality by supplanting a focus on class with a focus on ethnic identity. If we tend to think of people as occupying different cultural or ethnic enclaves, none superior to any other, rather than different classes with varying degrees of access to resources, then we have no reason to make those resources more widely available. Tolerance rather than redistribution becomes the solution to all of our conflicts.

Promoting cultural diversity and ethnic identity entails serious efforts to preserve history—a project central to Morrison's *Beloved*. But exacerbating the difficulties of such projects, according to Michaels, is the premium placed on subjective experience, which leads people to view history not merely as something you can learn about but as something you can either remember or forget, even if you were not alive during the events in question. Moreover, many proponents of ethnic pride, Morrison among them, suggest that members of a particular ethnicity enjoy a privileged access to the struggles and challenges their ancestors faced in history, as if they are somehow personally haunted by that history. The figure for this form of haunting in *Beloved* is the ghost, which visits Sethe's daughter Denver and grants her a subjective experience of events that occurred before she was born. But ghosts, Michaels maintains, do not exist. Nor can they serve as a symbol for a particular way of relating to history, because it is impossible to remember or forget things that we did not experience in the first place. We cannot, in other words, be personally haunted by history. In fact, it makes no sense to argue that the ghost in *Beloved* is a figure for historical memory, because the ghost is precisely the means by which

Morrison seeks to make a personal connection to history conceivable in the first place.[16]

Michaels, as Angus Fletcher and Michael Benveniste observe, traces the roots of present-day multiculturalism back to the New Critics—a plausible genealogy in their view, given that many contemporary scholars were in fact trained in New Critical methods and eventually applied these methods to areas beyond that of the literary work. Both New Critics and proponents of multiculturalism, according to Fletcher and Benveniste, tend to uphold heterogeneity as a good in itself ("Defending Pluralism"). They celebrate diversity, whether in the stylistic impulses of a given text, in the population of a school, or in the content of a syllabus, in other words, primarily because it is aesthetically pleasing, often without regard to its political utility. Though they dispute Michaels's conclusions, Fletcher and Benveniste agree that we should not embrace cultural diversity merely for its own sake, but must attend to the broader set of political consequences that it produces (664). Michaels's argument, in their account, represents a commendable effort to reject the residual retrograde aesthetics that continue to shape multiculturalism in favor of a commitment to progressive politics. While this description of what Michaels is doing helps bring to light the persistent influence of New Critical aesthetics over contemporary debates, Michaels's intervention might be better read not as a rejection of aesthetics in favor of politics but as a rejection of one aesthetic in favor of another.

The Shape of the Signifier generally reaffirms the position widely held within the academy today that it is impossible to understand aesthetics in isolation from politics. With daunting rigor, Michaels traces the hidden connections between seemingly disparate phenomena ranging from literary preferences to political affiliations. Indeed, the very beliefs that individuals hold about how to interpret marks on a page, Michaels contends, logically require them to subscribe to particular geopolitical positions. "To put the point in an implausible (but nonetheless, I will try to show, accurate) form, it means that if you hold, say, Judith Butler's view on resignification, you will also be required to hold, say, George W. Bush's view on terrorism—and, scarier still, if you hold Bush's view on terrorism, you must hold Butler's view on resignification" (13–14). Given the extraordinary breadth of distinct

subjects that turn out, under Michaels's inspection, to be mutually
constitutive, and given the obvious importance of the political goals
he seeks to promote, it might seem wrongheaded and irresponsible to
try to preserve the aesthetic as a distinct field or to suggest that
Michaels's arguments are at all invested in it.

And yet Michaels leaves open the possibility of upholding the very
divisions that he seems at times to undermine. He acknowledges, "Of
course I do not claim that very many people actually hold all the positions I do claim would follow from holding just one. This aspect of my
argument is very much more theoretical than historical, since it involves describing what people ought, if they were consistent, to believe
and to want in addition to (and sometimes instead of) describing what
they actually do believe and want" (14). In the actual world, remarkably enough, people do not necessarily abide by the logical imperatives
that Michaels describes. It is possible, he admits, to favor one kind of
literature and another kind of politics, to enjoy Toni Morrison but oppose George W. Bush's foreign policy, even though he would say that
the two positions are rationally incompatible. There is a difference, in
other words, in the experience of most people between literature and
politics. This of course does not mean that these categories are radically removed from each other. One can certainly influence the other—
in some cases in accordance with the logic that Michaels identifies.
But the link between a particular literary preference and a particular
political stance is not fixed or inevitable; it is subject to the vagaries of
human volition, and so there will necessarily be unforeseen alliances
and illogical discontinuities between the various positions and commitments specific to the two realms. The absolute inseparability of aesthetics and politics, often forwarded in the name of political activism
and in opposition to ivory-tower isolationism, turns out, as Michaels
admits, to be itself a purely theoretical construct.

Michaels's admission that his argument is theoretical rather than
historical raises questions about its usefulness as a political intervention. His systematic mapping of cross-situational homologies appears
to endow his claims for and against various cultural phenomena with
high stakes. And yet in deciding what stance to take on any of the specific subjects that Michaels invokes, ranging from deconstruction to
multiculturalism to identity politics to particular literary works such

as *Beloved*, it is absurd to worry that one is thereby subscribing to a much broader set of political commitments, since in practice, Michaels recognizes, this is not the case. To enjoy *Beloved*, for instance, or even to assign it in a course will not, thanks to the internal inconsistencies within people's beliefs, habits, and practices, lend support for neoconservative foreign policy or the perpetuation of economic inequality. Indeed Michaels's arguments against Morrison's novel, even if they are successful in changing his readers' opinion of it, will have little impact on their overall political perspective, just as his broader political argument will likely have little impact on their view of the book. And thus his brilliant syntheses turn out to be a series of purely logical exercises performed for their own sake—logic as a kind of aesthetic experience.

Michaels's attachment to pure logic helps to explain his dislike of *Beloved*. After all, by his own account, that novel and the subjectivist paradigm it exemplifies are so committed to a diversity of perspectives and the validity of contrary points of view that they deny the concept of contradiction altogether—the very foundation of logic. The formation that *Beloved* represents refigures any apparent contradiction between beliefs as simply a diversity of subjective feelings or identarian agendas, none of which can claim to be either right or wrong. Thus, *Beloved* and similar texts call into question precisely the logically rigorous modes of thinking that Michaels values most. In his rejection of the pluralism that he attributes to *Beloved*, Michaels is also rejecting the aesthetic criteria, centered on multiplicity, that have tacitly shaped literary and theoretical schools since New Criticism. His revolt against these criteria is apparent not only in his critique of *Beloved* but also in his own lucid style, which deviates significantly from the standard academic discourse, whose obscurity often parallels that of the literary works that it seeks to highlight—in that strategy known as "writing the difficulty." In his preference for linguistic clarity, singular truth, and logical rigor over semantic ambiguity, performative ambivalence, and epistemological uncertainty, and in his tendency to distill any particular text or philosophical movement down to a relatively straightforward position rather than to multiply its contradictory connotations and self-qualifications, Michaels seems to embrace an aesthetic reminiscent of the one against which New Criticism famously defined itself: the neoclassicism of the seventeenth and eighteenth centuries.[17] Given *Beloved*'s persistent centrality in our culture, it is not surprising that one of its only academic detractors would need to recover an utterly unfashionable aesthetic, one out of favor for two centuries, as support for his objections to the book.

Michaels's political views are common enough in contemporary debates; his audacity lies in his embrace and enactment of a radically unconventional aesthetic. Why, Michaels forces us to ask, do we automatically regard the ability to accommodate simultaneously multiple contradictory stances to be a sign of brilliance or a condition of aesthetic power? Should the suspension of conviction, the incessant negation of certainty, be the experience that we seek out, and when we deem this the quintessential effect of literature, are we foreclosing other, equally compelling responses or blinding ourselves to other aesthetic strategies? If a majority of critics, however methodologically trained, continue to identify a plurality of contradictory meanings or attitudes within the apparent unity of the literary work, the intellectual practice that Michaels models involves tracing a logical trajectory, indeed a unity, across a plurality of disparate phenomena. Michaels's argument demonstrates that paradox, irony, and ambiguity—all those devices aimed at producing multiplicity and self-division—do not exhaust the forms of aesthetically satisfying complexity that are available.

Michaels's attack on *Beloved* is uniquely compelling not because he is right and the other critics are wrong but because it inadvertently points literary scholarship in a new direction, asking us to question certain aesthetic principles that have been shielded by their own status as a disreputable subject of academic inquiry and have thereby become, strangely enough, axiomatic. To recognize the importance of Michaels's argument is not to reject categorically the aesthetic criteria proposed by the New Critics; it is simply to keep open the possibility of alternative criteria. Indeed, to subject our own tacit aesthetic assumptions to scrutiny, it may be necessary to reconsider dilemmas that the New Critics thought they had resolved several decades ago. What does it mean for a work to be complex or sophisticated or smart? Why do we find not only the indefinite suspension but also the incessant subversion of truth claims to be such an exhilarating cognitive experience? What other kinds of intellectual and emotional responses should we be encouraging? How can we make ourselves receptive to the range of effects that literature seeks to produce? To raise questions as basic as these is not to call for a wholesale return to purely formalist strategies of interpretation. Rather, it is simply to underscore, in response to the still pervasive tendency to regard the political as the only measure of literature's significance, that these questions are also important. One sign of their importance is that, in spite of whatever explicit priorities and commitments we have chosen to foreground, we have never actually stopped asking them.

CONCLUSION

Reading the Surface in the Distance

IT TURNS OUT THAT we cannot leave the ghost of *Beloved* behind just yet. If Toni Morrison's novel once galvanized an outpouring of anti-establishment critical fervor, its success in recent years has made it a ubiquitous cultural touchstone and thus an irresistible point of departure for those seeking to take academic literary studies in a new direction. In addition to Walter Benn Michaels, Heather Love has, in her already notorious essay "Close but Not Deep," used *Beloved* to launch an attack on contemporary scholarly tendencies and to propose an alternative. Simply put, the interpretive act she challenges is the search for depth beneath appearances. In *Beloved*, the depth is said to reside within the inner lives of the characters—a depth that refutes the dehumanizing portrayals of nineteenth-century African Americans and supplies that which is tragically missing from the historical archive. While Love does not discount the existence of such depth or the value of its articulation, she contends that an exclusive attention to it entails a failure to appreciate the novel's documentary power. In some moments, she maintains, *Beloved* captures the horror of slavery most effectively through its mere description of what is happening on the surface. Indeed, describing this horror in a "literal," "flat," and "objective" fashion, rather than attempting to identify a hidden poetry within the lives of its victims, is an effective means, argues Love, of acknowledging the inescapable fact of dehumanization (383–387).

Love maintains that "sometimes we have to let ghosts be ghosts," meaning we should not rush to treat Beloved as a symbol with a deeper meaning (387). One reason, perhaps, that her essay has aroused controversy is that such statements bear a disconcerting resemblance to remarks that students in literature classes make all the time: that is, *aren't we overreading this book?* The problem with this complaint is that if it is valid, then we, professional interpreters and teachers of literature, may be out of a job. Even more unsettling, Love's comment is actually an allusion to the same line in the equally influential essay by Stephen Best and Sharon Marcus introducing their 2009 special issue on surface reading, "The Way We Read Now," in *Representations* ("Surface Reading" 13). The critique of overinterpretation typically leveled by either unenthusiastic students or skeptical journalists reporting on academia's excesses is, in other words, now being made from within the discipline in a rigorous fashion by multiple intellectually serious figures.

In arguing for a new approach to literature, Love, Best, and Marcus are of course joining other major scholars, including Rita Felski, Bruno Latour, and Eve Sedgwick, in seeking an alternative to the hermeneutics of suspicion or symptomatic reading.[1] The latter strategy, as we have seen, presupposes that the text and other cultural gestures are the epiphenomenal, surface features of a deeper, ontologically prior reality. While influenced by the procedures of Freudian psychoanalysis, with its commitment to treating all variety of outward gestures as symptoms of unconscious psychic drives, suspicious reading generally seeks to uncover a hidden reality that is political in nature. But this reality, so the story goes, inevitably expresses itself, like the unconscious, in an oblique or deceptive manner; thus the job of the critic is to resist the literal meaning of the text, to read through or around it in order to expose the deeper reality, the true, foundational basis for its formal structures.

In refusing these premises, postcritical approaches deny the very distinction between depth and surface, arguing for a model of reality as a two-dimensional plane where various phenomena—some cultural, some material, some psychological, some scientific, some political, but none realer than any other—come into contact with and influence each other in multiple, unexpected ways. The critic's task, given this paradigm, is not to interrogate the cultural artifact so as to uncover its hidden meaning or unconscious determinants but simply to describe it as carefully as possible. This emphasis on description entails a departure from the skeptical view of empirical science that has prevailed within literary studies until fairly recently; thus Best, Marcus, and Love all present the digital humanities, with its data-driven approach to literature, championed most vocally by Franco Moretti, as an ally, another effort to abandon suspicious reading by means of a purportedly more neutral, objective mode of analysis.[2] Indeed, the latter may well prove more destabilizing to the discipline than the strategies favored by the self-declared surface readers, insofar as it represents an entirely new method—a way of putting postcritical theory into practice.

These interventions have already aroused much heated debate. My contribution here will be to consider what they might mean for aesthetic criticism—and my analysis will necessarily be provisional, given that the disciplinary impact of the interpretive schools that I am considering is still uncertain. It would be fairly easy to hypothesize that the newly emerging scientific aspirations within the discipline are tending toward a complete eradication of the aesthetic, accomplishing what earlier methodologies promised but failed to do. Without denying this possibility, I also want to suggest that postcritical approaches and the digital humanities may simply be offering a different mode of aesthetics, one founded on new criteria. The phrase "let the ghosts be ghosts" is a curious one, insofar as it seems, pace the empirical ambitions of Love, Best, and Marcus, to insist on preserving a belief in phenomena that resist a scientific worldview—that is, the weird, the surreal, the supernatural, the uncanny—all generally thought to be the province of literature. But the price critics must pay, it seems, for landmarking this endangered territory is to become quasi-scientists themselves, refusing to rethink, distort, or even interpret what they are seeking to document. In a peculiar way, this strategy is not altogether different from that of the New Critics, who also recognized, despite extreme misgivings, that poetry could be saved only if literary studies became more scientific. Nevertheless, they would undoubtedly regard the methods employed within the digital humanities as antithetical to everything that makes literary studies worthwhile. But would they be right? And does it matter? To put it another way, assuming that twenty-first-century approaches to literature let us keep our ghosts, exactly what experience of these ghosts will they allow us to have? And will this experience be enough to sustain the discipline in the decades to come?

Dense Surfaces

Before considering what these new methodologies have to offer, it is important to understand how they characterize what they are trying to replace. By working to relegate a seemingly disparate mix of older critical approaches to the discard pile, they point to underrecognized affinities between these approaches. Love notes the systematic effort to foster "rich" human experiences and to reaffirm humanistic values within literary studies—an agenda that she attributes not only to New Critical but also to deconstructive, Marxist, feminist, queer, African American, postcolonial, and diaspora studies ("Close but Not Deep" 371–372). Best and Marcus observe that both New Criticism and Marxist hermeneutics such as Fredric Jameson's present "freedom," or at least a vision of freedom, as the reward for strenuous engagement with the literary text ("Surface Reading" 14–15). Felski remarks, "Like the New Critic, the symptomatic reader is fascinated by ambiguity and equivocation" (*Limits of Critique* 63), adding that the hermeneutics of suspicion may be driven in part by the "aesthetic criteria of adroitness, ingenuity, sophistication, intricacy, and elegance" (111). And Moretti, who calls close reading a "secularized theology" (*Distant Reading* 67), remarks that both New Criticism and New Historicism err in the idiosyncratic and non-scientific methods they employ in selecting their materials: "very few texts" in the case of the former (67), and "the colourful anecdote" in the case of the latter (86). Whether promising depth, richness, freedom, sophistication, or transcendence, these older methodologies apparently all present literary study as an experiential gateway to something more, something other than flat empirical existence, a heightened, deeper, more vivid state of being unavailable elsewhere in the world.[3]

Postcritical reading and the digital humanities have been lambasted for abandoning the left and progressive ideals that have been central to the discipline in favor of interpretive practices that seem suspiciously at home within the current neoliberal order.[4] But it is also worth recognizing the ways in which these new methodologies may jeopardize a certain aesthetic experience. Though in general scholars seem to be far more worried about the turn away from politics, it is increasingly clear that the two potential casualties of postcritical thought are in fact allied, that a particular set of aesthetic values has, over the past several decades, served to sustain a particular mode of political interpretation and vice versa. The various forms of political critique have, in other words, as Love, Best, Marcus, and Felski suggest, gone hand in hand with experiences of richness, depth, and sophistication not dissimilar to what the New Critics had claimed to offer. No matter which has played the supporting role and which the lead, whether aesthetic pleasure has lent political critique an allure it would otherwise lack or political critique has lent a public rationale for moments of aesthetic satisfaction that would otherwise seem merely self-indulgent, it is clear that the two have been mutual bulwarks—which is why Love, Best, and Marcus have opted to confront them as if they represented a single, united front.

One lesson of this book, of course, is that in the perpetual contest of interpretive methodologies known as literary studies, interpretive habits inherited from one's predecessors are not always easy to break. A useful example is Anne Anlin Cheng's essay, "Skin, Tattoos, and Susceptibility," in Best and Marcus's special issue, an essay that not only performs a surface reading of Adolf Loos's building designs and Josephine Baker's theatrical poses but also uses these materials to consider what is at stake, what historically specific anxieties are invested in a concern for surfaces. In his early twentieth-century architectural theory, Loos apparently aligns an undue interest in ornamental surfaces with the purported primitivism of negroes, Arabs, rural peasants, women, and children (Cheng, "Skin" 102). While Cheng's intent is obviously to analyze, not reproduce, the racist, classist, and sexist discourse used to articulate this anxiety, her invocation of Loos's position nevertheless betrays an insecurity on her part about the project of surface reading. She seems, in other words, to recognize that, despite the aspirations of the methodology she is modeling, an attention to surfaces may make academic literary studies seem less rather than more scientific, confirming perceptions of it as an archaic, impractical pursuit, committed to superficial phenomena entirely marginal to modern modes of knowledge production and trajectories of historical progress.

Cheng's strategy for managing this anxiety is multipronged. First she challenges the schema that aligns science, modernity, and rationality with depth while identifying ornamentation, sensuality, and primitivism with surfaces, noting that Loos and other modernist architects do not argue for depth over surface; they simply argue for one kind of surface over another, a "clean" and "unadorned" surface over a highly decorated or ornamental one (103). Then she proceeds to deconstruct the binary between the ornamental and the functional, offering a variety of examples of Loos's designs in which "distinguishing unnecessary ornamentation from essential cladding" becomes virtually impossible (105). Her reading culminates in an analysis of the "vertiginous zebra stripes" in the plan for a house that Loos created for Baker, stripes that were both decorative and structural, since the model Loos made dictated that they be constructed out of black and white marble rather than painted on the surface, and that were at once primitive in their evocation of animalism and modernist in their geometric regularity (111). Cheng uses her reading of this building to raise a host of questions to do with race, gender, and power, while adding one further wrinkle, noting that its design may have been inspired by a striped dress that Baker wore, thus unsettling the sense of Loos's mastery over his own design while further complicating any attempt to read it as expressing either an ornamental or functional imperative (113–114).

Cheng opts to stay on the surface in her reading of both Loos's plans and Baker's poses in order to eschew merely "unearthing hidden ideology" (114)—ideology that would position the two figures within a predetermined structure of colonialist, masculinist power and subaltern, female victimhood. Thus she is able to attend to the "flexibility and receptiveness of the subject and object gripped in narratives of power" (100). Cheng's focus renders legible the spontaneity, playfulness, and desire purportedly foreclosed by symptomatic interpretation, but not by denying the ideological forces in response to which the surface games that she describes operate. She seems instead to rethink ideology, turning it into a malleable substance, responsive to the craft and whims of those caught within it, imagining a form of improvisation that exists by negotiating with rather than escaping from ideology. In so doing, she translates the kind of foundation that weighs things down and keeps them in place into the kind of foundation that can be rubbed onto the skin in order to mold identity and elicit desire—but without ever fully relinquishing its density, its status as something that matters.

Cheng's approach represents a gain in maneuverability, serendipity, and verve for both her subjects and her analysis of them, while simultaneously relocating on the surface all of the seriousness and substance that a postcritical methodology would otherwise risk relinquishing. While this might seem like an impossible gesture, a rhetorical sleight of hand aimed at getting more without having to pay for it, Cheng's gambit uncannily replays the rhetoric of the New Critics, who also feared that an emphasis on the surface features, the poetic form of literary works, would corroborate perceptions of their discipline as dealing with trivial subjects implicitly coded as feminine. The New Critics' answer was similar to Cheng's: the important substance of poetry exists precisely *on* the surface. Cleanth Brooks in "The Heresy of Paraphrase" (*Well-Wrought Urn* 192–214) and John Crowe Ransom in *The World's Body* both argued that poetry conveys a deep, palpable knowledge of reality, far denser and more descriptive than the abstractions of science, precisely *through* its surface textures—a knowledge that cannot be translated into a prose statement. That Cheng's defense echoes the New Critics' suggests significant affinities between the two methodologies; it also suggests that surface reading does not in fact surrender richness, either ideological or aesthetic, in favoring a flat ontology; it simply seeks to discover on the surface an intricacy as rewarding as the depth that it is claiming to surrender. To be sure, one might argue that Cheng is not the best representative of surface reading. As she acknowledges, her training in psychoanalytic theory makes her a peculiar spokesperson for an interpretive method dedicated to repudiating symptomatic interpretation. But, notwithstanding her own slippery rationale—that she is more interested in the "susceptible Freud" than the "symptomatic Freud"—her inclusion in the volume suggests a readiness on the part of the postcritical camp to incorporate the methods it is claiming to reject (100).[5]

Whether or not it represents a true departure, the attack launched by postcritical scholarship on both symptomatic and close reading, the decision to treat them as united by a commitment to textual "richness," raises a difficult question. Namely, if literature's aesthetic and political functions have served covertly to support each other, then is it advisable to disentangle them, as I have sought to do in this book? Can they survive in the absence of their unacknowledged alliance? Should we try to rid our acts of political interpretation of any residual investment in the heady pleasures of irony, paradox, and ambiguity? What would that kind of political criticism look like, and would it be compelling? To whom? Moreover, can our aesthetic pleasures endure in the absence of the more practical and political ends they have been required to serve? A central claim of this book is that aesthetic satisfaction has flourished over the past fifty years as an inefficient by-product of institutional and methodological endeavors organized around entirely other goals, indeed even as a part of interpretive projects explicitly opposed to aesthetic criticism. But is it possible that the aesthetic is paradoxically sustained by its location within this seemingly hostile context? Given the utilitarian ethos that tends to dictate priorities in higher education in the United States, is there any way to avoid embedding aesthetic experiences in processes aimed at serving more socially respectable goals? Might it be that aesthetic satisfaction, whose value is rooted in itself, somehow depends on being made to serve another end beyond itself? Do our aesthetic experiences need to maintain a grip on something else—whether it be history, or ethics, or politics—in order to be fulfilling? Would the pleasure of the text simply dissipate if it were the explicit goal, the same way the imperative to enjoy oneself inevitably backfires?

To be clear, in this book I have never argued that the aesthetic and the political should *not* be allied with each other or that such an alliance has been unproductive. I have simply advocated for distinguishing the two as carefully as possible in the moments when they get entangled. This too, of course, may represent a hazardous agenda, insofar as the aesthetic and the political functions of literature often seem to be at their most potent when they are not only allied but conflated, when nobody tries, for instance, to distinguish the immediate cognitive rewards produced by reading a given work from its potential to promote radical political change. That said, I would submit that there is some virtue in knowing what we are doing and why we are doing it, in being able to identify the multiple motives that mobilize our engagement with literature. Perhaps the challenge, then, is to forge new alliances between the aesthetic and the political that allow them to share resources without surrendering their specificity, to promote a kind of prickly but fruitful cooperation between the two, in which neither eclipses the other or assumes the role as the one justification for literary studies that really matters.

Moreover, as I have already suggested, efforts to distinguish the aesthetic from the political may make it easier to address certain important problems that have gotten buried under the weight of other agendas. Foregrounding the aesthetic, it is worth noting, means making it an object of scrutiny, not celebration. It may be time to question certain aesthetic values that we are not even aware we are still upholding. Recall, for instance, the controversy surrounding the New Critics' claim that all good poetry is complex. They won that argument, but were they right? Did Arthur Mizener have a point when he remarked that "attitudes can be relatively simple and valuable and they can be very complex and of little value" ("Desires" 468)? Are scholars today able to appreciate the aesthetic value of simplicity? Occasionally, perhaps, but almost always as a novelty, a momentary respite from the complexity that they relentlessly seek in every work and every archival artifact they interpret. What would it mean to consider simplicity in its own right? Might we discover multiple kinds of simplicity, some better and some worse, some that we find appealing and others that we do not? How might we discriminate between the two? On the basis of what formal or technical criteria?

Simplicity is of course just one example. In *The Rhetoric of Fiction*, Wayne Booth argued that a modernist attachment to ambiguity and complexity had made it hard for writers to produce and for critics to appreciate a myriad number of rhetorical effects—"tragic, or comic, or epic, or satiric" (49). That was in 1961. Are we any more equipped now to respond to the multiplicity of literary devices he identified? As Felski observes, "Individuals can be moved by different texts for very different reasons. This insight has often been lost to literary studies, thanks to a single-minded fixation on the merits of irony, ambiguity, and indeterminacy that leaves it mystified by other structures of value and fumbling to make sense of alternative responses to works of art" (*Uses of Literature* 21).[6] What aesthetic effects are we adept at analyzing, and which ones do we neglect? Which texts have we failed to appreciate or understand because our default attachment to particular aesthetic criteria is covertly dictating our responses, unbeknownst to us? In analyzing a wide range of rhetorical and poetic devices, New Formalist criticism is now addressing some of these questions, often with remarkable intelligence and sensitivity.[7] But it still tends to be hampered by the need to justify interest in the formal features it examines by invoking certain political ideals—ideals that, paradoxically enough, often have unexamined aesthetic criteria built into them.

We can all likely think of a passage whose aesthetic power we cannot explain. We search for ironies but find none. Or the ones we find fail to account for what we like about it. The text does not parody hegemonic structures. It does not subtly subvert its own apparent meaning. It does not baffle the intelligence. It does not appear to be fragmented, broken, ruptured, multiple, unstable, shifting, or opaque. Yet it resonates in our minds. Many of the qualities we are searching for to validate our admiration come to us as the features privileged by either New Criticism or deconstruction, and they have been freighted with additional virtues as the preferred forms of political subversion and thus have achieved a priority status that occludes other possibilities. Try as we might, we cannot find these features in the passage we are reading, and yet we like it; we think it is good. Why? Is there some principle of prosody, some rhetorical expertise that might explain what makes it effective? What new vocabularies do we need to develop, or what older vocabularies do we need to recover, in order to understand the variety of aesthetic effects that appeal to us?

Taking these questions seriously will also make for more effective political criticism. Ever since the New Critics outlawed the heresy of paraphrase, scholars have privileged texts in which the meaning cannot be disentangled from the formal devices used to deliver it, in which the language emphatically asserts its own presence, often deferring or disrupting, through strange metaphors or inscrutable ambiguities, the reader's ability to understand the meaning. But this preference has made it difficult to recognize the effectiveness of rhetorical strategies that foreground the content over the style—an understandable goal particularly for works that seek to make persuasive political arguments or appeal to the reader's emotions. To interpret such texts, it is important to note, literary scholars need not put aside their discursive orientation; they simply need to recognize that there is an artfulness in language that effaces itself in order to convey a clear and forceful message. To be sure, most political rhetoric is anything but transparent; and the foregrounding of form in various artistic experiments in the past century has obviously served as an effective means of challenging dominant ideologies. But criteria dictating an axiomatic preference for the latter have made it difficult to appreciate or assess other modes of rhetoric that may, in some circumstances, pose a more direct and legible challenge to power.

Finally, a reassertion of the specificity of the aesthetic may push us to confront several particularly hard questions about the goals of literary studies. Assuming the discipline could extricate the game of culture from the game of class, as John Guillory invites us to imagine (*Cultural Capital* 339–340)—assuming it could distribute aesthetic experiences on a much wider basis, so that these experiences no longer depend for their appeal on the social status they signify, then which kinds of aesthetic experience should it strive to disseminate and why? Political criticism has supplied one answer, arguing that we should teach literary works as a way of advancing the cause of justice, equality, tolerance, revolution, or collective well-being. But what if we suppose that certain aesthetic experiences are themselves among the goods that ought to be distributed more widely, among the things that everyone deserves to have, and not merely a means to some other end? How would we justify these experiences? On what basis are they more worthwhile than other experiences? Is their value context specific? Are they better responses to the needs produced by particular historical or personal situations? How so?

Aesthetic experiences of the kind promoted in English departments probably cannot be justified solely on the basis of the pleasure they produce. After all, junk food, dumb movies, pornography, and so forth can elicit more pleasure than literature. What makes reading a challenging novel or poem preferable? I. A. Richards believed he could answer this question with reference to the physical structure of the brain: good poetry, in his view, activates more neural impulses than other stimuli. Numerous scholars these days are following Richards's lead, using neurological findings to understand literature's function. But will this body of research provide satisfying answers, answers that confirm our intuitions about why literature deserves our time? Can we use quantitative measures to determine the value of aesthetic experiences, or do we also need qualitative distinctions? Are aesthetic descriptors such as the sublime and the beautiful sufficient to rationalize these experiences? Or is their inadequacy the reason we have felt compelled over the past forty years to invoke ethics and politics? Might it be possible to insert the ethical or political into the reading experience without dislodging the aesthetic? Is there a way, in other words, to recognize the practical and social uses of literature while also affirming a form of value that does not lead us beyond the moment of reading itself, that avoids making that experience subordinate to something else?

Unknowable Quantities

It may seem as if this book is excessively committed to the conservative thesis that even as various methodologies succeed each other, nothing much changes within the discipline of literary studies—that is, no matter what radically innovative approach is offered, certain deeply entrenched New Critical aesthetic principles will always continue to lurk somewhere in the background, dictating the shape of our interpretive work. While I would in fact argue that New Criticism has exerted a far greater influence and for longer than is generally acknowledged, I would underscore the relatively short period this book has covered: a mere eighty years—not an especially long time for a particular set of critical *doxa* to prevail. Moreover, this era may now finally be coming to an end with the emergence of the digital humanities. Unlike many of the other methodologies considered in this book, in other words, the latter seems to represent a true departure from both New Criticism's aesthetic values and its signature method, close reading.

Thus I want to conclude by considering how this new methodology might transform the way we experience literature and what it might mean for the future of the discipline.

I will focus on the Stanford Literary Lab because, while it cannot stand in for the diversity of digital humanities projects today, Moretti presents its work as an explicit rejection of New Critical close reading, and thus it speaks directly to the central concerns of this book. For those unfamiliar with this research, over the past decade Moretti and his colleagues have used computer technology in order to expand the scope of scholarly investigation well beyond the small corpus of titles that has constituted the literary canon, analyzing thousands of never-before-studied texts from several centuries, employing a method Moretti has called "distant reading." New software has allowed the lab to mine massive digital databases in order to discover both macroscopic and microscopic patterns: the growth and decline of particular genres and their corresponding stylistic markers across different geographic territories and time scales; the statistical frequency of syntactical or grammatical structures, lexical sequences, and word families within certain historical periods; the components of paragraphs in different modes of discourse, as measured by the variety of semantic fields they contain; the changing length of book titles within a huge sample size of literary works across multiple centuries; and so forth.[8]

This research distinguishes itself through its methods of analysis, through its dependence on collaborative research as opposed to single authorship, and through its visual presentation, offering information about literary trends that can be captured only through the use of intricate maps, diagrams, graphs, and charts, giving it an appearance on the page or screen utterly unlike that of typical literary scholarship. It also happens to require advanced coding skills (though not from all members of the lab), as well as innovations in statistical models and algorithmic methods. Thus, like much digital humanities scholarship, it lends itself to the critique voiced most emphatically by Richard Grusin, that its recent success depends on its capacity to develop marketable products and to cultivate highly transferable quantitative and technological skills akin to those promoted in STEM and business disciplines, in accordance with the increasingly neoliberal, profit-oriented mission of the contemporary university.[9] Nevertheless, as I have repeatedly asserted in this book, English departments have managed to promote noninstrumental aesthetic experiences as a paradoxical constituent of the more practical and utilitarian agendas they have adopted. It is worth considering, then, whether distant reading does the same—whether it serves to perpetuate or undermine this peculiar form of disciplinary resilience.

Perhaps the most telling sign of the radical nature of the Stanford Literary Lab's work is the frequency with which its representatives attempt to reassure potential critics. Moretti continuously strives to humanize his research: eagerly narrating the detective work performed by him and his colleagues, dramatizing their brainstorming sessions when faced with data that fail to make sense, announcing his hopes and frustrations, acknowledging the lab's frequent mistakes and disappointments, thus trying to underscore that even while they are teaching computers to read books, theirs is still a project conducted by actual people and still in dialogue with traditional scholarship in the humanities.[10] These rhetorical tactics cannot disguise but in fact betray an awareness of just how dramatic a shift Moretti is advocating. Indeed, the premise he is challenging by employing scientific and statistical methods, a premise once tirelessly defended by the New Critics, is that literature is ontologically distinct from other kinds of objects in the world and thus merits a mode of investigative procedure specific to its unique nature.[11] Ironically, of course, the method developed by the New Critics, close reading, has, as I have suggested throughout this book, been widely applied to many different nonliterary texts and artifacts. But the digital humanities represents a countervailing trend, with methods borrowed from other disciplines, most notably the sciences, now being used to analyze literature, thus potentially eroding any sense of its specificity.[12]

To be sure, the Stanford Literary Lab does not work to trivialize literature. Quite the opposite, while Moretti and his colleagues refuse the theological assumption that literature defies quantitative measurement, they nevertheless presuppose that it is important enough to merit analysis by means of expensive, cutting-edge technologies. In fact Moretti has remarked that he hopes his methods will restore an emphasis on literature, thus checking the "drift towards other discourses so typical of recent years" (*Graphs* 1). Moreover, while distant reading

is obviously an explicit repudiation of close reading, it represents anything but a rejection of formalism. Dubbing their approach "formalism
without close reading" (Moretti, *Distant Reading* 65) or "quantitative
formalism" (Allison, Heuser, et al., "Quantitative Formalism"), Moretti
and his colleagues are actually more focused than most other scholars
on understanding the function of small-scale rhetorical and formal
devices in determining the success or failure, the proliferation and reach
of literary works within particular populations and across different
geographic boundaries. Syntax, in their view, matters. The frequent conjunction of essayistic relative clauses and narrative independent clauses
in nineteenth-century realist fiction, for instance, is worth isolating
and studying insofar as it may be, according to the Stanford Literary
Lab's pamphlet 5 (Allison, Gemma, et al., "Style at the Scale"), what lends
that genre its remarkable power.

It is also worth noting the investment of distant reading in certain
privileged aesthetic experiences. As Alan Liu has noted, *design* is central to the presentation of work within the digital humanities
("Meaning" 416). The graphs and maps so prominently featured within
the lab's online pamphlets are visually arresting, mesmerizing both in
their meticulous, colorful visualization of what might otherwise elude
notice and in their capacity to present granular modes of knowledge in
an elegant manner. But perhaps even more significant than these polished, alluring visual presentations is the somewhat more unruly set
of feelings that serve as distant reading's raison d'être. Consider the
challenge Moretti lays out in his famous essay "Conjectures on World
Literature": "There are thirty thousand nineteenth-century British
novels out there, forty, fifty, sixty thousand—no one really knows, no
one has read them, no one ever will. And then there are French novels,
Chinese, Argentinian, American" (55). Moretti invokes what is probably the most common anxiety within the profession—how little one
has read—and renders it sublime. Indeed, the number of unread books
seems to grow, to double, even as he writes his sentence, proliferating
into an unconquerable infinity, becoming not merely incomprehensibly
large but in fact unknown.

Evocations of what Immanuel Kant called the "mathematically
sublime"—the encounter with an object whose magnitude refuses
comparison and resists comprehension—recur throughout Moretti's

recent work and the lab's pamphlets.[13] "You enter the archive," Moretti remarks, "and the usual coordinates disappear; all you can see are swarms of hybrids and oddities, for which the categories of literary taxonomy offer very little help. It's fascinating, to feel so lost in a universe one didn't even know existed" (*Distant Reading* 180). Pamphlet 1 conjectures what new software tools might accomplish: "One could give Docuscope and MFW [Most Frequent Words: an algorithm] thousands of texts of unknown generic affiliation, and see where they would fall in the gravitational field of better-known genres. One could envisage generation-by-generation maps of the literary universe, with galaxies, supernovae, black holes" (Allison, Heuser, et al., "Quantitative Formalism" 10). Encountering this uncharted cosmos, according to Moretti, is a "double lesson, of humility and euphoria at the same time" (*Graphs* 2)—two emotions repeatedly invoked throughout the lab's pamphlets and central to the experience of the sublime. While the tone of Moretti's texts and the pamphlets is generally cheerful, if not jaunty, a more tragic disposition necessarily infuses the entire project: an awareness of human limitation, of the impossibility of coming to terms with the material, of the shortness of available time and the finitude of one's own life span.

It might seem, then, that traditional scholars have nothing to fear from distant reading other than a reminder of their own mortality. It is a method, after all, that takes literature seriously, that pays careful attention to form, that democratically expands the canon, and that promotes aesthetic experiences with an eminent lineage. And yet, while all such defenses are viable, they do not fully take into account the strange logic of distant reading, the way it organizes the approach to literature so as to disrupt prevailing interpretive habits. The first, most obvious point to make is that in the lab's work the experience of the sublime comes at the beginning of the critical procedure, when one first encounters the vast constellation of books all demanding attention, rather than the end. The sublime is not the goal of distant reading, not the desired state, as it might be with other forms of interpretation, but the problem that needs to be solved. Moreover, it does not come from reading the text but rather from fearing the impossibly time-consuming task of reading that the text and the myriad others around it seem to demand. Admittedly, aesthetic fulfillment, as I have stressed in this book, has often assumed an obscure place within postwar academic literary criticism as an unintentional, even unlikely side effect of procedures ostensibly organized around more practical objectives. But what distinguishes distant reading from other methodologies is its tendency to cast the one recognizable aesthetic experience to which it most frequently and eloquently attests as something to be overcome.

This urge to solve, as it were, the problem of the sublime is actually symptomatic of a more thoroughgoing refusal of the value of experience itself within distant reading. This refusal reveals itself in various ways. Moretti acknowledges, "Objects that have no equivalent within lived experience: this is what *Graphs, Maps, Trees* is made of. The graph on the rise of the novel in five distinct countries, and the generational cycles of British literature; the circular patterns of village stories, and the tree of clues and free indirect discourse" (*Distant Reading* 157). His research, in other words, pursues patterns that exist entirely outside of and unavailable to human experience, patterns, in fact, that only a computer can detect. Even when the scale is smaller, when the lab investigates semantic and lexical structures within a given passage, the researchers are, in their need to justify their use of digital technology, drawn to phenomena that escape human perception. Certain information they hope to extract, such as the average number of topics or themes in the paragraphs of a handful of canonical novels, could in fact be determined through old-fashioned reading and analysis, but the lab nevertheless opts to use software, with a method that may in fact be more inexact than human effort, wherein word families (or semantic fields) detectable by a computer are indexed to particular subjects (Algee-Hewitt, Heuser, et al., "On Paragraphs"). Their motive, of course, is to test a method that will subsequently be used to process thousands of texts, which does require technology, but they also seem to believe that even when considering a single book or passage, a computer is preferable insofar as it can overcome the limitations of human readers. They open their discussion by noting that two of the closest readers who ever produced criticism, Ian Watt and Erich Auerbach, failed to recognize a paragraph as a paragraph and thus failed to explain how this particular textual unit works (4–5). But in seeking to correct the mistakes cf such readers and, by extension, all of the other less acute readers throughout history, to eradicate, in other words, the various biases, blind spots, and vagaries responsible for these mistakes, they are treating as an obstacle to knowledge everything that makes reading reading—that is, the various subjective moments that may well represent the defining feature of the human experience of books.

Practically every critic of course seeks to correct the mistakes of other, less careful readers, but the lab appears systematically committed to the almost total erasure of reading qua experience. Moretti wants to conquer what Margaret Cohen has called "the great unread" (qtd. in Moretti, "Conjectures" 55), a designation that eclipses the fact that most of these books probably were read by someone in their time. But even more significant than this inadvertent sleight to all of the reading experiences lost to the archive is Moretti's solution: to construct a kind of knowledge that will make the future reading of any fraction of this corpus unnecessary. That this knowledge always assumes a visual and spatial form is crucial. The diagrams Moretti uses to understand character networks in *Hamlet* are, he observes, "time turned into space" ("Network Theory" 3). His ambition, in other words, is to replace the temporal experience of reading, whose significance is dependent on its duration, with the spatial representation of knowledge, a form that can ideally be grasped in a single, instantaneous glimpse. Time, recall, is the enemy: its finitude is what inspires Moretti's initial moment of despair and the subsequent project of distant reading. His graphs, maps, and trees are an attempt to defeat time, but, as the romantic poets learned before him, he cannot succeed at this without also defeating all of the experiences that happen within time.

Though the lab repeatedly asserts its commitment to literature, even to understanding many of the same texts that critics have grappled with for centuries, it is in fact studying an entirely new object of its own making. "You *reduce* the text to a few elements," explains Moretti, "*abstract* them from the narrative flow, and construct a new, *artificial* object like the maps that I have been discussing" (*Graphs* 53). The reason that this represents a major disruption, despite Moretti's penchant for bringing his insights to bear on canonical texts, is that the bedrock for all literary studies, its underlying constant over the past eighty years, has not been a particular set of literary works. This is why the canon could expand, why scholars could consider nonliterary texts and other objects while still producing work that felt like literary scholarship. What has defined the field and served as the source of continuity through all variety of methodological interventions has been a particular aesthetic experience: to be precise, an experience of textual ambiguity or paradox, whose defining property is that it can never be fully translated into a fact, a truth, a statement, or a detachable form of knowledge. And it is this experience that the lab's quantitative and visual representations appear to disregard, if not erase.

Although they have been made to serve a variety of purposes, close reading and the encounter with ambiguity have always come with a built-in justification. For the New Critics, the purported unparaphrasability of this experience functioned as proof of its intrinsic value: it could not be converted into something external to itself; it was thus its own justification. Indeed, for reasons that scholars from Richards onward have struggled to articulate, this experience has been regarded as deeply fulfilling in its own right, satisfying a need whose frequent redefinition in the form of a variety of practical, scientific, social, political, and ethical urgencies actually suggests the existence of some less easily describable need that preexists these contingent worldly configurations. In abandoning close reading, then, the Stanford Literary Lab has discarded a decades-old, well-tested motive for engaging in literary studies. And thus it often struggles to explain the purpose of its various investigations. It discovers quantitative trends about literature that nobody has ever noticed before; it produces gorgeous models; it is clearly doing something exciting and innovative. But to what end exactly?

Moretti and his colleagues continuously wonder, What is the takeaway, what is the value of the patterns that they are detecting? "Do maps *add* anything, to our knowledge of literature?" he asks (*Graphs* 35). Noticing a remarkable geometric shape in one particular map, he concludes,

It is a sign that something is at work here—that something has *made* the pattern the way it is.
But what? (*Graphs* 56)

At one point the lab acknowledges that its quantitative study of syntax has in no way modified the preexisting understanding of the nineteenth-century novel (Allison, Gemma, et al., "Style at the Scale" 23). At another, Moretti realizes that his graph of *Antigone* has merely corroborated the critical consensus, remarking, "Corroboration is not nothing, but is also not much" ("'Operationalizing'" 11). The lab's rhetorical strategy on such occasions is generally to project the reward for their labor into the future, deferring it to some later date when they finally figure out how best to take advantage of the tools they are developing.[14] But how and whether this will happen remains unclear. In an especially telling moment of frustration, the lab's researchers ask, "How do we get from numbers to *meaning?*" (Heuser and Le-Khac, "Quantitative Literary History" 46), a question that has prompted Liu to assert that the digital humanities suffers from a "meaning problem" ("Meaning" 411).

Trying to assemble a digital archive of twentieth-century novels for pamphlet 8, Mark Algee-Hewitt and Mark McGurl confront this issue in a somewhat different way. In need of a method for winnowing the massive number of texts produced over the past hundred years into a more manageable list, Algee-Hewitt and McGurl ask whether they should choose novels that have achieved critical acclaim or just a random sample, thereby approaching twentieth-century literature "in its 'natural' state" and thus working to realize a "longstanding aspiration in the Lab" ("Between Canon and Corpus" 3). The question is obviously an important one. To put it another way, in building an archive, are they hoping to study the best that has been thought and said or simply a representative sampling of all the written stuff that humans have happened to produce during the twentieth century? Will their archive be a repository of values or facts? At first worried about "selection bias"—that is, allowing their own values to shape their choices—they eventually realize that they want their list to feature an element of canonicity. An entirely random set of titles "might suffer from a sense of *mere* arbitrariness, leaving out too many things—including most of the individual authors, certainly, and perhaps also whole genres and long phases of development—that scholars have come to care about" (3). Ultimately, then, they decide to construct an archive that reflects precisely what scholars have cared about—that reflects values to which they themselves subscribe. Far from seeking merely to observe the world of twentieth-century literature as they find it in scientific fashion, they eventually solicit suggestions from feminist and postcolonial scholars in order to correct the gender and ethnic imbalances in the lists they initially construct based on rankings from the Modern Library, the Radcliffe Publishing Course, Larry McCaffery's one hundred most important English works of fiction, and Publishers Weekly best sellers, thus actively shaping in advance the material they plan to investigate.

Purely random selection would potentially erase the aesthetic, ethical, and political values that have underwritten various critical appraisals of twentieth-century literature, destroying a certain legacy of a century of cultural effort, one significantly enmeshed with academic literary studies, in the name of a return to "nature." In eschewing this option and revealing that they still care about what scholars and critics have cared about, Algee-Hewitt and McGurl assert their loyalty to precisely the nonscientific methods of inquiry and evaluation that the digital humanities has at times seemed dedicated to replacing. In a profound understatement, they observe that their attention not merely to "sampling, representativeness, and quantifying" but also to "ranking and valuation" "does seem to carry with it concerns beyond what is typical of a digital humanities study" (20). In pushing back against the prevailing tendencies in this new field, Algee-Hewitt and McGurl endeavor to prevent their subject matter and their own work from collapsing into "*mere* arbitrariness." Their implicit suggestion here is that the digital humanities represents a systematic evacuation of "valuation." By quantitatively measuring, mapping, and graphing literature, in other words, the lab is engaged in a project of translating value into data. Its "meaning problem" is that it treats meaning as a problem.[15]

Ironically, however, this translation may be exactly what makes the digital humanities worthwhile and appealing; it may in fact represent not the eradication of aesthetic value but the introduction of a different aesthetic organized around a new kind of experience. Moretti is obsessed with human failure—his own and that of the authors and texts he studies. Explaining why the lab's pamphlets frequently report on its failures, he observes, "Failures *throw a unique light on the whole research process*. Failures take us all the way back to our starting points: to those unspoken assumptions that go 'without saying,' and thus easily escape critical scrutiny. . . . By frustrating our expectations, failed experiments 'estrange' our natural habits of thought, offering us a chance to transform them" ("Literature, Measured" 4). Though he spins failure as productive here, in pamphlet 11 he and his colleagues eloquently describe their fascination with failures that remain failures—that lead to nothing good or valuable.[16] One reason they want to study books far outside the canon is the same reason that most critics avoid this territory: "In part, it is the troubling nature of what forgotten authors force you to face: a vast wreck of ambitious ideals, very unlike the landscape literary historians are used to study. Learning to look at the wreck without arrogance—but also without pieties—is what the new digital archive is asking us to do; in the long run, it might be an even greater change than quantification itself" (Algee-Hewitt, Allison, et al., "Canon/Archive" 13). To look at the "vast wreck of ambitious ideals" is to grapple with the historical process through which attempted assertions of meaning and value become insignificant, returning, as they do, to "*mere* arbitrariness." The Stanford Literary Lab is thus hoping to find intellectual sustenance in the dissolution of value, a dissolution that its own procedures never seek to reverse or repair—hence the refusal of "pieties"—and in fact frequently seem to reinforce.

This again might be described as an instance of the sublime; but whereas most theorists have identified the latter with the confrontation with nonhuman entities—alps, oceans, night skies, and the like—the lab finds a tragically ironic basis for it precisely in the bafflingly enormous archive of efforts by humans to defeat or overcome a sense of their own insignificance. The lab's relentless invocation of the sheer number of texts out there underscores just how infinitesimal a fraction of the world's attention anyone's writing will claim, how statistically likely it is to go unnoticed, to fall into oblivion, dwarfed by the mountains of pulp around it. Moreover, the lab's commitment to discovering imperceptible structures, to considering books that have likely caused barely a ripple in other minds, and to viewing literature from the perspective of a computer reveals a desire, characteristic of much recent posthumanist scholarship, to imagine the world as it exists outside of human experience and its inevitable projection of meaning onto things. But if it uses human materials in order to produce this knowledge, distant reading also makes it into the basis for a perversely satisfying human experience—one that strives to conceive of its own extinction.

The promise of distant reading must be understood, then, as in absolute contrast to that of New Criticism. Though the latter also aimed to help readers escape from their own narrow point of view, it claimed to promote the expansion rather than the imagined obliteration of experience, to foster a way of reading that allowed one's consciousness to grow, to include within itself as many different, contradictory human perspectives as possible all at once, to achieve a kind of emphatic *meaningfulness* while stretching toward an infinity that might be thought to exist within the mind rather than outside it. It is hard to know which kind of aesthetic experience will prove more powerful, whether the digital humanities, if it succeeds at restructuring the discipline, will garner as much interest and win as many adherents as New Criticism did. It is hard to judge which is preferable, especially insofar as the two represent not only competing practices but also competing premises, each of which provides the very basis for judging what makes for a valuable intellectual experience.

One way of approaching this question is to consider the historical conditions responsible for the renewed attention to the aesthetic in the past couple of decades. A possible explanation, a way of situating without invalidating recent reassertions of the aesthetic, is that, notwithstanding the briefly seductive rhetoric of the Obama administration, scholars on the left have been living in a time of relative political hopelessness. To rehearse just a few of the most obvious problems: the humanities seem destined to go extinct; neoliberalism appears indestructible; while the U.S. political system has proved incapable of solving many of the most urgent problems its citizens face. Meanwhile, accelerating global climate change is beginning to destroy habitats, food sources, livelihoods, and communities across the globe. While they have not stopped looking for answers to these problems, intellectuals, along with everyone else, have also found themselves seeking solace and consolation. And the aesthetic, with its capacity to produce fulfillment here and now within compromised and constrained spaces, has thus become an especially attractive resource.[17] Indeed, the need for it may only increase as we struggle in the coming years both to resist and to cope with the present turn to far-right ethnonationalism and the risks it poses to democratic politics. But this raises an important question, one without an obvious answer. Namely, which kind of aesthetic experience is best equipped to serve us in these dark times? The kind that asserts its own significance, whose sheer density of human meaning would seem somehow to refute its own eventual disappearance, or the experience of imagining that very moment fading into nothingness and the world continuing on in its absence?

Notes

Introduction

1. George Levine offers a cogent summary of the methodological trends responsible for pushing aesthetic criticism to the margins:

   First, a shift in emphasis from interpretation to theory (which has, oddly, become a subject somehow independent of the literary texts it ostensibly works out of or against), from questions about what texts might "mean" to questions about the systems that contain them, about material conditions, hermeneutics, mediation, discourse, all of which tend to a new emphasis on self-reflexivity; second, a resistance to (or demystification of) the idea of literary value, particularly of literary greatness; third, an increasing emphasis on the necessity for interdisciplinary study; fourth, a virtually total rejection of, even contempt for, "formalism"; fifth, a determination that all things are political and hence that the function of literature and of literary study is primarily political; sixth, a view that the study of literature is not an adequately serious or important vocation—not only because literature divorced from its sociopolitical context serves in culture only as ornament or mystification, but because it is really indistinguishable from other forms of language (as against the dominant assumption of the now nefarious "New Criticism") and merely another part of culture; and finally, the movement to replace literary study with cultural studies. ("Introduction" 1–2)

2. For an extensive discussion of the ways in which the New Critics departed from aestheticism, see Foster, *New Romantics* 17–29.

3. Caroline Levine has observed a similar tendency, noting that "some of the most determinedly antiformalist scholars have necessarily depended on

219

organizing forms in their own arguments" (*Forms* 22). As Susan Wolfson puts it, "Exposing the fragile facticity of form and its incomplete cover-ups was the most powerful form-attentive criticism in the post- (and anti-) New Critical climate" ("Reading for Form" 3).

4. Marjorie Levinson summarizes and critiques some of these efforts in her 2007 essay "What Is New Formalism?" For examples of collections, special issues, books, and articles associated with this movement, see Theile and Tredennick, *New Formalisms*; Bogel, *New Formalist Criticism*; Wolfson and Brown, *Reading for Form* (which originally appeared as an *MLQ* special issue in 2000); Loesberg, *Return to Aesthetics*; Castronovo and Castiglia, "Aesthetics" (a special issue of *American Literature*); Joughin and Malpas, *New Aestheticism*; Clark, *Revenge of the Aesthetic*; Armstrong, *Radical Aesthetic*; Scarry, *On Beauty*; and G. Levine, *Aesthetics and Ideology*.

5. See Best and Marcus, "Surface Reading"; Love, "Close but Not Deep"; Latour, "Why Has Critique Run out of Steam?"; Felski, *Limits of Critique*; and Moretti, *Distant Reading*. Paul Ricoeur famously coined the term "the hermeneutics of suspicion" in *Freud and Philosophy* (356).

6. Joseph North has also made this point, noting the many figures within political criticism who have paid attention to form (*Literary Criticism* 145).

7. Sianne Ngai has perceptively noted how the category of the "interesting" can be a way of "making aesthetic evaluations on the sly" (*Our Aesthetic Categories* 110). She notes, "Skeptical as academic analysts of art and literature have grown since the late twentieth century about the role of aesthetic judgments in criticism, there is nonetheless one evaluation that continues to circulate promiscuously—if often, in a telling way, surreptitiously—in virtually all contemporary writing on cultural artifacts: 'interesting'" (110).

8. Several scholars have made similar arguments, though without drawing out the full implications of their own claims. Focusing on the economic rather than the political, Mary Poovey remarks, "First, I want to complicate the assumption of many literary critics that economic theory is the repressed truth of aesthetics by demonstrating that the reverse is also true" ("Aesthetics and Political Economy" 80). Oscar Kenshur has observed, "For we may ultimately decide that the reason we undertake ideological analyses of the symbolic structures that make up the fabric of our history is that we are motivated by principles that we find beautiful and valuable in themselves. And we may ultimately wish not to suppress this fact as sentimental and embarrassing, but to theorize these principles and make them an explicit part of our arguments" ("'Tumour'" 75). Rita Felski has noted that symptomatic reading may be motivated in part by certain aesthetic criteria (*Limits of Critique* 111). Finally, Dorothy Hale has remarked that the way in which cultural studies theorizes social and ethical responsibilities is indebted to theories of novelistic form that can be traced back to Henry James (*Social Formalism*).

9. See Jameson, *Political Unconscious*.

10. As Gerald Graff has noted,

The fact remains that first-generation New Critics were neither aesthetes nor pure explicators but cultural critics with a considerable "axe to grind" against the technocratic tendencies of modern mass civilization. Even when they minimized the social aspect of their work, their very way of doing so bespoke a social concern; for emphasizing the aesthetic over the directly social was a way of counteracting what the New Critics saw as the overly acquisitive and practical tenor of modern urban society. It was not merely that the taste of Eliot and the Southern New Critics for organically complex, overdidactically "Platonic" poetry reflected their admiration for organic, hierarchical societies over the abstractions of mechanistic industrialism, though this was in fact the case. These critics' very insistence on the disinterested nature of poetic experience was an implicit rejection of a utilitarian culture and thus a powerfully "utilitarian" and "interested" gesture. (*Professing Literature* 149)

I discuss the New Critics' relationship to a modern technocratic social order in more depth in Chapter 1.

11. As Catherine Gallagher puts it, "Against the homogenizing tendencies of the marketplace, the merely formal individualism of democratic politics, and the standardized consciousness produced by industrial workplaces and urban living, [the New Critics] counterposed a deeper, truer, and more qualitative selfhood" ("History of Literary Criticism" 134).

12. Best and Marcus argue, "When Jameson writes that 'the human adventure is one' (19), 'a single vast unfinished plot' (20), he seeks to return to human life a unity that Augustine found only in God" ("Surface Reading" 15).

13. Kant argues, "That a judgment of taste by which we declare something to be beautiful must not have an interest *as its determining basis* has been established sufficiently above. But it does not follow from this that, after the judgment has been made as a pure aesthetic one, an interest cannot be connected with it. This connection, however, must always be only indirect" (*Critique of Judgment* 163). Kant acknowledges that shared judgments of taste can end up promoting "sociability" and "moral feeling" (163–164), but he is careful to maintain a distinction between the aesthetic and moral faculties: "And hence it seems, not only that the feeling for the beautiful is distinct in kind from moral feeling (as indeed it actually is), but also that it is difficult to reconcile the interest which can be connected with the beautiful with the moral interest, and that it is impossible to do this by an [alleged] intrinsic affinity between the two" (165).

14. See Kant, *Critique of Judgment*, and Burke, *On Taste*.

15. See Genette, *Aesthetic Relation* 6–16, and Mukařovský, *Aesthetic Function* 1–23.

16. Nicholas Gaskill discusses the various meanings that literary form has been made to reference ("Close and the Concrete" 505). Underscoring the competing meanings of "form," Gallagher observes, "[Jameson and Genette] are engaged in the classical activity of displaying the overall shape, indeed the

symmetry or shapeliness, of these novels. However, the Russian formalists, as well as the more recent analysts of narrative discourse, often mean something different by *form:* they mean the style of the work, the grammar, syntax, verb modes, and tenses, and rhetoric" ("Formalism and Time" 306–307). Another central debate among critics is whether form can be understood as that which imposes coherence onto reality, thus concealing various contradictions, or whether form, through its immediacy and materiality, does the opposite, posing a challenge to theoretical abstractions and forcing the reader to confront the unassimilable, the heterogeneous, and the particular. The former position has often been associated with Terry Eagleton, particularly *Criticism and Ideology* and *The Ideology of the Aesthetic.* The New Formalists are generally committed to the latter position. See, for instance, Kaufman, "Everybody Hates Kant" and "Red Kant"; Rooney, "Form and Contentment"; Nemoianu, "Hating and Loving Aesthetic Formalism"; and Levao, *"Paradise Lost."*

17. See, for instance, Wolfson, "Reading for Form." Ellen Rooney offers a contrary view, questioning the equation of formalism and aesthetics, in "Form and Contentment."

18. Russian formalist Victor Shklovsky was one of the earliest critics to define literature in terms of its defamiliarizing effect in his 1917 essay "Art as Technique."

19. For some accounts of the university's function in twentieth-century America, see Donogue, *Last Professors;* Aronowitz, *Knowledge Factory;* and Kerr, *Uses of the University.*

20. See Bok, *Higher Education in America;* Geiger, *Research and Relevant Knowledge;* Washburn, *University, Inc.;* Readings, *University in Ruins;* and Kirp, *Shakespeare, Einstein and the Bottom Line.*

21. To be clear, I am focusing on how the specific aesthetic articulated by the New Critics came to define the discipline. But English studies obviously has a longer history of cultivating affective relationships to literature. In *Loving Literature,* Deirdre Lynch offers an illuminating examination of the complicated and sometimes ambivalent ways in which literary criticism and scholarship served in the eighteenth and early nineteenth centuries to constitute literature as an object of love, as a phenomenon whose study required an intense emotional attachment.

22. See Sedgwick, "Paranoid Reading and Reparative Reading" and *Touching Feeling;* Bersani, "Psychoanalysis and the Aesthetic Subject"; Berlant and Warner, "Sex in Public"; and Edelman, *No Future.*

23. Judith Halberstam also underscores Edelman's unacknowledged aesthetic commitments, noting the canonical authors he relies on and insisting: "If we want to make the antisocial turn in queer theory, we must be willing to turn away from the comfort zone of polite exchange to embrace a truly political negativity, one that promises, this time, to fail, to make a mess, to fuck shit up, to be loud, unruly, impolite, to breed resentment, to bash back, to speak up and out, to disrupt, assassinate, shock, and annihilate, and to abandon the neat, clever, chiasmic, punning emphasis on style and stylistic

order that characterizes both the gay male archive and the theoretical writing about it" ("Politics of Negativity" 824).

24. As North puts it, "Affect theory as emblematized by Berlant seems a case-in-point here, for the project, while clearly historicist/contextualist in its basic orientation toward cultural analysis, seems to have been homing in on something that strongly recalls the old aesthetic concerns" (*Literary Criticism* 177).

25. See Berlant, *Female Complaint* x, 3, 8, 27, 162, 164–165.

26. Marx and Friedrich Engels suggest that various modes of thought that seem removed from the political are in fact the expression of material and ideological conflicts most forcefully in *The German Ideology*. Obviously numerous other theorists, most famously Michel Foucault, have ascribed an ideological character to various ostensibly private realms and activities.

27. Jacques Rancière is the contemporary theorist who has most systematically tried to establish the radical power of the aesthetic, arguing that the re-ordering of sensory experiences—what he calls "the distribution of the sensible" (*Aesthetics and Its Discontents* 25)—brought about by various aesthetic practices can be conceived as a radical political transformation. See *Aesthetics and Its Discontents, Emancipated Spectator*, and *Politics of Aesthetics*. The recent proliferation of work on Theodor Adorno and the Frankfurt school more generally has also signaled, as Robert S. Lehman has noted, renewed interest in the radical political potential of formalist criticism. ("Formalism" 245). Felski has made a strong case for distinguishing between the shock value of certain aesthetic devices and their potential political functions, without disregarding the significance of either: "In both its utopian and elegiac versions, shock is frequently burdened with meanings it cannot sustain, thanks to what I have called an ethos of avant-gardism, a chain of programmatic beliefs about the necessary relations between aesthetic novelty, perceptual jolts, and impending social upheaval" (*Uses of Literature* 129). She adds, "That shock fails to unleash a social cataclysm does not render it less salient as an element of aesthetic response" (130).

28. Probably the two most famous arguments for the political power of parody and irony (repetition with a difference) are Judith Butler's *Gender Trouble* and Homi Bhabha's *Location of Culture*. In *Cool Characters*, Lee Konstantinou explores the reasons that postwar American intellectuals staked so much on irony as a tool of political subversion and the backlash this eventually produced. I consider Barbara Johnson's defense of ambiguity as a mode of feminist politics in Chapter 2.

29. Barbara Herrnstein Smith makes a similar argument in *Contingencies of Value*, observing, "Our experience of 'the value of the work' is equivalent to *our experience of the work in relation to the total economy of our existence*. And the reason our estimates of its probable value for other people may be quite accurate is that the total economy of *their* existence may, in fact, be quite similar to that of our own" (16).

30. As Jonathan Loesberg observes, "When Bourdieu argues, in *Distinction*, that a taste for autonomous non-utilitarian art is particular to the upper classes,

he does not think either that such a taste or that such art do not exist and are mere ideological delusions. Rather, his point is that, although the art and taste for it do exist, because they represent the value of a specific class, they have no transcendent value" (*Return to Aesthetics* 2).

31. This point was made most persuasively by the editors of *n + 1* in their statement "Too Much Sociology."

32. Guillory argues this point in *Cultural Capital*, remarking, "The strangest consequence of the canon debate has surely been the discrediting of judgment, as though human beings could ever refrain from judging the things they make" (xiv). Felski makes a similar claim, observing, "Evaluation is not optional: we are condemned to choose, required to rank, endlessly engaged in practices of selecting, sorting, distinguishing, privileging, whether in academia or in everyday life" (*Uses of Literature* 20).

CHAPTER 1 ❦ The Intellectual Critics and the Pleasures of Complexity

1. Catherine Gallagher also argues that the New Critics prepared the way for the schools that would replace them. She focuses on how their "cosmopolitanism" opened literary studies to all of the theories that could not find a home in other, more provincial disciplines—theories that would play such a major role in more recent methodologies, including deconstruction, psychoanalysis, Marxism, and so forth ("History of Literary Criticism" 140–141).

2. For a discussion of how the New Critics distinguish their approach from aestheticism, see Foster, *New Romantics* 17–29.

3. The conclusion to Walter Pater's *Renaissance*, the most famous fin de siècle statement of aestheticism next to Oscar Wilde's aphorisms, was, as Matthew Burroughs Price observes, "widely condemned as a seductive corrupter of young men" ("Genealogy" 648), and the New Critics obviously wanted to ensure that their work would avoid the same fate.

4. See also Brooks, *Modern Poetry* 40.

5. The New Critics describe this as the quintessential effect of poetry in many places. See, for instance, Brooks, *Well-Wrought Urn* 18–19; Wellek, *History of Modern Criticism* 3–4.

6. See Empson, *Seven Types of Ambiguity*; Ransom, *World's Body* and *New Criticism*; and Brooks, *Modern Poetry* and *Well-Wrought Urn*.

7. See Olson, "William Empson." See also Crane, "Critical Monism." Many traditional scholars argued against New Critical interpretations and the ambiguities they yielded by invoking the historical context or knowledge of the author's biography in order to delimit the meaning. See, for instance, Cunningham, *Tradition and Poetic Structure*; Bush, "New Criticism" and "Marvell's 'Horatian Ode'"; and Fogle, "Romantic Bards."

8. Richard Ohmann makes a similar argument, characterizing the positions of those who reject the need for a methodology of the kind developed by the New Critics as follows: "These are aristocratic positions, rooted in the pride of the natural-born critic (and, usually, poet) who needs no shared ways of

thinking, and whose advice to teachers would no doubt be 'look into your guts and write—if you dare.'" He adds, "It is not surprising that such views made little headway against the New Criticism, which at least aimed toward a democracy of critical ideas, available to all" (*English in America* 84–85).

9. Ohmann observes that a small number of essays and books written by Brooks, William Empson, R. P. Blackmur, and I. A. Richards "taught us how to write papers as students, how to write articles later on, and what to say about a poem to *our* students in a fifty-minute hour" ("Teaching and Studying Literature" 135). For histories of the New Critics and the role they played in establishing literary criticism as an academic discipline, see Graff, *Professing Literature* 145–161, 183–243; Winchell, *Cleanth Brooks*; Spilka, "Necessary Stylist"; Bradbury, *Fugitives*; D. Green, "Literature Itself"; Leitch, *American Literary Criticism*; and Eagleton, *Literary Theory*.

10. See, for instance, Graff, *Professing Literature* 173; Bush, "New Criticism" 13; and Barrett et al., "American Scholar Forum" 88.

11. See Graff, *Professing Literature* 55, 66–68, 78, 83–88. As Douglas Bush argues in his defense of traditional methods, the historical focus of scholars represents an "attempt to see a piece of writing through the minds of its author and its contemporaries" ("New Criticism" 13). Brooks's characterization of scholarly work is less generous; he concludes, quoting Robert Browning, that the effort to ascertain "what porridge had John Keats" does nothing to illuminate his poetry (*Well-Wrought Urn* 153). Ransom summarizes the reasons for the New Critics' dissatisfaction with literary scholarship somewhat more carefully in "Criticism, Inc." (*World's Body* 327–350). See also Ohmann, "Teaching and Studying Literature" 145; Foster, *New Romantics* 194; Wellek, "New Criticism" 614; and Leitch, *American Literary Criticism* 27. For a discussion of the early twentieth-century generalists, see Kazin, *On Native Grounds*, 265–311.

12. Ransom is quite explicit in asserting this as his goal in "Criticism, Inc." (*World's Body* 327–350).

13. For a concise summary of the New Critics' view of the relationship between poetry and an industrial, secular society, see Graff, *Professing Literature* 149.

14. The two most important examinations of the rise of managerial capitalism in the United States are Chandler, *Visible Hand*, and Yates, *Control through Communication*.

15. For descriptions of how the modern university arose in order to serve the needs of corporations, see Donogue, *Last Professors* 9–21, and Aronowitz, *Knowledge Factory* 15–37.

16. Florence Dore has persuasively argued that New Criticism was not a reactionary refusal of postwar capitalism but in fact shaped by the same market forces and responsive to the same desires as the mass cultural products, such as rock and roll, that it held in contempt ("The New Criticism").

17. Numerous historians and sociologists have explored the complex relationship between professional organizations and the free market. See, for instance, Larson, *Rise of Professionalism*; Brint, *Age of Experts*; and Perkin, *Third*

Revolution. Literary scholars, it is important to note, struggled to reconcile themselves with the professionalization of their discipline prior to the emergence of New Criticism. For a careful analysis of these earlier developments, see Glazener, *Literature in the Making*, 163, 210–217.

18. See, for instance, Charles Nelson's description of the humanistic role of the corporate manager in a 1958 essay for the *Harvard Business Review*. Nelson writes,

> Most executives' decisions at the top level affect other managers— their lives, their satisfactions in their work, and their ability to perform the kind of job they can be proud of. It is possible to organize a company in which the opposite occurs—in which men are almost of necessity made worse because of their association with the corporation. Executives have it within their power to frustrate the creative energies of most of the men under their direction or to help them to fulfill their capacities. It was the moral imperative of Immanuel Kant, the German philosopher, that every man must be treated as an end in himself. This means that men are not tools to be "handled," for tools are implements for some other end. ("Liberal Arts" 96)

19. In "Big Criticism," Evan Kindley traces the institutional and financial arrangements responsible for the growth of criticism's prestige in the postwar period. As large foundations came to support literary culture, they also required rational justification for the practices they were funding, and, according to Kindley, "Justification is, of course, what criticism has been historically good at, going back at least as far as Aristotle" (92).

20. Lee Konstantinou has made a similar observation about the New Critics: "At the same time, once it is encoded in an object, irony must replicate itself in the cognitive faculty of the discerning critic, who will need to cultivate the capacity to read doubly. Without the critic's taking up the normative mantle of ironic reading, irony will in some sense perish on the page" (*Cool Characters* 53–54).

21. In a fascinating analysis of Brooks's classroom materials, Rachel Sagner Buurma and Laura Heffernan explore just how connected Brooks's understanding of poetry was to his pedagogy ("Common Reader" 118–119).

22. Indeed, according to Buurma and Heffernan, Brooks's lecture notes indicate a far more provisional and open-ended sense of what constitutes poetic value than the proclamations he issues in his books (124).

23. Anxieties about the growth of science's influence recur regularly in almost all New Critical writings. Chicago formalist R. S. Crane faulted them for their "morbid obsession . . . with the problem of justifying and preserving poetry in an age of science" ("Critical Monism" 105). For an exploration of the New Critics' efforts to distinguish their practices from scientific procedures, see Gaskill, "Close and the Concrete."

24. See Graff, "Groping for a Principle of Order," in *Professing Literature* 145–161. See also Guillory, "Ideology and the Canonical Form," in *Cultural Capital* 134–175; and Schryer, "The Republic of Letters," in *Fantasies of the New Class* 29–54.

25. See "The Intentional Fallacy" 5–28, and "The Affective Fallacy" 21–39, in Wimsatt, *Verbal Icon*.

26. Or, as Brooks puts it in *Modern Poetry and the Tradition*, "The non-Platonic poet knows that he is not competing with [science]—is, as a matter of fact, dealing with another order of description from that in which science indulges" (47).

27. As Brooks writes, "If we allow ourselves to be misled by [the heresy of paraphrase], we distort the relation of the poem to its 'truth,' we raise the problem of belief in a vicious and crippling form, we split the poem between its 'form' and its 'content'—we bring the statement to be conveyed into an unreal competition with science or philosophy or theology" (*Well-Wrought Urn* 201).

28. Many scholars have accused the New Critics of denying referential powers to literature. See, for instance, Krieger, *New Apologists*, and Graff, *Poetic Statement*.

29. Graff reaches a similar conclusion about the premises of New Criticism in *Poetic Statement* when he observes: "There is thus an important sense in which the state of mind of the persona of a lyric *is itself* the 'context' of any statement made in the poem. It follows that the request for contextual or dramatic appropriateness is circular unless supported by a demand that the persona be in some sense reliable in his account of his objective situation, that is, unless an appeal is made to something outside the self-enclosed 'experience' of the poem itself" (98).

30. See Brooks, *Modern Poetry* 37–38.

31. Many scholars have noted the parallels between New Criticism and deconstruction. See Lentricchia, *After the New Criticism* 121, 169; Berman, *From New Criticism* 170; Martin, "Critical Response"; Bove, "Variations on Authority"; Fischer, *Does Deconstruction Make Any Difference?* 93; Cain, *Crisis in Criticism* 114; Hunter, "History of Theory" 107–108; and Loesberg, *Aestheticism and Deconstruction* 75.

32. Angus Fletcher and Michael Benveniste suggest that New Critical aesthetics have actually led to present-day multiculturalism ("Defending Pluralism").

33. I explore the New Historical turn to the archive in Chapter 3.

34. See, for instance, Bennett, *Vibrant Matter*; Harman, "Well-Wrought Broken Hammer"; and Macpherson, "Little Formalism."

CHAPTER 2 ❦ Appetite for Deconstruction

1. For a detailed account of these events, see Kampf and Lauter, introduction 34–39.

2. See Kampf and Lauter, introduction 19–21, 24–26, 41–42.

3. Derek Attridge characterizes deconstruction as the "Indian summer" of New Criticism (*Reading and Responsibility* 34).

4. For some New Critical reactions to deconstruction, see Wellek, "Destroying Literary Studies," and Brooks, "New Criticism." As we have seen, numerous scholars have pointed to parallels between New Criticism and deconstruction. See Chapter 1, n. 33.

5. For a discussion of deconstruction's connection to Tel Quel, see Leitch, *Deconstructive Criticism* 101–105; Rappaport, *Theory Mess* 12; and Mary Ann Caws, "Tel Quel."

6. François Cusset offers a helpful account of how the radicalism of U.S. campuses in the late 1960s and early 1970s made them hospitable to deconstruction (*French Theory* 27–28, 59–66).

7. For comprehensive accounts of deconstruction as a critical practice, see Leitch, *Deconstructive Criticism*; Culler, *On Deconstruction*; Norris, *Deconstruction*.

8. As Michael Fischer has noted, "It is no accident that deconstruction in particular first caught on at some of our most renowned universities, or that individuals thoroughly at home in the academic profession have switched their loyalty from Wimsatt or Frye to Jacques Derrida. Neither does the ease with which the university has assimilated deconstruction prove its capacity for tolerating dangerous ideas" (*Does Deconstruction?* 32). See also Ellis, *Against Deconstruction* 157. Other observers viewed deconstruction as either the symptom or the potential agent of the demise of literary studies. See Wellek, "Destroying Literary Studies," and Shaw, "Degenerate Criticism."

9. See Aronowitz, *Knowledge Factory* 2, and Menand, *Marketplace of Ideas* 54–64.

10. See Ohmann, *English in America* 209–254, and Berlin, *Rhetoric and Reality* 120–139.

11. See Donogue, *Last Professors* 24; Aronowitz, *Knowledge Factory* 36; and *2006 MLA Task Force* 17.

12. These problems obviously afflict many other departments in the humanities. The literature on this crisis is voluminous. See, for instance, Donogue, *Last Professors*; Aronowitz, *Knowledge Factory*; Kirp, *Shakespeare, Einstein, and the Bottom Line*; Cary Nelson, *No University*; Newfield, *Unmaking the Public University*; Bousquet, *How the University Works*; and G. Jay, "Hire Ed!"

13. See Donogue, *Last Professors* 40–52; Washburn, *University, Inc.* x–xv, 329–337; and Kerr, *Uses of the University* 199–200.

14. Cusset also notes that deconstruction's success coincided with an acceleration in the rhythm of academic publication in literary studies in the 1970s (*French Theory* 44).

15. That critics ought to embrace their role as creators, capable of producing the very aesthetic power that they claim to discover, is the central thesis of Geoffrey Hartman's *Criticism in the Wilderness*.

16. In *The Division of Literature*, Peggy Kamuf also notes that deconstruction allows for a doubleness in one's relationship to the discipline, which enables a radical critique from within (29).

17. See Graff, *Professing Literature* 240–243.

18. De Man returns to the example of using "giants" to describe other men in *Allegories of Reading*. Though, in his later analysis, he is less dismissive of this particular figure of speech, he uses it to make a similar point: "Meta-

phor is error because it believes or feigns to believe in its own referential meaning" (151).

19. Joseph Riddel famously argues that both de Man and J. H. Miller attempt to attribute a special status to literature, as that discourse uniquely aware of its own fictionality ("Miller's Tale"). Indeed, like de Man, Miller does unapologetically attribute special powers to literature. He remarks, "Another way to put this is to say that great works of literature are likely to be ahead of their critics. They are there already. They have anticipated explicitly any deconstruction the critic can achieve" ("Deconstructing the Deconstructors" 31).

20. For some useful summaries of structuralist thought, see Culler, *Structuralist Poetics*; Berman, *From New Criticism*; Jameson, *Prison-House of Language*; and Scholes, *Structuralism in Literature*.

21. Marc Redfield seems to suggest a similar function for the aesthetic in de Man's version of deconstruction: "Yet the aesthetic category of literature inevitably becomes exemplary of literariness as semiotic unrest—a mode of writing that can be incorporated into a humanist or national-aestheticist pedagogy only through ideological obfuscation. Aesthetics makes trouble for itself" (*Theory at Yale* 8).

22. According to some critics, including Fischer, Jeffrey Nealon, Robert Phiddian, and M. H. Abrams, the urge to produce aporia within American deconstruction is too automatic. In a manner that is all too predictable, they claim, deconstruction discovers semantic incoherence in every text it considers. See Fischer, *Does Deconstruction?* 54; Nealon, "Discipline of Deconstruction," 1274–1275; Phiddian, "Are Parody and Deconstruction?" 674; and Abrams, "Deconstructive Angel" 434–435.

23. See especially Barthes, *Pleasure of the Text*; *Sade, Fourier, Loyola*; and *Image, Music, Text*.

24. See Ransom, *New Criticism* 22, and *World's Body* 154–155.

25. See Lentricchia, *After the New Criticism* 185–189, 313; and Jameson, *Prison-House of Language* 185–194. For a history of the decline of deconstruction within the academy (and the role played by the discovery of de Man's pro-fascist, anti-Semitic journalist work in accelerating this decline), see J. Williams, "Death of Deconstruction." For a useful summary of the various characterizations of deconstruction as aestheticist, see Loesberg, *Aestheticism and Deconstruction* 3–10.

26. Miller acknowledges deconstruction's embattled position in the academy in his 1986 MLA presidential address.

27. For a lucid account of various efforts to bridge deconstruction and politics, see P. Jay, "Bridging the Gap." Probably the most explicit and organized attempt to underscore deconstruction's potential to intervene within politics is Anselm Haverkamp's 1995 collection, *Deconstruction Is/in America*.

28. In *The World's Body*, Ransom declares, "English might almost as well announce that it does not regard itself as entirely autonomous, but as a branch of the department of history, with the option of declaring itself occasionally a branch of the department of ethics" (335).

29. Eliot famously defends her aesthetic practices in the seventeenth chapter of *Adam Bede* 265–278.
30. Joyce's critique of Gates over the course of two separate essays includes all of these characterizations of deconstruction. See "Black Canon" 339–340, 342; and "'Who the Cap Fit'" 373, 378–379.
31. See, for instance, Gates, "'What's Love?'" 351.
32. See Gates, "Editor's Introduction" 3–4.
33. See Gates, *Figures* 28, 33, 39. Gates notes that the Black Arts movement actually asserts the same position as William Dean Howells, who once wrote, "I have sometimes fancied that perhaps the negroes *thought* black, and *felt* black: that they were racially so utterly alien and distinct from ourselves that there never could be common intellectual and emotional ground between us, and that whatever eternity might do to reconcile us, the end of time would find us far asunder as ever" (qtd. in Gates, *Figures* 22–23). Gates is quoting from Howells, "Majors and Minors" 630.
34. In *Of Grammatology*'s opening paragraph, Derrida famously identifies his enemies: "This triple exergue is intended not only to focus attention on the *ethnocentrism* which, everywhere and always, had controlled the concept of writing. Nor merely to focus attention on what I shall call *logocentrism*" (1).
35. Gates clearly feels particularly hamstrung by conceptions of blackness put forward by the Black Aesthetic movement. He observes, "If my analysis of the tautological dead end of their theories of black literature was accurate, then I felt that I could use non-black theories to detour, or step around, a position about black criticism that held no promise for my work" (*Figures* xxviii).
36. In *Social Formalism*, Dorothy Hale argues that Gates's emphasis on hearing the voices of black culture registers the influence of formalist Bakhtinian novel theory. See *Social Formalism* 199, 222–225. She observes, "The attempt to derive a theory of minority self-empowerment from an aesthetic tradition results not in a politicization of the aesthetic but in an aestheticization of the political" (222).
37. He credits Hartman with inspiring the book in the preface (ix).
38. Explaining how black people have actually signified on the very term *signifier*, Gates writes, "To revise the received sign (quotient) literally accounted for in the relation represented by *signified/signifier* at its most apparently denotative level is to critique the nature of (white) meaning itself, to challenge through a literal critique of the sign the meaning of meaning" (*Signifying Monkey* 47). Gates makes it clear that he is engaged in a similar kind of signifying when he observes, "This is the challenge of the critic of black literature in the 1980s: not to shy away from literary theory; rather, to translate it into the black idiom, *renaming* principles of criticism where appropriate, but especially *naming* indigenous black principles of criticism and applying these to explicate our own texts" ("'What's Love?'" 352).
39. For a careful argument for why there can be no necessary relationship between a particular aesthetic strategy and a particular mode of feminist poli-

tics, see Felski, *Beyond Feminist Aesthetics*. She reiterates this position in *Uses of Literature*, arguing that "political function cannot be deduced or derived from literary structure" (9.

CHAPTER 3 ❦ New Historicism and the Aesthetics of the Archive

1. Catherine Gallagher contends, "The new historicist, unlike the Marxist, is under no nominal compulsion to achieve consistency" ("Marxism" 46). Explaining the New Historicist method in *Learning to Curse*, Stephen Greenblatt writes, "But I am reluctant to confer upon any of these rubrics the air of doctrine or to claim that each marks out a quite distinct and well-bounded territory" (3).
2. For useful discussions of the major methodological assumptions of the New Historicists, see Thomas, *New Historicism*, and Veeser, *New Historicism*. Several essays in the latter volume offer a good summary of New Historicism, including Veeser's introduction; Greenblatt, "Toward a Poetics"; Gallagher, "Marxism"; and Fox-Genovese, "Literary Criticism." See also Greenblatt, *Representing*.
3. Joel Fineman and Brook Thomas both note that the very name New Historicism is designed to suggest a departure from New Criticism. See Fineman, "History" 50, and Thomas, "New Historicism" 183–184.
4. As Joseph North observes, New Criticism was no longer even a live target by the time New Historicism emerged (*Literary Criticism* 99). He cites Frank Lentricchia's observation that New Criticism was already "moribund" by 1957 (*After the New Criticism* 4).
5. See Newton, "History as Usual?" 153–154, and Porter, "Are We?" (1990) 30. In fact, Greenblatt and Gallagher acknowledge that feminist criticism cleared the way for New Historicism (*Practicing* 11).
6. Lentricchia offers a good summation of the multiple differences between New Historicism and old historicism in "Foucault's Legacy—A New Historicism?"
7. Stanley Fish offers a comedic analysis of a passage by a New Historicist (Jon Klancher) to show how perversely committed this school of criticism is to underscoring the shifting, unstable character of the things it describes:

> English Romantic writings are barely mentioned before they are said to be "staged," i.e. not there for our empirical observation, but visible only against a set of background circumstances that must be the new object of our attention; but before those circumstances are enumerated they are declared to be "unstable" and also an "ensemble" (not one particular thing); and then this instability itself is said to be "in crisis," but in a crisis that is only "emerging" (not yet palpable); and this entire staged, unstable, emerging and "ensembling" crisis is said to put pressure on "any act of cultural production." At this point it looks, alarmingly, as if there is actually going to be a reference to such an act, but anything so specific quickly disappears under a list of the

"institutional events" through which "it" is mediated; and finally, lest we carry away too precise a sense of those events (even from such large formulas as "the new media" and "radical dissent") they are given one more kaleidoscopic turn by the phrase "shifting modes." The question is, how long can one go on in *this* shifting mode? ("Young" 311–312)

8. Caroline Levine has also observed how historicist critics treat history like an aesthetic object. "Like the tidy art works beloved of the New Critics, historical periods operate as constructed wholes that give intelligible shape to complex cultural materials, enabling us to grasp significant interrelationships among their parts" (*Forms* 55). But she stops short of recognizing the degree to which the constructions of history forwarded by such scholars adhere to the particular aesthetic criteria championed by the New Critics and the deconstructionists.

9. Discussing the pleasures of earlier forms of literary historicism in the eighteenth century, Deirdre Lynch underscores the need to recognize the "particular—adamantly particularized—pleasures of laboriously recovered, recondite information" (*Loving Literature* 77)—a phrase that could easily describe the appeal of New Historicism.

10. See White, "New Historicism" 299; Pecora, "Limits" 270; and Liu, "Power of Formalism" 744.

11. Gallagher produces a similar interpretation in *Nobody's Story*, where the complexities of copyright laws and eighteenth-century conceptions of debt parallel and provoke complexities in the various eighteenth-century English novels that she considers.

12. Recognizing a similar moment of illogic in the desire to speak to the dead, Pieter Vermeulen argues that Greenblatt recognizes the impossibility of recovering the past, but this awareness allows him to make the engagement with history into a source of melancholy ("Greenblatt's Melancholy Fetish").

13. Christopher Lane argues that New Historicism is also not especially effective at handling literary works that resist mimeticism ("Poverty of Context"). Kevis Bea Goodman notes its overemphasis on reference to the exclusion of any concern for formal or aesthetic modifications of the material being explored ("Making Time"). In a similar vein, Laurence Lerner contends that New Historicists are not adept at handling certain formal patterns at work, for instance, in pastoral texts, which are motivated by long-standing genre conventions ("Against Historicism").

14. Dorothy Hale has noted how the historical turn has led to a privileging of novelistic form. She writes, "'Depriving' the literary object as such has only raised the stock of novels generally, making not just the 'literary' novel but any novel at all an object of serious critical attention. The novel seems to be revenging itself on the academy" (*Social Formalism* 4).

15. In Walter Benn Michaels's *The Gold Standard*, a book he produced while still in his New Historicist phase, money is an aesthetic object in its own right. Though he refuses to allow that great authors or their works might

occupy a place both within and opposed to capitalism, since such a position would be contradictory, he is eager to attribute to money the capacity for self-contradiction that he denies to literature, treating the latter as the truly complex phenomenon, the one worthy of fascination: "If money, by definition, is the desire for money, then money can never quite be itself" (34). Moreover, he takes very seriously the proposition suggested by several authors, including Henry James and H. G. Wells, that the love of money may represent the defining form of aesthetic appreciation: "Grounding the economic in the aesthetic, both writers imagine that our response to money is virtually physiological, on the order of our natural response to beauty" (155).

16. See Ransom, *New Criticism* 25, 85, 163, 174, 188, 190, 219.

17. See Kolodny, "Map for Rereading," 451.

18. Geoffrey Galt Harpham articulates this trend succinctly: "The paradoxical circumstance of trying to control the uncontrollable is played out in the New Historicism, whose central internal theoretical debate reproduces the question of 'containment' or 'subversion': the New Historicism insistently raises the question of whether dominant forces in culture are essentially totalizing, producing their own preco-opted subversions, or whether culture's power is incomplete and vulnerable to genuine destabilization" ("Foucault" 360).

19. Several scholars have noted the ahistorical character of this pattern. Edward Pechter argues, "What I am claiming, however, is that the histories being recovered are themselves transcendental signifieds (or sometimes, perhaps, transcendental ways of signifying) in the sense that their capacity to explain seems independent of many particulars" ("New Historicism" 298). Dimock, as we have seen, complains that they emphasize the synchronic patterns of history to the detriment of diachronic tendencies. See "Theory of Resonance" and "Feminism." See also Simpson, "Literary Criticism."

20. Numerous scholars have noted this consequence of the resistance/ co-optation paradigm. See, for instance, Liu, "New Historicism"; Eagleton, "Historian as Body-Snatcher"; Porter, "History"; and Jehlen, "Story of History."

21. See Tompkins, *Sensational Designs.*

22. For detailed descriptions of these developments, see Aronowitz, *Knowledge Factory*; Washburn, *University, Inc.*; Kirp, *Shakespeare, Einstein, and the Bottom Line*; Donogue, *Last Professors*; Cary Nelson, *No University*; Newfield, *Unmaking the Public University*; Bousquet, *How the University Works*; and G. Jay, "Hire Ed!"

23. As Aronowitz notes, between 1945 and 1960, the student population tripled (*Knowledge Factory* 3). A majority of college students today, he argues, "have little idea what they want to 'study.' In most cases, their choices of major and minor fields are informed (no, dictated) by a rudimentary understanding of the nature of the job market rather than by intellectual curiosity, let alone intellectual passion" (10). According to Donogue, "For several decades now, the college student population has been changing in significant ways, both demographically and ideologically. Though one can debate the factors prompting this change, the result is a cadre of students who both approach

college with more pragmatic aims and who are more willing to integrate the college experience into their work lives. We in the humanities have been losing students to other, occupation-oriented disciplines for a long time" (*Last Professors* 87). For descriptions of the administrative pressure to produce useful or marketable forms of knowledge, see Readings, *University in Ruins* 21–43; Bok, *Universities*; Kirp, *Shakespeare, Einstein, and the Bottom Line*; and Washburn, *University, Inc.*

24. For a description of the impact of Bayh-Dole on higher education, see Washburn, *University, Inc.* 59–70.

25. See Readings, *University in Ruins*; Aronowitz, *Knowledge Factory*; Washburn, *University, Inc.*; Kirp, *Shakespeare, Einstein, and the Bottom Line*; and North, *Literary Criticism*.

26. For a comprehensive collection of reports and interpretations from the Berkeley student revolt, see Lipset and Wolin, *Berkeley Student Revolt*.

27. See Newton, "History as Usual?" 153; Liu, "Power of Formalism" 745–748; and Thomas, *New Historicism* 41.

28. In "Surface Reading," Stephen Best and Sharon Marcus make a similar claim about the self-validating role of ideological critique as practiced by Jameson, arguing that it "presented professional literary criticism as a strenuous and heroic endeavor, one more akin to activism and labor than to leisure, and therefore fully deserving of remuneration" (6).

29. In a similar vein, Simon During has argued that literary criticism's residual conservativism might serve as a bulwark against the university's neoliberal turn, arguing that certain experiences promoted by the discipline represent "conservative storehouses for resistances to come" (*Against Democracy* 49).

CHAPTER 4   ◉   *Lolita* and the Stakes of Form

1. For New Critical readings, see Proffer, *Keys*; Rowe, *Nabokov's Deceptive World*; Stegner, *Escape into Aesthetics*; and Josipovici, "*Lolita*." For deconstructive readings, see Packman, *Vladimir Nabokov*; Bruss, "*Lolita*," in *Victims* 52–67; Ciancio, "Nabokov"; and Fraysse, "Worlds under Erasure." For New Historical readings, see Anderson, "Nabokov's Genocidal and Nuclear Holocausts"; Bowlby, "*Lolita*"; Mizruchi, "*Lolita* in History"; Whiting, "Strange Particularity"; and Brand, "Interaction of Aestheticism."

2. John Hollander, for instance, writes in *The Partisan Review*, "*Lolita*, if it is anything, 'really,' is the record of Nabokov's love affair with the romantic novel" ("Perilous Magic" 560). For a history of *Lolita*'s early reception, see de la Durantaye, *Style Is Matter* 15–17.

3. See Packman, *Vladimir Nabokov*; Bruss, "*Lolita*," in *Victims* 52–67; and Bader, *Crystal Land*.

4. For feminist readings of *Lolita*, see Kennedy, "White Man's Guest"; Kauffman, "Framing Lolita"; and Herbold, "Reflections on Modernism."

5. For other examples of misgivings about formalism in the early criticism, see Merrill, "Nabokov"; Rackin, "Moral Rhetoric"; Mitchell, "Mythic Seriousness"; M. Green, "Morality of Lolita"; and Harold, "*Lolita*."

6. At the end of his introduction, Appel repeats the phrase, maintaining that "the various 'levels' of Lolita are of course not the New Criticism's 'levels of meaning'" (lxxi).

7. Colin McGinn, who writes, "There is a light coating of the academy all over Lolita," is the only other critic to give this aspect of the novel any prominence ("Meaning and Morality" 31).

8. Scholars have not generally focused on Humbert's weakness. One notable exception is Andrew Hoberek, who reads Humbert as a representation of the postwar American "organization man"—a figure circumscribed by social norms and bureaucratic structures (Twilight 27–30).

9. For discussions of postwar middlebrow culture, see Rubin, Making, and Radway, Feeling for Books. Nabokov famously invented a derisory term to describe the tastes of middlebrow Americans: "poshlost." See Nabokov, interview by Herbert Gold (Strong Opinions 100–101).

10. In his Lectures on Literature, Nabokov declares, "A wise reader reads the book of genius not with his heart, not so much with his brain, but with his spine" (6). Nabokov makes this kind of remark in several different places. For a careful cataloging of all of them, see de la Durantaye, Style Is Matter 58.

11. Nabokov has made statements to this effect in many places. He observes, for instance, in an interview with Alvin Toffler,

> A work of art has no importance whatever to society. It is only important to the individual, and only the individual reader is important to me. I don't give a damn for the group, the community, the masses, and so forth. Although I do not care for the slogan "art for art's sake"—because unfortunately such promoters of it as, for instance, Oscar Wilde and various dainty poets, were in reality rank moralists and didacticists—there can be no question that what makes a work of fiction safe from larvae and rust is not its social importance but its art, only its art. (Strong Opinions 33)

Though he zeroes in on fiction at the end of this remark, he is clearly referring to works of art in general—all of which, in his view, perform the same function. He certainly makes no distinction between the purpose of fiction and that of poetry, referring in an interview with Alden Whitman for the New York Times to the "spinal twinge" as "the only valid reaction to a new piece of great poetry" (Strong Opinions 134).

12. See Brand, "Interaction of Aestheticism"; Winston, "Lolita"; R. Levine, "My Ultraviolet Darling"; Fowler, Reading Lolita; Jehlen, "Lolita"; and Blum, "Nabokov's Lolita," in Hide and Seek 201–245.

13. See Brand, "Interaction of Aestheticism"; Winston, "Lolita"; P. Levine, "Lolita"; Fowler, Reading Lolita; de la Durantaye, "Eichmann" and Style Is Matter; C. Williams, "Nabokov's Dialectical Structure"; Pifer, Nabokov; and Bullock, "Humbert the Character."

14. See Rorty, "The Barber of Kasbeam," in Contingency 141–168.

15. For critics who argue that Humbert elicits identification or sympathy, see Trilling, "Last Lover"; Booth, Rhetoric of Fiction 365–366; Fowler, Reading

Lolita; Phelan, "Estranging Unreliability"; Eylon, "Understand All"; Tamir-Ghez, "Art of Persuasion"; and Toker, *Nabokov.*

16. See Kauffman, "Framing Lolita"; Kennedy, "White Man's Guest"; and Harad, "Reviving Lolita."

17. As C. Namwali Serpell puts it, "Linking murder to style, the novel conjoins a question of morality to a question of form" (*Seven Modes* 1).

18. See Benson, "Augustinian Evil"; Rodgers, "*Lolita*'s Nietzschean Morality"; Phelan, "Estranging Unreliability"; Hustis, "Time Will Tell"; de la Durantaye, *Style Is Matter;* Eylon, "Understand All"; Nyegaard, "Poshlust and High Art"; Shelton, "'The Word Is Incest'"; Herbold, "Reflections on Modernism"; Rothstein, "*Lolita*"; Schweighauser, "Metafiction"; P. Levine, "*Lolita*"; de Vries, "'Perplex'd'"; Wood, "*Lolita* Revisited"; Tamir-Ghez, "Art of Persuasion"; Winston, "*Lolita*"; Appel, introduction; Toker, *Nabokov;* O'Rourke, "From Seduction to Fantasy," in *Sex* 167–190; R. Levine, "'My Ultraviolet Darling'"; McGinn, "Meaning and Morality"; Karshan, "Vladimir Nabokov's *Lolita*"; Pifer, *Nabokov;* Alexandrov, *Nabokov's Otherworld;* Harold, "*Lolita*"; Dawson, "Rare and Unfamiliar Things"; and Rackin, "Moral Rhetoric."

19. See, for instance, Rodgers, "*Lolita*'s Nietzschean Morality"; Hustis, "Time Will Tell"; Eylon, "Understand All"; Nyegaard, "Poshlust and High Art"; Rorty, "The Barber of Kasbeam," in *Contingency* 141–168; Wood, "*Lolita* Revisited"; McNeely, "'Lo' and Behold"; Tamir-Ghez, "Art of Persuasion"; de la Durantaye, *Style Is Matter;* Pifer, *Nabokov;* and Kennedy, "White Man's Guest."

20. See Toker, *Nabokov* 200; Trilling, "Last Lover"; and Booth, *Rhetoric of Fiction* 391.

21. See, for instance, de la Durantaye, "Eichmann"; Rorty, "The Barber of Kasbeam," in *Contingency* 141–168; Rodgers, "*Lolita*'s Nietzschean Morality"; Eylon, "Understand All"; Kauffman, "Framing Lolita"; and Rackin, "Moral Rhetoric."

22. This is what Nabokov seems to be getting at when he observes in his afterword, "I am neither a reader nor a writer of didactic fiction, and, despite John Ray's assertion, *Lolita* has no moral in tow" (*Annotated Lolita* 316).

23. See, for instance, Appel, "Springboard"; Dolinin, "Nabokov's Time Doubling"; de la Durantaye, *Style Is Matter* 76–77; and Frosch, "Parody and Authenticity."

24. Critics who read *Lolita* as serving some ethical purpose include Benson, "Augustinian Evil"; Rodgers, "*Lolita*'s Nietzschean Morality"; Walker, "Nabokov's *Lolita*"; de la Durantaye, *Style Is Matter;* Eylon, "Understand All"; Nyegaard, "Poshlust and High Art"; Rothstein, "*Lolita*"; Schweighauser, "Metafiction"; P. Levine, "*Lolita*"; de Vries, "'Perplex'd'"; Brand, "Interaction of Aestheticism"; Bullock, "Humbert the Character"; Connolly, "'Nature's Reality'"; Tamir-Ghez, "Art of Persuasion"; Toker, *Nabokov;* Stegner, *Escape into Aesthetics;* Jehlen, "*Lolita*"; C. Williams, "Nabokov's Dialectical Structure"; Pifer, *Nabokov;* Clifton, "Humbert"; Maddox, *Nabokov's Novels;* Seiden, "Nabokov and Dostoyevsky"; Dawson, "Rare and Unfamiliar Things"; Nemerov, "Review"; McGinn, "Meaning and Morality"; Alexandrov,

Nabokov's Otherworld; and Field, *Nabokov.* The number of those who read the book as purely aesthetic or removed from moral concerns is significantly smaller. It includes Tweedie, *"Lolita's* Loose Ends"; S. Butler, *"Lolita";* Bader, *Crystal Land;* Bruss, *"Lolita,"* in *Victims* 52–67; and Packman, *Vladimir Nabokov.*

25. Serpell observes that for early critics of the book, such as Lionel Trilling, "ambiguity . . . had become an unquestioned index of ethical value" (*Seven Modes* 13).

26. Very few scholars have viewed Humbert as an example of a paranoid reader. One who does make the connection is Fraysse in "Worlds under Erasure."

27. The most famous example is Appel's reading in his introduction. See also Proffer, *Keys;* Widiss, *Obscure Invitations;* Jehlen, *"Lolita";* Bader, *Crystal Land;* and Bruss, *"Lolita,"* in *Victims* 52–67.

28. Felski also remarks, "The hermeneutics of suspicion, in short, offers the promise of pleasure as well as knowledge" (*Limits of Critique* 108). Her insight echoes Eve Sedgwick's analysis of how the hermeneutics of suspicion can promote aesthetic pleasure. Sedgwick notes that D. A. Miller's paranoid reading style mobilizes "a wealth of tonal nuance, attitude, worldly observation, performative paradox, aggression, tenderness, wit, inventive reading, *obiter dicta,* and writerly panache," showing how "an insistence that everything means one thing somehow permits a sharpened sense of all the ways there are of meaning it" ("Paranoid Reading" 14).

29. See, especially, Wimsatt, "Affective Fallacy," in *Verbal Icon* 21–39. John Crowe Ransom offers a fairly extreme version of this position, claiming, "When you think of a thing as the cause of something else, you waive interest in it for itself" (*New Criticism* 15).

30. A large part of Felski's *The Limits of Critique* is dedicated to explaining why paranoid styles of interpretation are so appealing.

CHAPTER 5   ⊛   Why Is *Beloved* So Universally Beloved?

1. The most obvious example is the collection, edited by Marc C. Conner, *The Aesthetics of Toni Morrison.*

2. Angeletta KM Gourdine also raises this question. She writes, "Furthermore, I realized that I could not reconcile how *Beloved* could be so beloved when Beloved resists such affection; in fact, she vehemently articulates disaffection" ("Hearing Reading" 14).

3. See, for instance, Bowers, *"Beloved";* Sale, "Call and Response"; Christian, "Fixing Methodologies"; Khayati, "Representation"; Brivic, "American African Postmodernism in *Beloved,"* in *Tears of Rage* 144–192; and Harris, *Fiction and Folklore.*

4. See, for instance, Bell, *"Beloved";* Parrish, "Off Faulkner's Plantation," in *From the Civil War* 117–149; Davis, "'Postmodern Blackness'"; and Pérez-Torres, "Knitting and Knotting."

5. *Beloved* won the Pulitzer Prize, and Morrison won the Nobel Prize for Literature in 1993. In response to a 2006 survey put out by *New York Times*

Book Review editor Sam Tanenhaus, hundreds of writers, critics, and editors voted *Beloved* "the single best work of American fiction published in the last 25 years" ("What Is the Best Work?")

6. See, for instance, Henderson, "Toni Morrison's *Beloved*" 81.

7. C. Namwali Serpell also celebrates *Beloved* for its uncertainty, but she rejects the conclusion that this feature entails passivity or ethical quiescence. "Attention to literary uncertainty ought not paralyze us so completely" (*Seven Modes* 131). She has a point. As I have been suggesting throughout this book, there is no necessary, transhistorical link between particular aesthetic experiences and particular political or social dispositions or actions. That said, undecidability is a somewhat odd choice for scholars interested in underscoring the political efficacy of literary works, insofar as it seems unlikely to lend support for concrete political goals and can function as a mode of effective resistance only within specific political contexts. Thus it is my contention that, notwithstanding their justifications, many scholars are attracted to ambiguity, irony, and uncertainty for other reasons, namely for the aesthetic pleasure they generate.

8. See "Apostrophe, Animation, and Abortion," in *World of Difference* 184–200.

9. See, for instance, Rody, "Toni Morrison's *Beloved*"; Barnett, "Figurations of Rape"; Grewal, *Circles of Sorrow*; Horvitz, "Nameless Ghosts"; Rigney, "'Breaking the Back'" and *Voices*; Kreyling, "'Slave Life'"; and Christian, "Fixing Methodologies."

10. See the discussion in Chapter 3, as well as Ransom, *New Criticism* 25, 85, 163, 174, 188, 190, 219.

11. For a few examples, see Krumholz, "Ghosts of Slavery"; Rody, "Toni Morrison's *Beloved*"; Barnett, "Figurations of Rape"; Horvitz, "Nameless Ghosts"; Carden, "Models of Memory"; and Fultz, *Toni Morrison*.

12. See, for instance, Bowers, "*Beloved*"; Lawrence, "Fleshly Ghosts"; Grewal, *Circles of Sorrow*; Krumholz, "Ghosts of Slavery"; and Bouson, *Quiet as It's Kept*. Serpell has also noted the tendency of scholars to domesticate *Beloved*'s uncertainty so as to enlist the book in an unambiguous ethical or political project (*Seven Modes* 119–120).

13. See, for instance, Peterson, "The (Im)Possibility of Historical Recovery in *Beloved*," in *Against Amnesia* 60–69; Jesser, "Violence"; Krumholz, "Ghosts of Slavery"; Heinze, *Dilemma of "Double Consciousness"*; Ramadanovic, "'You Your Best Thing'"; Victoria Smith, "Generative Melancholy"; and Raynaud, "Poetics of Abjection." Dean Franco offers a useful summation and critique of the psychoanalytic responses to *Beloved* in "What We Talk about When We Talk about *Beloved*."

14. Such attempts at yoking the deconstructive and the ethical have been fairly numerous. Psychoanalytic critics, for instance, often suggest that the healing process remains incomplete, as the specter of Beloved, symbolizing the repressed traumatic aftermath of slavery, returns to haunt the final pages of the book, thus complicating any clear recipe for psychological healing. See Krumholz, "Ghosts of Slavery"; Bouson, *Quiet as It's Kept*; and Carden, "Models of Memory." And some deconstructionists position the very rejec-

tion of truth—a Western construct in most accounts—as the unequivocal moral of the book and the means of promoting human happiness. See, for instance, Sitter, "Making of a Man." Valerie Smith offers a helpful exploration of the tensions between the poststructuralist and ethical readings of the book ("'Circling the Subject'").

15. Bill Brown offers a powerful reading of postmodern theory in order to identify its postsecular impulses in "The Dark Wood of Postmodernity." See also McClure, *Partial Faiths*.

16. One possibility that Michaels does not consider is that the ghost is a figure for the *desire* to be able to remember slavery and its casualties. As Kathryn Bond Stockton puts it, *"Beloved*, too, offers a count—'60 million and more'—in its dedication. These, like the Holocaust, are inconceivable extensions of meaning, along with lost futures. Which means, in the case of chain-linked death (and slavery was surely always that), we are forced to tame a richness we may never have seen. But how does one regulate an epistemic hunger for bodies that haven't been around to feed it?" ("Prophylactics and Brains" 66).

17. See Wimsatt and Brooks, "Rhetoric and Neo-classic Wit," in *Literary Criticism* 221-251. Whether it is possible to reappropriate the Enlightenment's stylistic ideals, as Michaels appears to, without also supporting the racist taxonomies that it upheld is an important question. For a discussion of Morrison's critical attitude toward Enlightenment rationality, see Tally, *Toni Morrison's "Beloved."* See also Morrison, "Site of Memory." Michaels would suggest that a rejection of multiculturalism and an affirmation of deracinated rationality can produce radical egalitarianism. One might also observe that the embrace of a particular aesthetic need not, at least in practice, entail a specific form of racial politics—a point Michaels, at least in moments, seems to acknowledge.

Conclusion

1. See Felski, *Limits of Critique;* Latour, "Why Has Critique?"; and Sedgwick, "Paranoid Reading."

2. See Love, "Close but Not Deep" 373-374, and Best and Marcus, "Surface Reading" 17.

3. Characterizing prevailing views of literature in the academy today, Felski articulates what unites aesthetic and political modes of interpretation as follows: "The literary work enables an encounter with the extraordinary, an imagining of the impossible, an openness to pure otherness, that is equipped with momentous political implications" (*Uses of Literature* 5).

4. See, for instance, Rooney, "Live Free"; Bartolovich, "Humanities of Scale"; Grusin, "Dark Side"; and Allington et al., "Neoliberal Tools."

5. Jennifer Fleissner has also noted the indebtedness of surface reading to the methodology its proponents claim to be rejecting, observing, "It is striking, then, to note the degree to which the essays in the issue [the 2009 special issue of *Representations*], despite the ritual denunciations of Jameson, in fact retain a historicist framework—indeed, the degree to which they might even be said to *hyperbolize* it" ("Historicism Blues" 700).

6. Disputing the position forwarded by Felski, C. Namwali Serpell argues that we have not come close to exhausting the possibilities of ambiguity or what she terms "uncertainty." The problem, she avers, is that we have reduced literary uncertainty to a limited and predictable set of effects. (*Seven Modes* 7, 20). While Serpell's readings persuasively demonstrate the need to revisit ambiguity so as to broaden our sense of its possibilities, her argument should not prevent us from also looking beyond the family of aesthetic devices denoted by this category to consider entirely different devices and rhetorical strategies.

7. See especially Serpell, *Seven Modes of Uncertainty*; D. A. Miller, *Jane Austen*; James, "Critical Solace"; Eccles, "Formalism and Sentimentalism"; Ferguson, "Jane Austen"; Ngai, *Our Aesthetic Categories*; and Bogel, *New Formalist Criticism*.

8. For the results of this research, see Stanford Literary Lab, "Pamphlets."

9. N. Katherine Hayles lauds the digital humanities for just this reason, noting that it offers useful training for work in our media-saturated world (*How We Think* 10).

10. Thus far, the Stanford Literary Lab has been relatively inseparable from Franco Moretti's outsize personality, despite its emphasis on collaboration. His distinctive voice is ubiquitous in the early pamphlets, and he is the sole author of four of the first sixteen pamphlets that the lab has produced. Thus his essays are useful as one attempt to articulate what digital humanities research has accomplished so far and to predict how it might change the discipline in the years to come. Already an emeritus professor, he may now disappear from view, particularly with the emergence of several allegations of rape and sexual harassment against him as reported by the *Stanford Daily* and the *Chronicle of Higher Education*. See Fangzhou Liu and Hannah Knowles, "Harassment"; Mangan, "Two Women Say."

11. As Nicholas Gaskill puts it, "[The New Critics'] entire project turned on the belief that aesthetic objects and scientific objects were radically different sorts of phenomena that could only be grasped through radically different methods" ("Close and the Concrete" 506).

12. Leah Price makes a similar observation: "Where the humanistic social sciences once borrowed literary-critical tricks to interpret nontextual objects, literary critics today mine other disciplines—bibliography, history of science, even archaeology—for a vocabulary in which to describe the nontextual aspects of a particular category of material object: books. Instead of 'reading'" sewer systems, critics now smell leather bindings" ("From the *History of a Book* to a 'History of the Book'" 121).

13. For Kant's definition of the "quantitatively sublime,"see *Critique of Judgment*, 103–106.

14. As Moretti puts it in an interview with Melissa Dinsman, "Somehow digital humanities has managed to secure for itself this endless infancy, in which, it is always a future promise" (Dinsman, "Digital").

15. Moretti makes the lab's adversarial relationship to meaning explicit, remarking: "Now, meaning is not one of the things literary critics study; it is

the thing. Here lies the great challenge of computational criticism: thinking about literature, removing meaning to the periphery of the picture" ("Patterns" 2).

16. They share this belief in the value of failure with the larger community of digital humanities scholars. As Lisa Spiro puts it, "Failure is accepted as a useful result in the digital humanities, since it indicates that the experiment was likely high risk and means that we collectively learn from failure rather than reproducing it (assuming that the failure is documented)" ("'This Is Why'" 29).

17. For a suggestive analysis of how the aesthetic dimensions of contemporary literature can serve as a consolation for the bleak political realities that it depicts, see James, "Critical Solace."

Works Cited

Abel, Darrel. "Intellectual Criticism." *American Scholar* 12 (1943): 414–428.

Abrams, M. H. "The Deconstructive Angel." *Critical Inquiry* 3 (1977): 425–438.

Alexandrov, Vladimir E. *Nabokov's Otherworld.* Princeton, NJ: Princeton University Press, 1991.

Algee-Hewitt, Mark, Sarah Allison, Marissa Gemma, Ryan Heuser, Franco Moretti, and Hannah Walser. "Canon / Archive: Large-Scale Dynamics in the Literary Field." *Stanford Literary Lab*, pamphlet 11 (2016): 1–13. https://litlab.stanford.edu/LiteraryLabPamphlet11.pdf.

Algee-Hewitt, Mark, Ryan Heuser, and Franco Moretti. "On Paragraphs. Scales, Themes, and Narrative Form." *Stanford Literary Lab*, pamphlet 10 (2015): 1–22. https://litlab.stanford.edu/LiteraryLabPamphlet10.pdf.

Algee-Hewitt, Mark, and Mark McGurl "Between Canon and Corpus: Six Perspectives on 20th-Century Novels." *Stanford Literary Lab*, pamphlet 8 (2015): 1–27. https://litlab.stanford.edu/LiteraryLabPamphlet8.pdf.

Allington, Daniel, Sarah Brouillette, and David Golumbia. "Neoliberal Tools (and Archives): A Political History of Digital Humanities." *Los Angeles Review of Books*, May 1, 2016. https://lareviewofbooks.org/article /neoliberal-tools-archives-political-history-digital-humanities.

Allison, Sarah, Marissa Gemma, Ryan Heuser, Franco Moretti, Amir Tevel, and Irena Yamboliev. "Style at the Scale of the Sentence." *Stanford Literary Lab*, pamphlet 5 (2013): 1–29. https://litlab.stanford.edu /LiteraryLabPamphlet5.pdf.

Allison, Sarah, Ryan Heuser, Matthew Jockers, Franco Moretti, and Michael Witmore. "Quantitative Formalism: An Experiment." *Stanford Literary Lab*, pamphlet 1 (2011): 1–27. https://litlab.stanford.edu /LiteraryLabPamphlet1.pdf.

Anderson, Douglas. "Nabokov's Genocidal and Nuclear Holocausts in *Lolita*." *Mosaic: A Journal for the Interdisciplinary Study of Literature* 29 (1996): 73–90.

Appel, Alfred, Jr. Introduction to Nabokov, *Annotated Lolita*, xv–lxxi.

———. "The Springboard of Parody." *Wisconsin Journal of Contemporary Literature* 8 (1967): 204–241.

Arac, Jonathan, Wlad Godzich, and Wallace Martin, eds. *The Yale Critics: Deconstruction in America*. Minneapolis: University of Minnesota Press, 1983.

Armstrong, Isobel. *The Radical Aesthetic*. Oxford: Blackwell, 2000.

Aronowitz, Stanley. *The Knowledge Factory: Dismantling the Corporate University and Creating True Higher Learning*. Boston: Beacon, 2000.

Attridge, Derek. *Reading and Responsibility: Deconstruction's Traces*. Edinburgh: Edinburgh University Press, 2010.

Bader, Julia. *Crystal Land: Artifice in Nabokov's English Novels*. Berkeley: University of California Press, 1972.

Barnett, Pamela E. "Figurations of Rape and the Supernatural in *Beloved*." *PMLA* 112 (1997): 418–427.

Barrett, William, Kenneth Burke, Malcolm Cowley, Robert Gorham Davis, and Hiram Haydn. "American Scholar Forum: The New Criticism." *American Scholar* 20 (1950–1951): 86–104.

Barthes, Roland. *Image, Music, Text*. Translated by Stephen Heath. New York: Hill and Wang, 1978.

———. *The Pleasure of the Text*. Translated by Richard Miller. New York: Hill and Wang, 1975.

———. *Sade, Fourier, Loyola*. Translated by Richard Miller. New York: Hill and Wang, 1976.

Bartolovich, Krystal. "Humanities of Scale: Marxism, Surface Reading—and Milton." *PMLA* 127 (2012): 115–121.

Baumgarten, Alexander Gottlieb. *Reflections on Poetry*. Translated by Karl Aschenbrenner and William B. Holther. Berkeley: University of California Press, 1954.

Bell, Bernard W. "*Beloved*: A Womanist Neo-slave Narrative; or Multivocal Remembrances of Things Past." *African American Review* 26 (1992): 7–15.

Bennett, Jane. *Vibrant Matter: A Political Ecology of Things*. Durham, NC: Duke University Press, 2010.

Benson, Sean. "Augustinian Evil and Moral Good in *Lolita*." *Renascence: Essays on Values in Literature* 64 (2012): 353–367.

Berger, James. "Ghosts of Liberalism: Morrison's *Beloved* and the Moynihan Report." *PMLA* 111 (1996): 408–420.

Berlant, Lauren. *The Female Complaint*. Durham, NC: Duke University Press, 2008.

Berlant, Lauren, and Michael Warner. "Sex in Public." *Critical Inquiry* 24 (1998): 547–566.

Berle, Adolf A., and Gardiner C. Means. *The Modern Corporation and Private Property*. New York: Harcourt, 1932.

Berlin, James A. *Rhetoric and Reality: Writing Instruction in American Colleges, 1900–1985*. Carbondale, IL: Southern Illinois University Press, 1987.

Berman, Art. *From New Criticism to Deconstruction: The Reception of Structuralism and Post-Structuralism*. Urbana: University of Illinois Press, 1988.

Bersani, Leo. "Psychoanalysis and the Aesthetic Subject." *Critical Inquiry* 32 (2006): 161–174.

Bérubé, Michael. *Employment of English: Theory, Jobs, and the Future of Literary Studies*. New York: New York University Press, 1997.

Best, Stephen, and Sharon Marcus. "Surface Reading: An Introduction." *Representations* 108 (2009): 1–21.

———, eds. "The Way We Read Now." Special issue, *Representations* 108 (2009).

Bhabha, Homi. *The Location of Culture*. New York: Routledge, 1994.

Bloom, Harold, Paul de Man, Jacques Derrida, Geoffrey Hartman, and J. Hillis Miller. *Deconstruction and Criticism*. New York: Seabury, 1979.

Blum, Virginia L. *Hide and Seek: The Child between Psychoanalysis and Fiction*. Champaign: University of Illinois Press, 1995.

Bogel, Fredric. *New Formalist Criticism*. Basingstoke, UK: Palgrave, 2013.

Bok, Derek. *Higher Education in America*. Princeton, NJ: Princeton University Press, 2013.

———. *Universities in the Marketplace: The Commercialization of Higher Education*. Princeton, NJ: Princeton University Press, 2003.

Booth, Wayne C. "'Preserving the Exemplar': or, How Not to Dig Our Own Graves." *Critical Inquiry* 3 (1977): 407–423.

———. *The Rhetoric of Fiction*. 2nd ed. Chicago: University of Chicago Press, 1983.

Bourdieu, Pierre. *Distinction: A Social Critique of the Judgement of Taste*. Translated by Richard Nice. Cambridge, MA: Harvard University Press, 1984.

———. "The Field of Cultural Production, or: The Economic World Reversed." *Poetics* 12 (1983): 311–356.

Bouson, J. Brooks. *Quiet as It's Kept: Shame, Trauma, and Race in the Novels of Toni Morrison*. Albany: State University of New York Press, 2000.

Bousquet, Marc. *How the University Works: Higher Education and the Low-Wage Nation*. New York: New York University Press, 2008.

Bove, Paul A. "Variations on Authority: Some Deconstructive Transformations of the New Criticism." In Arac, Godzich, and Martin, *Yale Critics*, 3–19.

Bowers, Susan. "*Beloved* and the New Apocalypse." *Journal of Ethnic Studies* 18 (1990): 59–77.

Bowlby, Rachel. "*Lolita* and the Poetry of Advertising." *Vladimir Nabokov's "Lolita": A Casebook*, edited by Ellen Pifer, 155–179. Oxford: Oxford University Press, 2003.

Boyer, Ernest L. *Scholarship Reconsidered: Priorities of the Professoriate*. San Francisco: Carnegie Foundation for the Advancement of Teaching, 1990.

Bradbury, John M. *The Fugitives*. Chapel Hill: University of North Carolina Press, 1958.

Brand, Dana. "The Interaction of Aestheticism and American Consumer Culture in Nabokov's *Lolita*." *Modern Language Studies* 17 (1987): 14–21.

Braudel, Fernand. *Capitalism and Material Life, 1400–1800*. Translated by Miriam Kochan. New York: Harper, 1973.

Brint, Steven. *In an Age of Experts: The Changing Role of Professionals in Politics and Public Life*. Princeton, NJ: Princeton University Press, 1994.

Brivic, Shelly. *Tears of Rage: The Racial Interface of Modern American Fiction—Faulkner, Wright, Pynchon, Morrison*. Baton Rouge: Louisiana State University Press, 2008.

Brooks, Cleanth. *Modern Poetry and the Tradition*. Chapel Hill: University of North Carolina Press, 1939.

———. "The New Criticism." *Sewanee Review* 87 (1979): 592–607.

———. *The Well-Wrought Urn: Studies in the Structure of Poetry*. New York: Harcourt, 1947.

Brooks, Cleanth, and Robert Penn Warren. *Understanding Poetry*, 3rd ed. New York: Holt, Rinehart, and Winston, 1960.

Brouillette, Sarah. *Literature and the Creative Economy*. Stanford, CA: Stanford University Press, 2014.

Brown, Bill. "The Dark Wood of Postmodernity (Space, Faith, Allegory)." *PMLA* 120 (2005): 734–750.

Bruss, Paul. *Victims: Textual Strategies in Recent American Fiction*. Lewisburg, PA: Bucknell University Press, 1981.

Bullock, Richard H. "Humbert the Character, Humbert the Writer," *Philological Quarterly* 63 (1984): 187–204.

Burke, Edmund. *On Taste; On the Sublime and the Beautiful; Reflections on the French Revolution; A Letter to a Noble Lord*. New York: P. F. Collier, 1909.

Bush, Douglas. "Marvell's 'Horatian Ode.'" *Sewanee Review* 60 (1952): 363–376.

———. "The New Criticism: Some Old-Fashioned Queries." In supplement, *PMLA* 64, pt. 2 (1949): 13–21.

Butler, Judith. *Gender Trouble: Feminism and the Subversion of Identity*. New York: Routledge, 1990.

Butler, Steven H. "*Lolita* and the Modern Experience of Beauty." *Studies in the Novel* 18 (1986): 427–437.

Buurma, Rachel Sagner, and Laura Heffernan. "The Common Reader and the Archival Classroom: Disciplinary History for the Twenty-First Century." *New Literary History* 43 (2012): 113–135.

Cain, William E. *The Crisis in Criticism: Theory, Literature, and Reform in English Studies.* Baltimore: Johns Hopkins University Press, 1984.

Carden, Mary Paniccia. "Models of Memory and Romance: The Dual Endings of Toni Morrison's *Beloved.*" *Twentieth Century Literature* 45 (1999): 401–427.

Castronovo, Russ, and Christopher Castiglia, eds. "Aesthetics and the End(s) of American Cultural Studies." Special issue, *American Literature* 76 (2004).

Caws, Mary Ann. "Tel Quel: Text and Revolution." *Diacritics* 3 (1973): 2–8.

Chandler, Alfred D. *The Visible Hand: The Managerial Revolution in American Business.* Cambridge, MA: Belknap Press of Harvard University Press, 1977.

Cheng, Anne Anlin. "Skin, Tattoos, and Susceptibility." *Representations* 108 (2009): 98–119.

Christian, Barbara. "Fixing Methodologies: *Beloved.*" *Cultural Critique* 24 (1993): 5–15.

Ciancio, Ralph A. "Nabokov and the Verbal Mode of the Grotesque." *Contemporary Literature* 18 (1977): 509–533.

Clark, Michael P. *Revenge of the Aesthetic: The Place of Literature in Theory Today.* Berkeley: University of California Press, 2000.

Cleaveland, Bradford. "Education, Revolutions, and Citadels." In Lipset and Wolin, *Berkeley Student Revolt*, 81–93.

Clifton, Gladys M. "Humbert Humbert and the Limits of Artistic License." In Rivers and Nicol, *Nabokov's Fifth Arc*, 153–170.

Coleridge, Samuel Taylor. *Biographia Literaria or Biographical Sketches of My Literary Life and Opinions.* London: J. M. Dent, 1906.

Conner, Marc C., ed. *The Aesthetics of Toni Morrison: Speaking the Unspeakable.* Jackson: University of Mississippi Press, 2000.

Connolly, Julian W. "'Nature's Reality' or Humbert's 'Fancy': Scenes of Reunion and Murder in *Lolita.*" *Nabokov Studies* 2 (1995): 41–61.

Crane, R. S. "The Critical Monism of Cleanth Brooks." In Crane, *Critics and Criticism*, 83–107.

———, ed. *Critics and Criticism: Ancient and Modern.* Chicago: University of Chicago Press, 1952.

Culler, Jonathan. *On Deconstruction: Theory and Criticism in the 1970s.* Ithaca, NY: Cornell University Press, 1982.

———. *Structuralist Poetics: Structuralism, Linguistics, and the Study of Literature.* Ithaca, NY: Cornell University Press, 1975.

Cunningham, J. V. *Tradition and Poetic Structure*. Denver: Alan Swallow, 1960.

Cusset, François. *French Theory: How Foucault, Derrida, Deleuze, & Co. Transformed the Intellectual Life of the United States*. Translated by Jeff Fort with Josephine Berganza and Marion Jones. Minneapolis: University of Minnesota Press, 2008.

Davis, Kimberly Chabot. "'Postmodern Blackness': Toni Morrison's *Beloved* and the End of History." *Twentieth Century Literature* 44 (1998): 242–260.

Dawson, Kellie. "Rare and Unfamiliar Things: Vladimir Nabokov's 'Monsters.'" *Nabokov Studies* 9 (2005): 115–131.

De la Durantaye, Leland. "Eichmann, Empathy, and Lolita." *Philosophy and Literature* 30 (2006): 311–328.

———. *Style Is Matter: The Moral Art of Vladimir Nabokov*. Ithaca, NY: Cornell University Press, 2007.

De Man, Paul. *Allegories of Reading: Figural Language in Rousseau, Nietzsche, Rilke, and Proust*. New Haven, CT: Yale University Press, 1979.

———. *Blindness and Insight: Essays in the Rhetoric of Contemporary Criticism*. 2nd, rev. ed. Minneapolis: University of Minnesota Press, 1983.

Derrida, Jacques. "Living On." In Bloom et al., *Deconstruction and Criticism*, 75–176.

———. *Of Grammatology*. Translated by Gayatri Spivak. Baltimore: Johns Hopkins University Press, 1976.

———. "Positions." *Diacritics* 2 (1972): 35–43.

———. "Structure, Sign, and Play in the Discourse of the Human Sciences." In Macksey and Danato, *Structuralist Controversy*, 247–265.

De Vries, Gerard. "'Perplex'd in the Extreme': Moral Facets of Vladimir Nabokov's Work." *Nabokov Studies* 2 (1995): 135–152.

Dimock, Wai-Chee. "Feminism, New Historicism, and the Reader." *American Literature* 63 (1991): 601–622.

———. "A Theory of Resonance." *PMLA* 112 (1997): 1060–1071.

Dinsman, Melissa. "The Digital in the Humanities: An Interview with Franco Moretti." *Los Angeles Review of Books*, March 2, 2016. https://lareviewof books.org/article/the-digital-in-the-humanities-an-interview-with-franco -moretti.

Dolinin, Alexander. "Nabokov's Time Doubling: From *The Gift* to *Lolita*." *Nabokov Studies* 2 (1995): 3–40.

Donogue, Frank. *The Last Professors*. New York: Fordham University Press, 2008.

Dubey, Madhu. "The Politics of Genre in *Beloved*." *Novel* 32 (1999): 187–206.

During, Simon. *Against Democracy: Literary Experience in the Age of Emancipations*. New York: Fordham University Press, 2012.

Eagleton, Terry. *Criticism and Ideology: A Study in Marxist Literary Theory*. London: Verso, 1976.

———. "The Historian as Body-Snatcher." *Times Literary Supplement*, January 18, 1991, 7.

———. *The Ideology of the Aesthetic*. Cambridge, MA: Basil Blackwell, 1990.

———. *Literary Theory: An Introduction*. Minneapolis: University of Minnesota Press, 1983.

Eastman, Max. *The Literary Mind: Its Place in an Age of Science*. New York: Scribner, 1931.

Eccles, Anastasia. "Formalism and Sentimentalism: Victor Schlovsky and Laurence Sterne." *New Literary History* 47 (2016): 525–545.

Edelman, Lee. *No Future: Queer Theory and the Death Drive*. Durham, NC: Duke University Press, 2004.

Eliot, George. *Adam Bede*. Edinburgh: Blackwood, 1877–1880.

Eliot, T. S. "The Metaphysical Poets." In *Selected Prose of T. S. Eliot*, edited by Frank Kermode, 59–67. New York: Harcourt, 1975.

Ellis, John M. *Against Deconstruction* Princeton, NJ: Princeton University Press, 1989.

Empson, William. *Seven Types of Ambiguity*. London: Chatto and Windus, 1930.

Eylon, Yuval. "Understand All, Forgive Nothing: The Self-Indictment of Humbert Humbert." *Philosophy and Literature* 30 (2006): 158–173.

Felski, Rita. *Beyond Feminist Aesthetics: Feminist Literature and Social Change*. Cambridge, MA: Harvard University Press, 1989.

———. *The Limits of Critique*. Chicago: University of Chicago Press, 2015.

———. *Uses of Literature*. Malden, MA: Blackwell, 2008.

Ferguson, Frances. "Jane Austen, *Emma*, and the Impact of Form." *Modern Language Quarterly* 61 (2000): 157–181.

Field, Andrew. *Nabokov, His Life in Art: A Critical Narrative*. Boston: Little, Brown, 1967.

Fineman, Joel. "The History of the Anecdote: Fiction and Fiction." In Veeser, *New Historicism*, 49–76.

Fischer, Michael. *Does Deconstruction Make Any Difference? Poststructuralism and the Defense of Poetry in Modern Criticism*. Bloomington: Indiana University Press, 1985.

Fish, Stanley. "The Young and the Restless." In Veeser, *New Historicism*, 303–316.

Fleissner, Jennifer. "Historicism Blues." *American Literary History* 25 (2013): 699–717.

Fletcher, Angus, and Michael Benveniste. "Defending Pluralism: The Chicago School and the Case of *Tom Jones*." *New Literary History* 41 (2010): 653–667.

Fogle, Richard H. "Romantic Bards and Metaphysical Reviewers." *English Literary History* 12 (1945): 221–250.

Foster, Richard. *The New Romantics: A Reappraisal of the New Criticism.* Bloomington: Indiana University Press, 1962.

Foucault, Michel. *Discipline and Punish: The Birth of the Prison.* Translated by Alan Sheridan. New York: Pantheon, 1977.

Fowler, Douglas. *Reading Lolita.* Ithaca, NY: Cornell University Press, 1974.

Fox-Genovese, Elizabeth. "Literary Criticism and the Politics of The New Historicism." In Veeser, *New Historicism,* 213–224.

Franco, Dean. "What We Talk about When We Talk about *Beloved.*" *Modern Fiction Studies* 52 (2006): 415–439.

Fraysse, Suzanne. "Worlds under Erasure: *Lolita* and Postmodernism." *Cynos* 12 (1995): 93–100.

Frosch, Thomas R. "Parody and Authenticity in *Lolita.*" In Rivers and Nicol, *Nabokov's Fifth Arc,* 171–187.

Fultz, Lucille. *Toni Morrison: Playing with Difference.* Urbana: University of Illinois Press, 2003.

Gallagher, Catherine. "Formalism and Time." In Wolfson and Brown, *Reading for Form,* 305–327.

———. "The History of Literary Criticism." *Daedalus* 126 (1997): 133–153.

———. *The Industrial Reformation of English Fiction: Social Discourse and Narrative Form, 1832–1867.* Chicago: University of Chicago Press, 1985.

———. "Marxism and The New Historicism." In Veeser, *New Historicism,* 37–48.

———. *Nobody's Story: The Vanishing Acts of Women Writers in the Marketplace, 1670–1820.* Berkeley: University of California Press, 1994.

Gaskill, Nicholas. "The Close and the Concrete: Aesthetic Formalism in Context." *New Literary History* 47 (2016): 505–524.

Gates, Henry Louis, Jr. "Editor's Introduction: Writing 'Race' and the Difference It Makes." In *"Race," Writing, and Difference,* edited by Henry Louis Gates Jr., 1–20. Chicago: University of Chicago Press, 1985.

———. *Figures in Black: Words, Signs, and the "Racial" Self.* New York: Oxford University Press, 1987.

———. *The Signifying Monkey: A Theory of African-American Literary Criticism.* New York: Oxford University Press, 1988.

———. "Talkin' That Talk." In *'Race,' Writing, and Difference,* edited by Henry Louis Gates Jr., 402–409. Chicago: University of Chicago Press, 1985.

———. "'What's Love Got to Do with It?': Critical Theory, Integrity, and the Black Idiom." *New Literary History* 18 (1987): 345–362.

Geiger, Roger L. *Research and Relevant Knowledge: American Research Universities since World War II.* New Brunswick, NJ: Transaction, 2004.

Genette, Gérard. *The Aesthetic Relation.* Translated by G. M. Goshgarian. Ithaca, NY: Cornell University Press, 1999.

Glazener, Nancy. *Literature in the Making: A History of U.S. Literary Culture in the Long Nineteenth Century.* New York: Oxford University Press, 2016.

Goodman, Kevis Bea. "Making Time for History: Wordsworth, the New Historicism, and the Apocalyptic Fallacy." *Studies in Romanticism* 35 (1996): 563–577.

Gourdine, Angeletta KM. "Hearing Reading and Being 'Read' by Beloved." *NWSA Journal* 10 (1998): 13–31.

Graff, Gerald. *Literature against Itself: Literary Ideas in Modern Society.* Chicago: University of Chicago Press, 1979.

———. *Poetic Statement and Critical Dogma.* Evanston: Northwestern University Press, 1970.

———. *Professing Literature: An Institutional History.* Chicago: University of Chicago Press, 1987.

Green, Daniel. "Literature Itself: The New Criticism and Aesthetic Experience." *Philosophy and Literature* 27 (2003): 62–79.

Green, Martin. "The Morality of Lolita." *Kenyon Review* 28 (1966): 352–377.

Greenblatt, Stephen. *Learning to Curse: Essays in Early Modern Culture.* New York: Routledge, 1990.

———. *Renaissance Self-Fashioning: From More to Shakespeare.* Chicago: University of Chicago Press, 1980.

———, ed. *Representing the English Renaissance.* Berkeley: University of California Press, 1988.

———. *Shakespearean Negotiations: The Circulation of Social Energy in Renaissance England.* New York: Clarendon, 1988.

———. "Toward a Poetics of Culture." In Veeser, *New Historicism,* 1–14.

Greenblatt, Stephen, and Catherine Gallagher. *Practicing New Historicism.* Chicago: University of Chicago Press, 2000.

Grewal, Gurleen. *Circles of Sorrow, Lines of Struggle: The Novels of Toni Morrison.* Baton Rouge: Louisiana State University Press, 1998.

Grusin, Richard. "The Dark Side of the Digital Humanities: Dispatches from Two Recent MLA Conventions." *differences: A Journal of Feminist Cultural Studies* 25 (2014): 79–92.

Guillory, John. *Cultural Capital: The Problem of Literary Canon Formation.* Chicago: University of Chicago Press, 1993.

Halberstam, Judith. "The Politics of Negativity in Recent Queer Theory." *PMLA* 121 (2006): 823–824.

Hale, Dorothy J. *Social Formalism: The Novel in Theory from Henry James to the Present.* Stanford, CA: Stanford University Press, 1998.

Harad, Alyssa. "Reviving Lolita; or, Because Junior High Is Still Hell." In *Catching a Wave: Reclaiming Feminism for the Twenty-First Century*, edited by Rory Dicker and Alison Piepmier, 81–98. Lebanon, NH: Northeastern University Press.

Harman, Graham. "The Well-Wrought Broken Hammer: Object-Oriented Literary Criticism." *New Literary History* 43 (2012): 183–203.

Harold, Brent. "*Lolita:* Nabokov's Critique of Aloofness." *Papers on Language and Literature* 11 (1975): 71–82.

Harpham, Geoffrey Galt. "Foucault and the New Historicism." *American Literary History* 3 (1991): 360–375.

Harris, Trudier. *Fiction and Folklore: The Novels of Toni Morrison*. Knoxville: University of Tennessee Press, 1991.

Hartman, Geoffrey H. *Criticism in the Wilderness*. New Haven, CT: Yale University Press, 1980.

———. Preface to Bloom et al., *Deconstruction and Criticism*, vii–ix.

Hartman, Saidiya V. *Scenes of Subjection: Terror, Slavery, and Self-Making in Nineteenth-Century America*. New York: Oxford University Press, 1997.

Haverkamp, Anselm, ed. *Deconstruction Is/in America: A New Sense of the Political*. New York: New York University Press, 1995.

Hayles, N. Katherine. *How We Think: Digital Media and Contemporary Technology*. Chicago: University of Chicago Press, 2012.

Heinze, Denise. *The Dilemma of "Double Consciousness": Toni Morrison's Novels*. Athens: University of Georgia Press, 1993.

Henderson, Mae G. "Toni Morrison's *Beloved:* Re-membering the Body as Historical Text." In *Comparative American Identities: Race Sex, and Nationality in the Modern Text*, edited by Hortense J. Spillers, 62–86. New York: Routledge, 1991.

Herbert, Christopher. "The Conundrum of Coherence." *New Literary History* 35 (2004): 185–206.

Herbold, Sarah. "Reflections on Modernism: *Lolita* and Political Engagement: or, How the Left and the Right Both Have It Wrong." *Nabokov Studies* 3 (1996): 145–150.

Heuser, Ryan, and Long Le-Khac. "A Quantitative Literary History of 2,958 Nineteenth-Century British Novels: The Semantic Cohort Method." *Stanford Literary Lab*, pamphlet 4 (2012): 1–66. https://litlab.stanford.edu/LiteraryLabPamphlet4.pdf.

Hoberek, Andrew. *The Twilight of the Middle Class: Post–World War II American Fiction and White-Collar Work*. Princeton, NJ: Princeton University Press, 2005.

Hollander, John. "The Perilous Magic of Nymphets." *Partisan Review* 23 (1956): 557–560.

Horvitz, Deborah. "Nameless Ghosts: Possession and Dispossession in *Beloved.*" *Studies in American Fiction* 17 (1989): 157–167.

Howells, William Dean. "*Majors and Minors.*" *North American Review,* June 27, 1886, 630.

Hunter, Ian. "The History of Theory." *Critical Inquiry* 33 (2006): 78–112.

Hustis, Harriet. "Time Will Tell: (Re)Reading the Seductive Simulacra of Nabokov's *Lolita.*" *Studies in American Fiction* 35 (2007): 89–111.

James, David. "Critical Solace." *New Literary History* 47 (2016): 481–504.

Jameson, Fredric. *The Political Unconscious: Narrative as a Socially Symbolic Act.* Ithaca, NY: Cornell University Press, 1981.

———. *The Prison-House of Language: A Critical Account of Structuralism and Russian Formalism.* Princeton, NJ: Princeton University Press, 1972.

Jay, Gregory. "Hire Ed! Deconstructing the Crises in Academe." *American Quarterly* 63 (2011): 163–178.

Jay, Paul. "Bridging the Gap: The Position of Politics in Deconstruction." *Cultural Critique* 22 (1992): 47–74.

Jehlen, Myra. "*Lolita:* A Beautiful, Banal, Eden Red Apple." In *Five Fictions in Search of Truth,* 103–132. Princeton, NJ: Princeton University Press, 2008.

———. "The Story of History Told by New Historicism." In *Reconstructing American Literary and Historical Studies,* edited by Günter H. Lenz, 308–323. New York: St. Martin's, 1990.

Jesser, Nancy. "Violence, Home, and Community in Toni Morrison's *Beloved.*" *African American Review* 33 (1999): 325–345.

Johnson, Barbara. *The Critical Difference: Essays in the Contemporary Rhetoric of Reading.* Baltimore: Johns Hopkins University Press, 1980.

———. *A World of Difference.* Baltimore: Johns Hopkins University Press, 1987.

Josipovici, Gabriel. "*Lolita:* Parody and the Pursuit of Beauty." *Critical Quarterly* 6 (1964): 35–48.

Joughin, John J., and Simon Malpas, eds. *The New Aestheticism.* Manchester: Manchester University Press, 2003.

Joyce, Joyce Ann. "The Black Canon: Reconstructing Black American Literary Criticism." *New Literary History* 18 (1987): 335–344.

———. "A Tinker's Damn: Henry Louis Gates, Jr., and 'The Signifying Monkey' Twenty Years Later." *Callaloo* 31 (2008): 370–380.

———. "'Who the Cap Fit': Unconsciousness and Unconscionableness in the Criticism of Houston A. Baker, Jr., and Henry Louis Gates, Jr." *New Literary History* 18 (1987): 371–384.

Kampf, Louis, and Paul Lauter. Introduction to Kampf and Lauter, *Politics of Literature,* 3–54.

———, eds. *The Politics of Literature: Dissenting Essays on the Teaching of English.* New York: Pantheon, 1972.

Kamuf, Peggy. *The Division of Literature, or, The University in Deconstruction.* Chicago: University of Chicago Press, 1997.

Kant, Immanuel. *The Critique of Judgment.* Translation J. H. Bernard. New York: Hafner, 1968.

———. *The Groundwork of the Metaphysic of Morals.* Translated by H. J. Paton. New York: Harper, 1964.

Karshan, Thomas. "Vladimir Nabokov's *Lolita* and Free Play." In *Reading America: New Perspectives on the American Novel,* edited by Elizabeth Boyle and Anne-Marie Evans, 97–113. Newcastle upon Tyne, UK: Cambridge Scholars, 2008.

Kauffman, Linda. "Framing Lolita: Is There a Woman in the Text?" In *Refiguring the Father: New Feminist Readings of Patriarchy,* edited by Patricia Yaeger and Beth Kowaleski-Wallace, 131–152. Carbondale: Southern Illinois University Press, 1989.

Kaufman, Robert. "Everybody Hates Kant: Blakean Formalism and the Symmetries of Laura Moriarity." In Wolfson and Brown, *Reading for Form,* 203–230.

———. "Red Kant, or the Persistence of the Third *Critique* in Adorno and Jameson." *Critical Inquiry* 26 (2000): 682–724.

Kazin, Alfred. *On Native Grounds: An Interpretation of Modern American Prose Literature.* New York: Reynal and Hitchcock, 1942.

Kennedy, Colleen. "The White Man's Guest, or Why Aren't More Feminists Rereading *Lolita.*" In *Narrative and Culture,* edited by Janice Carlisle and Daniel R. Schwarz, 46–57. Athens: University of Georgia Press, 1994.

Kenshur, Oscar. "'The Tumour of Their Own Hearts': Relativism, Aesthetics, and the Rhetoric of Demystification." In George Levine, *Aesthetics and Ideology,* 57–78.

Kerr, Clark. *The Uses of the University.* 5th ed. Cambridge, MA: Harvard University Press, 2001.

Khayati, Abdellatif. "Representation, Race, and the 'Language' of the Ineffable in Toni Morrison's Narrative." *African American Review* 33 (1999): 313–324.

Kindley, Evan. "Big Criticism." *Critical Inquiry* 38 (2011): 71–95.

Kirp, David L. *Shakespeare, Einstein and the Bottom Line: The Marketing of Higher Education.* Cambridge, MA: Harvard University Press, 2003.

Klein, Richard. "Prolegomenon to Derrida." *Diacritics* 2 (1972): 29–34.

Kolodny, Annette. "A Map for Rereading: or, Gender and the Interpretation of Literary Texts." *New Literary History* 11 (1980): 451–467.

Konstantinou, Lee. *Cool Characters: Irony and American Fiction.* Cambridge, MA: Harvard University Press, 2016.

Kreyling, Michael. "'Slave Life; Freed Life—Everyday Was a Test and a Trial': Identity and Memory in *Beloved.*" *Arizona Quarterly* 63 (2007): 109–136.

Krieger, Murray. *The New Apologists for Poetry.* Minneapolis: University of Minnesota Press, 1956.

Krumholz, Linda. "The Ghosts of Slavery: Historical Recovery in Toni Morrison's *Beloved.*" *African American Review* 26 (1992): 395–408.

Laden, Sonja. "Recuperating the Archive: Anecdotal Evidence and Questions of Historical Realism." *Poetics Today* 25 (2004): 1–28.

Lane, Christopher. "The Poverty of Context: Historicism and Nonmimetic Fiction." *PMLA* 118 (2003): 450–469.

Larson, Magali Sarfatti. *The Rise of Professionalism: A Sociological Analysis.* Berkeley: University of California Press, 1977.

Latour, Bruno. "Why Has Critique Run Out of Steam? From Matters of Fact to Matters of Concern." *Critical Inquiry* 30 (2004): 225–248.

Lawrence, David. "Fleshly Ghosts and Ghostly Flesh: The Word and the Body in *Beloved.*" *Studies in American Fiction* 19 (1991): 189–201.

Lee, Maurice S. "Searching the Archives with Dickens and Hawthorne: Databases and Aesthetic Judgment after the New Historicism." *English Literary History* 79 (2012): 747–771.

Lehman, Robert S. "Formalism, Mere Form, and Judgment." *New Literary History* 48 (2017): 245–263.

Leitch, Vincent B. *American Literary Criticism from the Thirties to the Eighties.* New York: Columbia University Press, 1988.

———. *Deconstructive Criticism: An Advanced Introduction.* New York: Columbia University Press, 1983.

Lentricchia, Frank. *After the New Criticism.* Chicago: University of Chicago Press, 1980.

———. "Foucault's Legacy—A New Historicism?" In Veeser, *New Historicism,* 231–242.

Lerner, Laurence. "Against Historicism." *New Literary History* 24 (1993): 273–292.

Levao, Ronald. "*Paradise Lost* and the Forms of Intimacy." In Wolfson and Brown, *Reading for Form,* 100–128.

Levine, George, ed. *Aesthetics and Ideology.* New Brunswick, NJ: Rutgers University Press, 1994.

———. "Introduction: Reclaiming the Aesthetic." In George Levine, *Aesthetics and Ideology,* 1–28.

Levine, Peter. "*Lolita* and Aristotle's Ethics." *Philosophy and Literature* 19 (1995): 32–47.

Levine, Robert T. "'My Ultraviolet Darling': The Loss of Lolita's Childhood." *Modern Fiction Studies* 25 (1979): 471–479.

Levinson, Marjorie. "Reflections on the New Historicism." *European Romantic Review* 23 (2012): 355–362.

———. "What Is New Formalism?" *PMLA* 122 (2007): 558–569.

Lipset, Seymour Martin, and Sheldon S. Wolin, eds. *The Berkeley Student Revolt: Facts and Interpretations.* Garden City, NJ: Anchor Books, 1965.

Liu, Alan. "The Meaning of the Digital Humanities." *PMLA* 128 (2013): 409–423.

———. "The New Historicism and the Work of Mourning." *Studies in Romanticism* 35 (1996): 553–562.

———. "The Power of Formalism: The New Historicism." *English Literary History* 56 (1989): 721–771.

Liu, Fangzhou, and Hannah Knowles. "Harassment, Assault Allegations Against Moretti Span Three Campuses." *Stanford Daily,* November 16, 2017. https://www.stanforddaily.com/2017/11/16/harassment-assault-allegations-against-moretti-span-three-campuses/.

Loesberg, Jonathan. *Aestheticism and Deconstruction: Pater, Derrida, and De Man.* Princeton, NJ: Princeton University Press, 1991.

———. *A Return to Aesthetics: Autonomy, Indifference, and Postmodernism.* Stanford, CA: Stanford University Press, 2005.

Love, Heather. "Close but Not Deep: Literary Ethics and the Descriptive Turn." *New Literary History* 41 (2010): 371–391.

Lynch, Deirdre Shauna. *Loving Literature: A Cultural History.* Chicago: University of Chicago Press, 2015.

Macksey, Richard, and Eugenio Danato, eds. *The Structuralist Controversy: The Languages of Criticism and the Sciences of Man.* Baltimore: Johns Hopkins University Press, 1970.

Macpherson, Sandra. "A Little Formalism." *English Literary History* 82 (2015): 385–405.

Maddox, Lucy. *Nabokov's Novels in English.* Athens: University of Georgia Press, 1983.

Mangan, Katherine. "Two Women Say Stanford Professors Raped Them Years Ago." *Chronicle of Higher Education,* November 11, 2017. https://www.chronicle.com/article/2-Women-Say-Stanford/241749.

Martin, Wallace. "Critical Response: Literary Critics and Their Discontents: A Response to Geoffrey Hartman." *Critical Inquiry* 4 (1977): 397–406.

Marx, Karl, and Friedrich Engels. *The German Ideology.* Translated by S. Ryazanskaya. Moscow: Progress, 1964.

McClure, John A. *Partial Faiths: Postsecular Fiction in the Age of Pynchon and Morrison.* Athens: University of Georgia Press, 2007.

McGinn, Colin. "The Meaning and Morality of *Lolita.*" *Philosophical Forum* 30 (1999): 31–41.

McNeely, Trevor. "'Lo' and Behold: Solving the *Lolita* Riddle." *Studies in the Novel* 21 (1989): 182–199.

Menand, Louis. *The Marketplace of Ideas: Reform and Resistance in the American University.* New York: Norton, 2010.

Merrill, Robert. "Nabokov and Fictional Artifice." *Modern Fiction Studies* 25 (1979): 439–462.

Michaels, Walter Benn. *The Gold Standard and the Logic of Naturalism: American Literature at the Turn of the Century.* Berkeley: University of California Press, 1987.

———. *The Shape of the Signifier: 1967 to the End of History.* Princeton, NJ: Princeton University Press, 2004.

———. "'You Who Never Was There': Slavery and the New Historicism—Deconstruction and the Holocaust." In *The Americanization of the Holocaust,* edited by Hilene Flanzbaum, 181–197. Baltimore: Johns Hopkins University Press, 1999.

Miller, D. A. *Jane Austen, or, The Secret of Style.* Princeton, NJ: Princeton University Press, 2003.

Miller, J. Hillis. "Deconstructing the Deconstructors." *Diacritics* 5 (1975): 24–31.

———. *The Ethics of Reading: Kant, de Man, Eliot, Trollope, James, and Benjamin.* New York: Columbia University Press, 1987.

———. *Fiction and Repetition: Seven English Novels.* Cambridge, MA: Harvard University Press, 1982.

———. *The Linguistic Moment: From Wordsworth to Stevens.* Princeton, NJ: Princeton University Press, 1985.

———. "Presidential Address 1986: The Triumph of Theory, the Resistance to Reading, and the Question of the Material Base." *PMLA* 102 (1987): 281–291.

Mitchell, Charles. "Mythic Seriousness in *Lolita.*" *Texas Studies in Literature and Language* 5 (1963): 329–343.

Mizener, Arthur. "The Desires of the Mind." *Sewanee Review* 55 (1947): 460–469.

Mizruchi, Susan. "*Lolita* in History." *American Literature* 75 (2003): 629–652.

Montrose, Louis. "Professing the Renaissance: The Poetics and Politics of Culture." In Veeser, *New Historicism,* 15–36.

———. "Renaissance Literary Studies and the Subject of History." *English Literary Renaissance* 16 (1986): 5–12.

Moretti, Franco. "Conjectures on World Literature." *New Left Review* 1 (2000): 54–68.

———. *Distant Reading.* New York: Verso, 2013.

———. *Graphs, Maps, Trees: Abstract Models for a Literary History.* New York: Verso, 2005.

———. "Literature, Measured." *Stanford Literary Lab,* pamphlet 12 (2016): 1–7. https://litlab.stanford.edu/LiteraryLabPamphlet12.pdf.

———. "Network Theory, Plot Analysis." *Stanford Literary Lab,* pamphlet 2 (2011): 1–31. https://litlab.stanford.edu/LiteraryLabPamphlet2.pdf.

————. "'Operationalizing': or, The Function of Measurement in Modern Literary Theory." *Stanford Literary Lab*, pamphlet 6 (2013): 1–13. https://litlab.stanford.edu/LiteraryLabPamphlet6.pdf.

————. "Patterns and Interpretation." *Stanford Literary Lab*, pamphlet 15 (2017): 1–10. https://litlab.stanford.edu/LiteraryLabPamphlet15.pdf.

Morrison, Toni. *Beloved*. 1987. Reprint, New York: Vintage, 2004.

————. "The Pain of Being Black: An Interview with Toni Morrison." By Bonnie Angelo. In *Conversations with Toni Morrison*, edited by Taylor Danielle-Guthrie, 255–261. Jackson: University of Mississippi Press, 1994.

————. "Rootedness: The Ancestor as Foundation." In *Black Women Writers (1950–1980): A Critical Evaluation*, edited by Mari Evans, 339–345. New York: Doubleday, 1984.

————. "The Site of Memory." In *Inventing the Truth*, edited by Mari Evans, 185–200. Boston: Houghton Mifflin, 1998.

Mukařovský, Jan. *Aesthetic Function, Norm and Value as Social Facts*. Translated by Mark E. Suino. Ann Arbor: University of Michigan Press, 1970.

Muller, Herbert J., and Cleanth Brooks, "The Relative and the Absolute: An Exchange of Views." *Sewanee Review* 57 (1949): 357–377.

Nabokov, Vladimir. *The Annotated Lolita*. Edited by Alfred Appel Jr. New York: McGraw-Hill, 1970.

————. Interview by Anne Guérin. *L'Express*, January 26, 1961, 26–27.

————. *Lectures on Literature*. Edited by Fredson Bowers. New York: Harcourt, 1980.

————. *Strong Opinions*. New York: McGraw, 1973.

Nealon, Jeffrey T. "The Discipline of Deconstruction." *PMLA* 107 (1992): 1266–1279.

Nelson, Cary. *No University Is an Island: Saving Academic Freedom*. New York: New York University Press, 2010.

Nelson, Charles A. "The Liberal Arts in Management." *Harvard Business Review* 36 (1958): 91–99.

Nemerov, Howard. "Review of *Lolita*." *Kenyon Review* 19 (1957): 313–314, 316–321.

Nemoianu, Virgil. "Hating and Loving Aesthetic Formalism." In Wolfson and Brown, *Reading for Form*, 49–65.

Newfield, Christopher. *Unmaking the Public University: The Forty-Year Assault on the Middle Class*. Cambridge, MA: Harvard University Press, 2008.

Newton, Judith Lowder. "History as Usual? Feminism and the 'New Historicism.'" In Veeser, *New Historicism*, 152–167.

Ngai, Sianne. *Our Aesthetic Categories: Zany, Cute, Interesting*. Cambridge, MA: Harvard University Press, 2012.

Norris, Christopher. *Deconstruction: Theory and Practice.* New York: Methuen, 1982.

North, Joseph. *Literary Criticism: A Concise Political History.* Cambridge, MA: Harvard University Press, 2017.

Nyegaard, Ole. "*Poshlust* and High Art: A Reading of Nabokov's Aesthetics." *Orbis Litterarum: International Review of Literary Studies* 59 (2004): 341–365.

Ohmann, Richard. *English in America: A Radical View of the Profession.* New York: Oxford University Press, 1976

———. "Teaching and Studying Literature at the End of Ideology." In Kampf and Lauter, *Politics of Literature,* 130–159.

Olson, Elder. "William Empson, Contemporary Criticism, and Poetic Diction." In Crane, *Critics and Criticism,* 45–82.

O'Rourke, James. "From Seduction to Fantasy: 'Lolita, or the Confession of a White Widowed Male.'" In *Sex, Lies, and Autobiography,* 167–190. Charlottesville: University of Virginia Press, 2006.

Packman, David. *Vladimir Nabokov: The Structure of Literary Desire.* Columbia: University of Missouri Press, 1982.

Parrish, Timothy. "Off Faulkner's Plantation: Toni Morrison's *Beloved* and *Song of Solomon.*" In *From the Civil War to the Apocalypse: Postmodern History and American Fiction,* 117–149. Amherst: University of Massachusetts Press, 2008.

Pease, Donald. "J. Hillis Miller: The Other Victorian at Yale." In Arac, Godzich, and Martin, *Yale Critics,* 66–89.

Pechter, Edward. "The New Historicism and Its Discontents: Politicizing Renaissance Drama." *PMLA* 102 (1987): 292–303.

Pecora, Vincent P. "The Limits of Local Knowledge." In Veeser, *New Historicism,* 243–276.

Pérez-Torres, Rafael. "Knitting and Knotting the Narrative Thread—*Beloved* as Postmodern Novel." *Modern Fiction Studies* 39 (1993): 689–707.

Perkin, Harold James. *The Third Revolution: Professional Elites in the Modern World.* London: Routledge, 1996.

Peterson, Nancy J. *Against Amnesia: Contemporary Women Writers and the Crises of Historical Memory.* Philadelphia: University of Pennsylvania Press, 2001.

Phelan, James. "Dual Focalization, Retrospective Fictional Autobiography, and the Ethics of Lolita." In *Narrative and Consciousness: Literature, Psychology and the Brain,* edited by Gary D. Fineman, Ted E. McVay Jr., and Owen J. Flanagan 129–145. Oxford: Oxford University Press, 2003.

———. "Estranging Unreliability, Bonding Unreliability, and the Ethics of *Lolita.*" *Narrative* 15 (2007): 222–238.

Phiddian, Robert. "Are Parody and Deconstruction Secretly the Same Thing?" *New Literary History* 28 (1997): 673–696.

Pifer, Ellen. *Nabokov and the Novel.* Cambridge, MA: Harvard University Press, 1980.

Poovey, Mary. "Aesthetics and Political Economy in the Eighteenth Century: The Place of Gender in the Social Constitution of Knowledge." In George Levine, *Aesthetics and Ideology,* 79–105.

Porter, Carolyn. "Are We Being Historical Yet?" *South Atlantic Quarterly* 87 (1988): 743–786.

———. "Are We Being Historical Yet?" In *The States of "Theory": History, Art, and Critical Discourse,* edited by David Carroll, 27–62. New York: Columbia University Press, 1990.

———. "History and Literature: 'After the New Historicism.'" *New Literary History* 21 (1990): 253–272.

Price, Leah. "From the *History of a Book* to a 'History of the Book.'" *Representations* 108 (2009): 120–138.

Price, Matthew Burroughs. "A Genealogy of Queer Detachment." *PMLA* 130 (2015): 648–665.

Proffer, Carl R. *Keys to Lolita.* Bloomington: Indiana University Press, 1968.

Rackin, Donald. "The Moral Rhetoric of Nabokov's *Lolita.*" *Four Quarters* 22 (1973): 6–19.

Radway, Janice. *A Feeling for Books: The Book-of-the-Month Club, Literary Taste, and Middle-Class Desire.* Chapel Hill: University of North Carolina Press, 1997.

Ramadanovic, Petar. "'You Your Best Thing, Sethe': Trauma's Narcissism." *Studies in the Novel* 40 (2008): 178–188.

Rancière, Jacques. *Aesthetics and Its Discontents.* Translated by Steven Corcoran. Cambridge, UK: Polity, 2009.

———. *The Emancipated Spectator.* Translated by Gregory Elliot. London: Verso, 2011.

———. *The Politics of Aesthetics: The Distribution of the Sensible.* Translated by Gabriel Rockhill. London: Continuum, 2006.

Ransom, John Crowe. *The New Criticism.* Norfolk, CT: New Directions, 1941.

———. *The World's Body.* Baton Rouge: Louisiana State University Press, 1938.

Rappaport, Herman. *The Theory Mess: Deconstruction in Eclipse.* New York: Columbia University Press, 2001.

Raynaud, Claudine. "The Poetics of Abjection in *Beloved.*" In *Black Imagination and the Middle Passage,* edited by Maria Diedrich, Henry Louis Gates Jr., and Carl Pedersen, 70–85. Oxford: Oxford University Press, 1999.

Readings, Bill. *The University in Ruins.* Cambridge, MA: Harvard University Press, 1996.

Redfield, Marc. *Theory at Yale: The Strange Case of Deconstruction in America.* New York: Fordham University Press, 2015.

Richards, I. A. *Principles of Literary Criticism.* 1924. Reprint, New York: Harcourt, 1959.

Ricoeur, Paul. *Freud and Philosophy: An Essay on Interpretation.* Translated by Denis Savage. New Haven, CT: Yale University Press, 1970.

Riddel, Joseph N. "A Miller's Tale." *Diacritics* 5 (1975): 56–65.

Rigney, Barbara Hill. "'Breaking the Back of Words': Language, Silence, and the Politics of Identity in *Beloved.*" In *Critical Essays on Toni Morrison's Beloved,* edited by Barbara H. Solomon, 138–147. New York: G. K. Hall, 1998.

———. *The Voices of Toni Morrison.* Columbus: Ohio State University Press, 1991.

Rivers, J. E., and Charles Nicol, eds. *Nabokov's Fifth Arc: Nabokov and Others on His Life's Work.* Austin: University of Texas Press, 1982.

Rodgers, Michael. "*Lolita*'s Nietzschean Morality." *Philosophy and Literature* 35 (2011): 104–120.

Rody, Caroline. "Toni Morrison's *Beloved:* History, 'Rememory,' and a 'Clamor for a Kiss.'" *American Literary History* 7 (1995): 92–119.

Rooney, Ellen. "Form and Contentment." In Wolfson and Brown, *Reading for Form,* 25–48.

———. "Live Free or Describe: The Reading Effect and the Persistence of Form." *differences: A Journal of Feminist Cultural Studies* 21 (2010): 112–139.

Rorty, Richard. *Contingency, Irony, and Solidarity.* Cambridge: Cambridge University Press, 1989.

Rothstein, Eric. "*Lolita:* Nymphet at Normal School." *Contemporary Literature* 41 (2000): 22–55.

Rowe, William Woodin. *Nabokov's Deceptive World.* New York: New York University Press, 1971.

Rubin, Joan Shelley. *The Making of Middlebrow Culture.* Chapel Hill: University of North Carolina Press, 1992.

Russo, John Paul. "The Tranquilized Poem: The Crisis of New Criticism in the 1950s." *Texas Studies in Language and Literature* 30 (1988): 198–229.

Sale, Maggie. "Call and Response as Critical Method: African-American Oral Traditions and *Beloved.*" *African American Review* 26 (1992): 41–50.

Scarry, Elaine. *On Beauty and Being Just.* Princeton, NJ: Princeton University Press, 1999.

Scholes, Robert. *Structuralism in Literature: An Introduction.* New Haven, CT: Yale University Press, 1974.

Schryer, Stephen. *Fantasies of the New Class: Ideologies of Professionalism in Post–World War II American Fiction.* New York: Columbia University Press, 2011.

Schweighauser, Philipp. "Metafiction, Transcendence, and Death in Nabokov's *Lolita*." *Nabokov Studies* 5 (1998–1999): 99–116.

Seiden, Melvin. "Nabokov and Dostoyevsky." *Contemporary Literature* 13 (1972): 423–444.

Sedgwick, Eve Kosofsky, ed. *Novel Gazing: Queer Readings in Fiction.* Durham, NC: Duke University Press, 1997

———. "Paranoid Reading and Reparative Reading; or, You're So Paranoid, You Probably Think This Introduction Is about You." In Sedgwick, *Novel Gazing*, 1–37.

———. *Touching Feeling: Affect, Pedagogy, Performativity.* Durham, NC: Duke University Press, 2003.

Serpell, C. Namwali. *Seven Modes of Uncertainty.* Cambridge, MA: Harvard University Press, 2014.

Shaw, Peter. "Degenerate Criticism: The Dismal State of English Studies." *Harper's*, October 1979, 93–99.

Shelton, Jen. "'The Word Is Incest': Sexual and Linguistic Coercion in *Lolita*." *Textual Practice* 13 (1999): 273–294.

Shklovsky, Victor. "Art as Technique." In *Russian Formalist Criticism: Four Essays*, translated by Lee T. Lemon and Marion J. Reiss, 3–24. Lincoln: University of Nebraska Press, 1965.

Simpson, David. "Literary Criticism and the Return to 'History.'" *Critical Inquiry* 14 (1988): 721–747.

Sitter, Deborah Ayer. "The Making of a Man: Dialogic Meaning in *Beloved*." *African American Review* 26 (1992): 17–29.

Smith, Barbara Herrnstein. *Contingencies of Value: Alternative Perspectives for Critical Theory.* Cambridge, MA: Harvard University Press, 1988.

Smith, Valerie. "'Circling the Subject': History and Narrative in *Beloved*." In *Toni Morrison: Critical Perspectives Past and Present*, edited by Henry Louis Gates Jr. and K. A. Appiah, 342–355. New York: Amistad, 1993.

Smith, Victoria L. "Generative Melancholy: Women's Loss and Literary Representation." *Mosaic* 41 (2008): 95–110.

Spilka, Mark. "The Necessary Stylist: A New Critical Revision." *Modern Fiction Studies* 6 (1960–1961): 283–297.

Spiro, Lisa. "'This Is Why We Fight': Defining the Values of the Digital Humanities." In *Debates in the Digital Humanities*, edited by Matthew Gold, 16–35. Minneapolis: University of Minnesota Press, 2012.

Stanford Literary Lab. "Pamphlets." Accessed April 9, 2018. https://litlab .stanford.edu/pamphlets/.

Stanton, Donna C., Michael Bérubé, Leonard Cassuto, Morris Eaves, John Guillory, Donald E. Hall, and Sean Latham. "MLA Task Force on Evaluating Scholarship for Tenure and Promotion." *Profession* 2007.

Stegner, Page. *Escape into Aesthetics: The Art of Vladimir Nabokov*. New York: Dial, 1966.

Stockton, Kathryn Bond. "Prophylactics and Brains: *Beloved* in the Cybernetic Age of AIDS." In Sedgwick, *Novel Gazing*, 41–73.

Tally, Justine. *Toni Morrison's "Beloved": Origins*. New York: Routledge, 2009.

Tamir-Ghez, Nomi. "The Art of Persuasion in Nabokov's *Lolita*." *Poetics Today* 1 (1979): 65–83.

Tanenhaus, Sam. "What Is the Best Work of American Fiction of the Last Twenty Five Years?" *New York Times*, May 21, 2006, section 7, 16.

Tate, Allen. *Reason in Madness: Critical Essays*. New York: Putnam, 1941.

Theile, Verena, and Linda Tredennick, eds. *New Formalisms and Literary Theory*. Basingstoke, UK: Palgrave, 2013.

Thomas, Brook. *The New Historicism and Other Old-Fashioned Topics*. Princeton, NJ: Princeton University Press, 1991.

———. "The New Historicism and Other Old-Fashioned Topics." In Veeser, *New Historicism*, 182–203.

Toker, Leona. *Nabokov: The Mystery of Literary Structures*. Ithaca, NY: Cornell University Press, 1989.

Tompkins, Jane. *Sensational Designs: The Cultural Work of American Fiction, 1790–1860*. New York: Oxford University Press, 1985.

"Too Much Sociology." *N+1* 16 (2013). https://nplusonemag.com/issue-16/the-intellectual-situation/too-much-sociology.

Trilling, Lionel. "The Last Lover: Vladimir Nabokov's 'Lolita.'" *Encounter* 16 (1958): 9–18.

Tweedie, James. "*Lolita*'s Loose Ends: Nabokov and the Boundless Novel." *Twentieth Century Literature* 46 (2000): 150–170.

Veeser, H. Aram. Introduction to Veeser, *New Historicism*, ix–xvi.

———, ed. *The New Historicism*. New York: Routledge, 1989.

Vermeulen, Pieter. "Greenblatt's Melancholy Fetish: Literary Criticism and the Desire for Loss." *Textual Practice* 24 (2010): 483–500.

Walker, Steven F. "Nabokov's *Lolita* and Goethe's *Faust:* The Ghost in the Novel." *Comparative Literature Studies* 46 (2009): 512–535.

Wall, Cheryl. "On Freedom and the Will to Adorn: Debating Aesthetics and/as Ideology in African American Literature." In George Levine, *Aesthetics and Ideology*, 283–303.

Washburn, Jennifer. *University, Inc.: The Corporate Corruption of American Higher Education*. New York: Basic Books, 2004.

Wellek, René. "Destroying Literary Studies." *New Criterion* 2 (1983): 1–8.

———. *A History of Modern Criticism, 1750–1950*. Vol. 1, *The Later Eighteenth Century*. New Haven, CT: Yale University Press, 1955.

———. "The New Criticism: Pro and Contra." *Critical Inquiry* 4 (1978): 611–624.

White, Hayden. "New Historicism: A Comment." In Veeser, *New Historicism*, 293–302.

Whiting, Frederick. "'The Strange Particularity of the Lover's Preference': Pedophilia, Pornography, and the Anatomy of Monstrosity in *Lolita*." *American Literature* 70 (1998): 833–862.

Widiss, Benjamin Leigh. *Obscure Invitations: The Persistence of the Author in Twentieth-Century American Literature*. Stanford, CA: Stanford University Press, 2011.

Williams, Carol T. "Nabokov's Dialectical Structure." In *Nabokov: The Man and His Work*, edited by L. S. Dembo, 165–182. Madison: University of Wisconsin Press, 1967.

Williams, Jeffrey. "The Death of Deconstruction, the End of Theory, and Other Ominous Rumors." *Narrative* 4 (1996): 17–35.

Wimsatt, William K., Jr. *The Verbal Icon: Studies in the Meaning of Poetry*. Lexington: University of Kentucky Press, 1954.

Wimsatt, William K., Jr., and Cleanth Brooks. "Rhetoric and Neo-classic Wit." In *Literary Criticism: A Short History*, 221–251. 1957. Reprint, London: Routledge, 1970.

Winchell, Mark Royden. *Cleanth Brooks and the Rise of Modern Criticism*. Charlottesville: University of Virginia Press, 1996.

Winston, Mathew. "*Lolita* and the Dangers of Fiction." *Twentieth Century Literature* 21 (1975): 421–427.

Wolfson, Susan J. "Reading for Form." *MLQ* 61 (2000): 1–16.

Wolfson, Susan J., and Marshall Brown, eds. *Reading for Form*. Seattle: University of Washington Press, 2006.

Wood, Michael. "*Lolita* Revisited." *New England Review: Middlebury Series* 17 (1995): 15–43.

Yates, Joanne. *Control through Communication: The Rise of System in American Management*. Baltimore: Johns Hopkins University Press, 1989.

Žižek, Slavoj. *The Fragile Absolute, or, Why Is the Christian Legacy Worth Fighting For?* London: Verso, 2000.

Acknowledgments

I STARTED WORKING on *Guilty Aesthetic Pleasures* while on sabbatical during the 2011–2012 academic year, and I am grateful to Baruch College for giving me the time necessary to do my initial research. I was also supported during the 2012–2013, 2013–2014, 2015–2016, and 2016–2017 academic years by research grants from PSC-CUNY. Chapter 1 touches on some aspects of the argument proposed in "The Discipline of Feeling: The New Critics and the Struggle for Academic Legitimacy," *REAL: Yearbook of Research in English and American Literature,* vol. 31, edited by Winfred Fluck, Günter Leypoldt, and Philipp Löffler (Tübingen: Narr Francke Attempto, 2015), 127–140. Portions of Chapter 5 are reprinted from "Why Is *Beloved* so Universally Beloved? Uncovering Our Hidden Aesthetic Criteria," by Timothy Aubry in *Criticism: A Quarterly for Literature and the Arts,* vol. 58, no. 3, copyright © 2016 Wayne State University Press, with the permission of Wayne State University Press.

Many people have helped me along the way. I would especially like to thank Jon Baskin, John Brenkman, Sarah Brouillette, Marshall Brown, Florence Dore, Sorin Cucu, Rita Felski, Stephanie Hershinow, Mary McGlynn, Sandra Parvu, Rick Rodriguez, Michael Sayeau, Trysh Travis, and Nancy Yousef for reading parts of the manuscript and / or responding critically (and in a few cases, enthusiastically) to the ideas contained in it. My anonymous reviewers offered meticulous and generous feedback, which proved immensely helpful. I am grateful to my editors, Lindsay Waters and Joy Deng, for supporting the project over the past year and a half and ably steering it toward completion. Thank you to Beth Blum and the other participants at UPenn's Modernism and Twentieth Century Studies Group for inviting me to offer a very early, as yet undercooked version of my chapter on Toni Morrison's *Beloved*. I would also like to thank Günter Leypoldt and the remarkable group of scholars he assembled for the 2013 University of Heidelberg conference on "Acquired Taste" for hearing me out on New Criticism, as well as Douglas Manson, Stephen Marsh, and Daniel Nutters for joining me for a spirited session on midcentury formalism at NEMLA in 2017. And I would like to thank Deborah Blocker, Jin Chang, Josephine Donovan, Katherine Fry, Oleg Gelikman, Regina Martin, Ludwig Schmitz, Geoffrey Wildanger, and Arielle Zibrak for responding to my paper on New Historicism at a 2016 ACLA panel devoted to aesthetics.

I should also say that I could never have finished this project without the love and support of my friends and family over the last half decade or so, several of whom served as informal interlocutors, whether knowingly or not, for the arguments I wanted to make here. I am grateful to many of them for asking me how my book was going and, at certain moments, for *not* asking me about it. Thanks also of course to my unstoppably rambunctious, endlessly distracting son Julian, who was actually learning to read while I was merely trying to learn to read differently. And thank you last of all to Tala, whose confidence in me has never wavered and whose imitation of academic language keeps getting more eerily accurate with every passing year, thus betraying—I cannot help speculating—a certain affection, if not for the work, then at least for the person doing the work.

Index

Abel, Darrel, 31, 32, 50
Abolitionists, 131, 132
Aesthete(s), 34; Humbert as, 145, 150; New Historicists as, 114; use of term, 33
Aesthetic: autonomy of, 110; of beautiful, 103; *Beloved* and, 167–168, 169–177; as category, 10; commitment to, 155; of contemporary liberalism, 176; critique of as tacit defense, 158; danger of in *Lolita*, 159; defined, 9–10; derision of, 106; disavowal of, 134; distinguishing political from, 22; ethics' relationship with, 152–159, 160, 161, 205; impure, 19–20, 43; inability to exist in isolation, 20, 201; Johnson's repudiation of, 99; Kant's use of, 9; Miller's commitment to, 86; New Criticism's, influence of, 189; operating within political constraint, 170; opposition to, 1; paradoxical conception of, 148; poetic equated with, 150; political critique of, 3, 103; political hopelessness and, 216–217; politics and, 91, 189, 201–202, 205; as resource for those lacking agency, 19; respecting specificity of, 20–21, 204; slaves' turn to, 134; social power of, 159; subcategories of, 10; of sublime, 103; survival of, 5; suspicion of, 2; uses of, 20

Aesthetic appreciation: vs. close reading, 57–58; New Historicism and, 110, 111–112
Aesthetic bliss, 141, 151, 153, 160, 161
Aesthetic commitments, 16; acknowledging, 14; of New Critics, 61–63
Aesthetic criteria: changes in, 23; Hartman's, 130–131, 132; historical developments and, 23–27; ideological premises in, 24–26; of New Critics, 192; persistence of, 181; privileged, 23; sharing, 24. *See also* Aesthetic value
Aesthetic criticism, 12, 165; covert practice of, 3; defining, 11; formalist criticism and, 11; as future oriented, 165; institutionally acceptable form, 33 (*see also* New Criticism/New Critics); New Criticism's rejection of, 33–34
Aesthetic education, 36, 41. *See also* English departments; Humanities; Liberal arts
Aesthetic experience: defined, 10; in English departments, 204–205; identifying social purpose for, 14; logic as kind of, 191; low-intensity, 12; offered by deconstruction, 102; offered by Jameson, 9; postcritical reading, 198; privileging, 168, 204; rationalizing, 205

Eastman, Max, 35
Edelman, Lee, 15, 163–165
Education, aesthetic, 36, 41. *See also*
  English departments; Humanities;
  Liberal arts; Universities
Efficiency, prioritization of, 38
Eliot, George, 86–88
Eliot, T. S., 38, 49
Elizabethan Club, 109
Employees, white collar, 40–41
Empson, William, 35, 68, 77
English departments: aesthetic
  experiences in, 204–205; deconstruc-
  tion and, 67, 68–69, 70; function of,
  41; job market in, 67, 69, 70;
  knowledge offered by, 26; making
  relevant, 37; perceptions of, 137;
  position of, 70–71; value of, 52.
  See also Humanities; Liberal arts;
  Literary studies; Universities
English studies: as form of job training,
  138; New Historicism as advocate
  for, 138–139. *See also* Education,
  aesthetic; English departments;
  Humanities; Literary studies
Enlightenment rationality, return to,
  187
Escape into Aesthetics (Stegner), 142
*Essai sur l'origine des connaissances
  humaines* (Rousseau), 72, 73
Ethical criticism, relation to New
  Criticism, 184
Ethical language, de Man on, 86
Ethics/ethical, 83–89; aesthetic's
  relation to, 152–159, 160, 161, 205;
  Beloved and, 169, 183–184, 186;
  deconstruction and, 81, 89; language
  of, 83–85; as product of grammar, 84;
  reading and, 83, 84, 88
Ethics of Reading, The (Miller), 82–89
Ethnic pride, 188
Ethnocentrism, 93
Exegesis, preference for, 95
Experiences: accounting for value of,
  12–13; nonpolitical modes of, 21

Felski, Rita, 2, 163, 195, 197, 198,
  202–203
Female Complaint, The (Berlant), 17
Female consumers, 147
Femininity, New Critics' view of, 63

Feminism: agency of, 123; New
  Historicism and, 120; second-wave,
  21
"Feminism, New Historicism, and the
  Reader" (Dimock), 120–124
Feminist criticism: early, 123; gender
  categories in, 122; Lolita and, 152,
  154; of "Yellow Wallpaper," 120–122
Feminist politics, 98
Field, Andrew, 142
"Field of Cultural Production, The"
  (Bourdieu), 25
Fineman, Joel, 117, 119
Fischer, Michael, 68
Fletcher, Angus, 189
Folk traditions, 96–97, 176, 183
Form: appreciation of, 3; attention to, 11;
  foregrounding of, 204; hazards of
  overcommitment to, 143; ignoring, 92
Formalism, 4, 11–12, 173; calls for
  return to, 83, 167; close reading
  identified with, 2; deconstruction
  and, 65, 71; desire to rebrand, 145;
  limitations of, 145; Lolita and,
  141–142, 144; New Criticism and, 58,
  63; New Historicism and, 114;
  rejection of, 129; relationship to
  aesthetic criticism, 11; similarities to
  political criticism, 4; sociopolitical
  blindness of, 109; struggle to
  discredit, 65; survival of, 71;
  uncertainty about interpretive
  principles., 144. *See also* Deconstruction; New Criticism/New Critics
Formalists, Chicago, 36
Forms (Levine), 14–15
Forms, tension with ideology, 110
Foucauldian criticism, 165
Foucault, Michel, 127–128, 130
Fragile Absolute, The (Žižek), 184–187
Fragmentation, 5, 6, 38, 40, 57
Frankfurt School, 93
Free-market mentality, 136
Functional, vs. ornamental, 199
Future, 163–164, 165, 166

Gallagher, Catherine, 108, 110, 112, 113,
  114–115, 116, 117, 119, 123, 137, 139
Garner, Margaret, 186
Gates, Henry Louis Jr., 81, 90–97, 107,
  183

www.ingramcontent.com/pod-product-compliance
Lightning Source LLC
Chambersburg PA
CBHW021829090426

42811CB00032B/2089/J